Belshazzar

A Tale of the Fall of Babylon

William Stearns Davis

Alpha Editions

This edition published in 2024

ISBN : 9789367244050

Design and Setting By
Alpha Editions
www.alphaedis.com
Email - info@alphaedis.com

As per information held with us this book is in Public Domain.
This book is a reproduction of an important historical work. Alpha Editions uses the best technology to reproduce historical work in the same manner it was first published to preserve its original nature. Any marks or number seen are left intentionally to preserve its true form.

Contents

CHAPTER I BABYLON THE GREAT ....- 1 -

CHAPTER II ....- 8 -

CHAPTER III ....- 18 -

CHAPTER IV ....- 28 -

CHAPTER V ....- 35 -

CHAPTER VI ....- 44 -

CHAPTER VII ....- 57 -

CHAPTER VIII ....- 70 -

CHAPTER IX ....- 78 -

CHAPTER X ....- 92 -

CHAPTER XI ....- 100 -

CHAPTER XII ....- 108 -

CHAPTER XIII ....- 117 -

CHAPTER XIV ....- 126 -

CHAPTER XV ....- 136 -

CHAPTER XVI ....- 145 -

CHAPTER XVII ....- 156 -

CHAPTER XVIII ....- 168 -

CHAPTER XIX ....- 176 -

CHAPTER XX ....- 184 -

CHAPTER XXI ....- 193 -

CHAPTER XXII ....- 203 -

CHAPTER XXIII ....- 211 -

CHAPTER XXIV ....- 220 -

CHAPTER XXV ....- 230 -

CHAPTER XXVI ....- 236 -

CHAPTER XXVII ....- 245 -

FOOTNOTES ....- 254 -

NOTE TO THE READER ....- 255 -

CHAPTER I
BABYLON THE GREAT

On a certain day in the month Airu, by men of after days styled April, a bireme was speeding down the river Euphrates. Her swarthy Phœnician crew were bending to the double tier of oars that rose flashing from the tawny current; while the flute-player, perched upon the upcurved prow, was piping ever quicker, hastening the stroke, and at times stopping the music to cry lustily, "Faster, and faster yet! Thirty furlongs to Babylon now, and cool Helbon wine in the king's cellars!" Whereupon all would answer with a loud, "Ha!"; and make the bireme leap on like a very sea-horse. Under the purple awning above the poop, others were scanning the flying waves, and counting the little mud villages dotting the river-banks. A monotonous landscape;—the stream, the sky, and between only a broad green ribbon, broken by clumps of tassel-like date palms and the brown thatched hamlets. Four persons were on the poop, not counting as many ebony-skinned eunuchs who squatted silently behind their masters. Just as the flute-player blew his quickest, a young man of five and twenty rose from the scarlet cushions of his cedar couch, yawned, and stretched his muscular arms.

"So we approach Babylon?" he remarked in Chaldee, though with a marked Persian accent. And Hanno the ship-captain, a wiry, intelligent Phœnician in Babylonian service, answered:—

"It is true, my Lord Darius; in another 'double-hour' we are inside the water-gate of Nimitti-Bel."

The first speaker tossed his head petulantly: "Praised be Ahura the Great, this river voyage closes! I am utterly weary of this hill-less country. Surely the Chaldees have forgotten that God created green mountain slopes, and ravines, and cloud-loved summits."

Hanno shrugged his shoulders.

"True; yet this valley is the garden of the earth. The Nile boasts no fairer vineyards nor greater yield of corn-land. He who possesses here a farm has a treasure better than a king's. Gold is scattered; the river yields eternal riches. Four thousand years, the tablets tell, has the river been a mine of things more precious than gems. And we approach Babylon, rarest casket in all this vast treasure-house."

"All men praise Babylon!" quoth the Persian lightly, yet frowning downward.

"Yes, by Astarte! I have seen India and the Tin Isles, the chief wonders of the world. Yet my heart beats quicker now. A hundred strokes brings us to the first view of the mistress of cities."

But Darius did not answer—only scowled in silence at the foam-eddy under the flying stern. As he stood, a stranger could have noted that his tight leathern dress set off a figure short, but supple as a roe's, with the muscles of a leopard. Fire sparkled in his steel-blue eyes; the smile on his lips, from under his curling, fair beard, was frank and winsome. His crisp blond hair and high forehead were pressed by a gray felt cap, and upon his untanned jacket hung his sole ornament, a belt of gold chains, whence dangled a short sword in an agate sheath. Here was a man of power, the first glance told.

After no short silence the young man turned to his companions. Upon one of the couches lounged a handsome elderly nobleman, dressed in a flowing white and purple robe, and with a felt cap like Darius's; on the next a lady, clad also in the loose "Median" mantle, beneath which peeped low boots of crimson leather. But her face and shoulders were quite hidden by an Indian muslin veil. Without speaking, Darius stood beside her for so long a time that she broke the silence in their own musical Persian:—

"My prince, you grow dumb as a mute. Does this piping desert breeze waft all your thoughts after it? By Mithra! Pharnaces"—with a nod to the old nobleman—"has been a wittier travelling companion."

And, as if to gain a better view, the lady lowered the veil, showing a face very white, save as the blood of health crimsoned behind it, and deep-blue eyes, and hair bound by a gold circlet, though not more golden than the unruly tresses it confined. The lines of her face were soft; but despite the banter on her lips none was in her eyes. Upon her breast burned a single great topaz, such as only kings' daughters wear.

There was no levity in Darius's voice when he answered:—

"Princess Atossa, you do well to mock me. Let Ahura grant forgetfulness of that night in the gardens at Ecbatana, when we stood together, and heard the thrushes sing and the fountains tinkle, and said that which He alone may hear. And now we near Babylon, where Belshazzar will hail you as his bride. In Babylon they will proclaim you 'Lady of the Chaldees,' and I Darius, son of Hystaspes, must obey Cyrus, your father—must deliver you up, as pledge of peace betwixt Persia and Babylon; must sit at your marriage feast"—with a pause—"must return to Susa, and forget Atossa, daughter of the Great King."

The lady drew back the veil and answered softly: "Cyrus is King; his word is law and is right. Is he not called 'the father of his people'?"

"Yes, verily, more a father to his people than to his friends," was the bitter reply. "In my despair when you were promised to the Babylonian I went to him, and he professed great sorrow for us both. But 'he were unworthy to rule if he set the joy of a daughter and a friend above the peace of his kingdom.' Then he bade me ask any boon I wished, saving your hand; I should have it, though it be ten satrapies. And I asked this—'to go as the envoy that should deliver you to Belshazzar.' He resisted long, saying I made the parting more bitter; but I was steadfast. And now"—hesitating again—"we are close to Babylon."

Atossa only looked away, and repeated, "Better to have parted in Susa! We should be learning a little how to forget."

Darius had no answer, but Hanno, who could not hear her, cried from the steering oar, "Look, my lords and my lady! Babylon!" He was pointing southward.

The river bent sharply. Just above the topmost plumes of the palms on the promontory thus formed hung a glitter as of fire, pendent against the cloudless blue.

"Flame!" exclaimed Darius, shaken out of his black mood.

"Gold!" answered Hanno, smiling; "the crest of the queen of *ziggurats*, the uppermost shrine of Bel-Marduk, the greatest temple-tower of the twenty in Babylon." And Darius, fresh from the splendours of Susa, marvelled, for he knew the wondrous shining was still a great way off.

But even without this bright day-beacon they would have known they approached the city. The shores were still level as the stream, but the palm-groves grew denser. They saw great cedars and tamarisks, blossoming shrubs, strange exotic trees in pleasant gardens, and the splendour of wide beds of flowers. Tiny canals drained away inland. The villages were larger, and beyond them scattered white-walled, rambling farm-houses. They saw dirty-fleeced sheep and long-horned kine; and presently Hanno pointed out a file of brown camels swaying along the river road—a Syrian caravan, doubtless, just safe across the great desert.

But never in her mountain home had Atossa seen a sight like that upon the river. For the Euphrates seemed turned to life. Clumsy barges loaded with cattle were working with long sweeps against the current; skiffs loaded with kitchen produce were drifting southward; and especially huge rafts, planks upborne by inflated skins, and carrying building-stone and brick, were creeping down-stream towards Babylon. In and out sculled little wicker boats, mere baskets, water-tight, which bore a goodly cargo. And, as the bireme swept onward, the boatman gave many a hail of good omen. "Marduk favour you! Samas shine on you!" While others, who guessed the royal passenger, shouted, "Istar shed gladness on the great lady Atossa!"

So for the moment the young Persians forgot all cares, admiring river and land. All the time the tower of Bel shone with growing radiance. They could see its lower terraces. Around it other *ziggurats*, nearly as high, seemed springing into being, their cone-shaped piles of terraces glowing with the glazed brickwork,—gold, silver, scarlet, blue,—and about them rose masses of walls and buildings, stretching along the southern horizon almost as far as the eye could traverse.

Hanno stood smiling again at the wonderment of the Persians.

"Babylon the Great!" he would cry. "Babylon that endures forever!"

And truly Darius and Atossa thought his praise too faint, as they saw those ramparts springing up to heaven, worthy to be accounted the handiwork of the gods.

"Do you say now," asked Hanno, "that the Chaldees have forgotten the hills? Elsewhere the gods make the mountains; in Babylonia men vie with the lords of heaven! You can see yonder the green feathers of the trees in the Hanging Gardens. The great Nebuchadnezzar once wedded Amytis the Mede, who wept for her native uplands. In fifteen days, such was her husband's love and might, he reared for her this mountain upon arches, and covered it with every fruit and tree. And this paradise shall be yours, O Lady Atossa!"

"Verily," cried Darius, half bitterly, "on this earth you will enjoy the delights of Ahura's *Garo-nmana*, 'the Abode of Song.'"

But Atossa, shuddering, answered, "Not so; in *Garo-nmana* there is no such word as 'farewell.'" And for a moment her eyes went back to the river. But now Hanno was thundering to his men to back water. A crimson pennant was being dipped on the staff before an ample country house by the river bank, and as the Phœnicians stroked slowly backward, a six-oared barge shot out towards the bireme. Behind the white liveries of the rowers one could see two figures sitting in the stern, and Hanno, with his hawk's eyes, cried again, "I am not deceived. The 'civil-minister' Daniel and the chief of the eunuchs, Mermaza, are coming aboard, as escort of honour, before we reach the city."

Darius appeared puzzled. "Daniel?" he asked. "That is not a Babylonian name."

"You are right. His official name is Belteshazzar, but he is by birth a Jew; one from the petty kingdom Nebuchadnezzar destroyed. He has held very high office in these parts. All men honour him, for he is justice and faithfulness itself. The priests hate him because he clings to the worship of his native god Jehovah; but the government continues him, old as he is, as 'Rabsaris,' the 'civil-minister.' His popularity strengthens the dynasty."

"And the eunuch with him?"

The captain laughed significantly. "There must be like pretty serpents at Cyrus's court. He was born a Greek. Men say he is soft-voiced and soft-mannered, yet with a brain sharp enough to outwit Ea, god of wisdom. But he is nothing to dread; never will dog run more obediently at your heels than will he."

The boat was near. The two figures in the stern rose, and the elder hailed, "God favour you, Hanno! Is the Lady Atossa aboard?"

"May Baal multiply your years! She is here and the Lords Darius and Pharnaces."

Then, while the boat drew alongside, the younger of the strangers, who was beringed and coiffured in half-feminine fashion, burst into a flowery oration, praising every god and goddess for the safety of the princess, for the sight of whose face the King Belshazzar waited impatient as the hungering lion. The need of clambering upon the bireme cut short the flow of his eloquence. Darius had only good-natured indifference for the eunuch, who was, as Hanno said, quite one of his kind—handsome, according to a vulgar mould, rouged, pomaded, and dressed in a close-fitting robe of blue, skilfully embroidered with red rosettes; gold in his ears, gold chains about his neck, gold on his white sandals; the whole adorned with a smile of such imperturbable sweetness that Darius wondered if he were a god, and so removed above mortal hate and grief.

But the Jew was far otherwise. The Persians saw a man of quite seventy, yet still unbowed by his years, his hair and beard white as the wave-spray; in his dark eyes a fire; strength, candour, and wisdom written on his sharp Semitic features. His dress was the plainest—a white woollen robe that fell with hardly a fold, a simple leathern girdle, around the feet a fringe of green tassels. He was barefoot, his hair was neatly dressed, but he wore no fillet. Upon his breast hung his badge of office, a cylinder seal of carved jasper, bored through the centre for the scarlet neck-cord.

Daniel had salaamed respectfully; Mermaza brushed his purple fillet on the very deck. The salutations once over, Darius began with a question:—

"And is it true, the report we heard at Sippar, that my Lord Nabonidus, the father of my Lord Belshazzar, has been so grievously stricken with madness that he can never hope to be made whole, and that his son must rule for him, as though he were dead?"

Daniel's answer came slowly, as if he were treading on delicate ground. "The rumour is too true. So it has pleased the All-Powerful. Nabonidus is hopelessly mad, the chiefs of the Chaldeans declare. He lies in his palace at Tema. Belshazzar has, seven days since, as the saying is, 'taken the hands of Bel,' and become sole Lord of Babylon."

"And I trust, with Ahura's grace," replied the prince formally, "soon to stand before him, and in my master's name wish his reign all manner of prosperity."

Then, when the ceremonies of greeting were ended, formality fled, and the talk drifted to the wonders of the approaching city.

"And was it your own villa that your boat left?" asked Darius; to which the minister answered affably: "My own. As Hanno may have told, I am by birth a Jew; yet our God has blessed me in this land of captivity. I possess a passing estate; it will be a fair marriage portion to my daughter."

"Your daughter? Does God refuse a son?" A shiver and sigh seemed to sweep over Daniel at the question.

"I had three sons. All perished in the conspiracy when the young king Labashi-Marduk fell. They are in Abraham's bosom. Now, in my evening, Jehovah sends me one ewe lamb, Ruth, who now waits for me in Babylon. But alas! her mother is dead."

"Ahura pity you, good father," protested the Persian, thrilling in sympathy; "in Persia there is no greater woe than to lack a son. You have much to mourn."

But the other answered steadily, "And much to rejoice over." Then, raising his head, he pointed forward. "See! We are before the great water-gate of the outer wall. The king waits in his yacht inside the barrier. We are sighted from the walls; they raise flags and parade the garrison in honour of the daughter of Cyrus."

Darius gazed not forward, but upward; for though not yet within the fortifications, the walls of brown brick lowered above his head like beetling mountains. The mast of the bireme was dwarfed as it stood against the bulwark. Steep and sheer reared the wall; a precipice, so high that Darius could well believe Hanno's tale that the city folk boasted its height two hundred cubits. At intervals square flanking towers jutted and rose yet higher, faced with tiles of bright blue and vermilion; and behind this "rampart of the gods" rose a second, even loftier; while Daniel professed that inside of this ran still a third, not so high, yet nigh impregnable. As the current swept them nearer they saw the water-gates, ponderous cages of bronze, hung from the towers by ingenious chainwork, ready to drop in a twinkling, and seal all ingress to the "Lady of Kingdoms."

Then, while Darius looked, suddenly the sun flashed on the armour of many soldiers pacing the airy parapets. He heard the bray of trumpets, the clangor of kettle-drums, the tinkling of harps, and soft flutes breathing; while, as the vessel sped between the guardian towers, a great shower of blossoms rained upon her deck, of rose, lily, scarlet pomegranate; and a cheer out-thundered "Hail, Atossa! Hail, Queen of Akkad! Hail, Lady of Babylon!"

Daniel knelt at the princess's feet. "My sovereign," said he, with courtly grace, "behold your city and your slaves. We have passed the water-gate of Nimitti-Bel; before us lies the inner barrier of Imgur-Bel. Except Belshazzar order otherwise, your wish is law to all Babylon and Chaldea."

And at sight of this might and glory, Atossa forgot for a moment her father and the love of Darius. "Yes, by Mithra!" cried she in awe, "this city is built, not by man, but by God Most High."

But Daniel, while he rose, answered softly, as if to himself, "No, not by God. Blood and violence have built it. And Imgur-Bel and Nimitti-Bel shall be helpless guardians when Jehovah's will is otherwise."

Another shout from Hanno, and Daniel cut short his soliloquy.

"My lady," said the Jew, in a changed tone, "the royal galley comes to greet us. Prepare to meet Belshazzar."

CHAPTER II

While Hanno's bireme glided betwixt the portals of Nimitti-Bel, a yet more magnificent galley had been flying up-stream to meet her. On the poop, where the polished teak and ivory glittered, stood a group of officers, in array glorious as the orb of Samas. Here stood Sirusur, the *Tartan*, commander of the host; here Bilsandan, the *Rabsaki*, grand vizier; here, proudest of all, Avil-Marduk, whose gray goatskin across his shoulders proclaimed him chief priest of Bel,[1] highest pontiff of the kingdom. Tall, handsome men were they all, worthy rulers of the city of cities. But at their centre was no less a person than Belshazzar himself, sovereign lord of "Sumer and Akkad," as myriads hailed him. The monarch sat while his ministers stood round him; yet even on his gold-plated chair Belshazzar seemed nearly as tall as they. The royal dress differed from that of the nobles' only as the embroideries on the close-fitting robes blazed with more than common splendour, and the gems on the necklet would have drained the revenues of a petty kingdom. Upon the carefully curled hair perched the royal tiara, white and blue, threaded with gold, cone-shaped, but the top slightly flattened. There was majesty and force stamped upon his aquiline features; force—and it might be passion—glittered in his dark eye, and shone from the white teeth half hid by the thick black beard. In brief, no diadem was needed to proclaim Belshazzar lord.

Avil-Marduk, a gaunt, haughty man, with a strident voice, was speaking to Sirusur, while the eunuchs behind the king flapped their ostrich fans to keep the flies away from majesty.

"I would give much," quoth he, "to know how long Cyrus will remain blind. We must dissemble to the envoys; chatter peace. By Istar! I wish the Egyptian treaty were signed! Pharaoh's envoy is timorous as a wild deer."

Sirusur laughed dryly. "I have less fear. There are two envoys—Pharnaces, an old nobleman, but the chief is the young Prince Darius. They say his eyes are only for hunts and arrow-heads, after these Persian barbarians' fashion. We will give him a great fête, and show all courtesy. He will return to Susa dazzled, and tell Cyrus that Belshazzar is friendly as his own son."

"Nevertheless," answered Avil, cautiously, "be guarded. The Persians forgive twelve murders sooner than one lie. If Darius dreams we ask the marriage treaty but to gain time for an Egyptian alliance and war—"he broke off—"then, my gallant *Tartan*, you may have chance to prove your valour."

Sirusur shrugged his shoulder. "The power of Cyrus is great. Media and Lydia were both swallowed by him; but Babylon, Bel grant, shall prove over large in his maw!"

"The ship of the princess approaches," announced Bilsandan. And even Belshazzar arose as the vessel of Hanno swept alongside. The king stepped to the bulwarks, the purple parasol of royalty held above his head by a ready nobleman. The nimble Phœnicians lashed the two vessels together, and laid a railed gangway between. Of the Persians Atossa crossed first, followed by her eunuchs; and as she knelt at the king's feet, she unveiled. Her face was very pale, but marvellously fair in the eyes of the Chaldeans, accustomed to the darker beauty of their own race.

Belshazzar spoke to her, his voice deep, melodious, penetrating. "Rise, daughter of Cyrus. Istar grant that the white rose of Persia shall bud with new beauty in the gardens of Chaldea!"

Atossa stood with downcast eyes. "I am content to find grace in the sight of my lord," was all she said. Then Darius followed, bowed himself before the king, and delivered the good wishes of his master, to which Belshazzar made friendly reply. After these compliments were ended, and the Babylonians had salaamed before Atossa, Belshazzar commanded the Persians to sit beside him, and affably pointed out each new building as they entered the city.

"Before us, on the left, rises the citadel of Nebuchadnezzar; yonder flashes the brass of the great Gate of Istar; beside the mighty *ziggurat* of Bel rises that, scarce smaller, of his consort Beltis. These brick quays on either bank extend ten furlongs, yet do not suffice for the shipping. The high walls to the right are of the royal palace, a city in itself, and the forest of the Hanging Gardens is close by. Though all the rest of Babylon were taken," Belshazzar spoke proudly, "a host might rage against the palace in vain."

Darius could only wonder and gaze. The quays were a forest of masts. The houses that crowded the water-front rose three and four stories high, and were flat-roofed, walled with plastered wicker brightly painted. The windows were very small, and all the buildings were closely thrust together.

"By Ahura!" cried the Persian, "do your people forget the smell of pure air?"

To which Belshazzar answered, laughing: "If one would live in Babylon, one must pay his price. Happy the man so rich as to possess a little garden in the midst of the city. As you go south, you find vineyards and country houses inside the walls."

"Verily," declared Darius, "better a reed hut in the forest, and good hunting, than a thousand talents and life in Babylon!"

The frankness and good nature of the Persian seemed contagious. Belshazzar laughed again, heartily.

"Now, by Marduk! you will never covet my kingdom. Tell me, do you love to follow the lion?"

The prince's eyes flashed fire. "What are the joys of Ahura's paradise without a lion hunt before the feasting? Understand, O king, that the name men call me by in Persia is the 'King of the Bow,' for I boast that I have no peer in archery."

"Then, by Nergal, lord of the hunting," swore the monarch, "you shall face the fiercest lions and wild bulls in my preserves in the marshes! And I will learn if a Persian can conquer a king of Babylon in the chase."

"Excellent," exclaimed the Persian. "Babylon and Persia are at peace; they shall test their might on the lord of beasts. And if I am not Cyrus's self, next to him there is none other of my nation that calls me vassal."

But now the water-gate of Imgur-Bel was passed, and while on the left the cone of Bel-Marduk lifted its series of diminishing terraces to a dizzy height, on the right spread the royal palace, a vast structure, surrounded by a dense park, and all girded by a wall. On the river side the buildings closely abutted the shores, rising from a lofty brick-faced embankment, themselves of brick, but splendid with the gilding on the battlements, with the sculptured winged bulls that flanked the many portals, and the bright enamel upon the brickwork. Out of the masses of walls sprang castellated towers crowned with gaudy flags, and toward the centre reared a *ziggurat*, the private temple of the king.

For an instant Darius was at Atossa's side as she gazed, and no one watched them.

"This is the dwelling of Belshazzar," said he softly, "a great king. Joy to be his wife." But the lady shivered behind her veil.

"He is a great king, but they will never call him, like Cyrus, 'the father of his people.'"

"You will soon forget Persia, happy as mistress in this wondrous city."

"When I have lived ten thousand years I shall forget—perhaps." Then she added very softly, "I am afraid of Belshazzar; his lips drop praise, his heart is cold and hard as the northern ice. I shall always dread him."

"You wrong the king," Darius vainly strove to speak lightly; "the ways of Babylon are not those of Persia. But there will come a day when you will feel that the Chaldees are your own people. Belshazzar is a splendid man; he will delight to honour you."

But Atossa only held down her head, and answered in a whisper Darius might not hear.

They had no time for more. A vast multitude was upon the embankment before the palace—white-robed priests, garlanded priestesses, the glittering body-guard, all manner of city folk. A shout of welcome drifted over the river.

"Hail, King Belshazzar! Hail, Lady Atossa! May your years exceed those of Khasisadra the Ancient!" Then, amid tinkling harps, many voices raised the hymn of praise to Marduk, the conductor of the royal bride:—

"O merciful one among the gods,

Marduk, king of heaven and earth,

Mankind, the black-headed race,

All creatures, and the spirits of the sky,

Bow down before thee!"

The royal galley headed toward the landing. The great orchestra of eunuchs and playing-girls raised a prodigious din; yet all their music was drowned by the shoutings of the people. The staid citizens brandished their long walking-staffs, and cheered till the heavens seemed near cracking. But a large corps of the body-guard had cleared a portion of the royal quay, and the party disembarked between two files of soldiers. Close to the landing waited the chariots—the six-spoked wheels all glistening with the gilding, more gilding on the panels of the body, the pole, and the harness, and jewels and silver bells braided into the manes of the prancing bay Elamites. For Atossa was ready a four-wheeled coach, adorned as richly as the chariots, drawn by two sleek gray mules, and with a closed body, that the daughter of Cyrus might rest on her cushions within, undisturbed by the vulgar ken. Belshazzar ceremoniously waited upon the princess, till Mermaza closed the door upon her. Then the king beckoned to Darius to mount one of the chariots, while he leaped himself into another. "To the palace," was the royal command; but just as the charioteers upraised their lashes, the steeds commenced to plunge and rear almost beyond control.

Along the brick-paved terrace tugged several lumbering wains, for which great and small made way. As the wagons approached, a low rumble proceeded from them, which set all the chariot horses prancing, and the women and timid burghers uttered low cries and began to mutter incantations. The eyes of Darius commenced to sparkle. The meaning of that rumble he knew right well.

"Lions?" demanded he of his chariot-driver.

"Yes, lord," the man answered, scarce reining the horses, "twelve bull-lions just taken, being sent to Kutha for the king's preserves."

The Persian's nostrils dilated like a charger scenting battle. And as if in answer to his half-breathed prayer, lo! one of the oxen, stung by the goad and fretted by the roarings, commenced to shake his yoke, halting obstinately, and lifting a full-voiced bellow. Instantly his mates answered; the lions' thunders doubled; the wagon-train was halted.

Belshazzar called fiercely to the chief wagoner, "Quiet instantly, or fifty stripes!"

His voice was drowned in the roar. The teams were so near now that one could look into the cages, and see the great beasts pent up behind the stout wooden bars; bars that seemed all too frail at this moment, as lion after lion, frightened and enraged by the din of the oxen, the multitude, and his own fellows, began to claw at the bars, digging out huge splinters with tooth and talon, and roaring louder, ever louder.

Belshazzar's voice sounded now above all the noise. "Clear away this rabble!" he was ordering Sirusur, "Master of the Host." "The man who sent the lion-train this way shall face me to-night. Silence the beasts, and get off with them!"

But not the lord of Babylon and all his guards could still those oxen and their maddened freight.

Sirusur did as bidden. His men pushed on the crowd with their sword-scabbards, but truth to tell the press was so close, and the exits from the quay so cramped, the soldiers could accomplish little. The panic was spreading swiftly enough, however. The goads on the oxen had only driven them into deeper obstinacy.

"Look! In Nergal's name, look!" cried Darius's charioteer; and before the prince's half-terrified, half-exulting eyes he saw the lion within the nearest cage leaping to and fro, trebly maddened now by all the growing tumult. The wagon swayed on its wheels. The wooden bars gave a crash every instant.

"Three more leaps and he is free!" the prince was shouting, transported by his excitement.

"Danger! The wagon topples!" was the howl of the people, and at last they began to give way indeed.

Sirusur, having abandoned his hopeless effort to restore order and silence, hurried men to form before the chariots, while others ran to aid the despairing drivers. Late—the unruly oxen strained their chains. Darius saw the heavy cage totter, fall—a crash, a murk of dust, a noise that thrilled the stoutest, hard wood giving way under harder talons and teeth, then a roar of triumph. Out of the dust he saw a kingly lion bounding, in all his panoply of tawny mane. As the beast leaped, drivers and soldiers sped back like leaves before a gale. The multitude was shrinking, trampling.

"The lion! The lion! Loose! Escape!"

Belshazzar's curse was heard above all else. "Take him alive, or, by Marduk, you are all flayed!" Some guardsmen sprang forward, but the lion, crafty brute, did not fling himself against those breasts of steel. There were bowmen present, but the king stayed their arrows. "Not a shaft. Better ten killed than have him butchered!" The soldiers stood impotent, while the lion ran with low bounds straight into the helpless crowd, that recoiled as at the touch of fire. Belshazzar was in a towering rage. "Nets and hot irons from the palace!" he thundered. "Impalement to all if he escapes!"

The people were screaming, panic-struck; priests were trampling down women; the noise grew indescribable. The other lions dashed against their cages. The brute ran like a great cat down the lane opened through the multitude. A moment, and he would have broken clear and ranged the streets. But from his own side Darius heard a cry of mortal fear.

"Jehovah, have mercy! Ruth! My daughter!"

In the next chariot stood Daniel, covering his face with his hands. The Persian glanced toward the lion. In the centre of the lane, before the escaping monster, stood a white-clad girl, terrified, shivering, her eyes upon the lion, fascinated by his gaze, held helpless as a dove before the snake. How she came there, what fate ordained that she alone of those thousands should be left to confront the monster, that was no time to know. But present she was, and before her the lion. The whole scene passed in less time than the telling. The beast had instantly forgotten his own perils. Keepers, soldiers, multitude, all ignored. He seemed again in his forest—fair prey! That was all he knew!

The lion sank low upon the earth, and crept by little leaps nearer, nearer. The charming fire in the eyeballs Darius saw not, but he saw the red, lolling tongue, the bristling mane, the great tail undulating at the tip, the paws fit to crush an ox. Daniel was turning away his face.

"Arrows, O king! Shoot! My only one!" pleaded he; but Belshazzar flung back, "What is a maid beside a royal lion! Too far—no bow can carry!"

"Darius had proved his title, 'King of the Bow.'"

Many an archer's fingers tightened around his bow, but the king's eye was on them. Not a shaft flew. There was a moment's silence, lions and oxen hushed. A low moan seemed rising from the people. The lion had covered twenty of the thirty paces betwixt him and his prey. The maid was quaking, yet her feet seemed turned to stone. Belshazzar stood in his car, no god more splendid, more merciless.

"Pity me, O king!" was Daniel's last appeal. He had leaped down, and grovelled as a worm before the royal car.

"Too late," came the answer, "only Bel's bolt now can save!" What joy to the king to see those lithe limbs in the monster's clutch! But a great cry had broken from Darius.

"No, in the name of Ahura the merciful!" Few saw him, bounding from his chariot, pluck bow and quiver from a soldier. The lion coiled his limbs for the final leap; men saw his body spring as a stone from a catapult; heard a twitter of a bow, and right at the bound the shaft entered the shoulder, cunningly sped. A roar of dying agony, the body dashed upon the pavement at the girl's feet. No second shaft needed—a twitch, a great bestial groan. Darius had proved his title, "King of the Bow."

But Belshazzar, who had seen the shot but not the archer, blazed out in blind fury, "As Marduk rules, who shot? Impale him!"

Darius stepped beside the royal chariot; his pose was very haughty. "My lord," said he, "I give proof we Persians are fair huntsmen."

Belshazzar's hand went to his sword-hilt, but Darius met the flame in his eyes unflinchingly. By a great effort the king controlled himself, but did not risk speech. The drivers had mastered the oxen, the lions grew still. The people were shouting in delight, "Glory to Nergal! The Persian is peer to the hero Gilgamesh!"

Daniel was kissing Darius's shoes, his voice too choked for thanks. But a young man with a forceful, frank face, a manly form, dressed like Daniel, very simply, came and kissed, not the shoes, but the dust at Darius's feet.

"For life I am your slave, O prince! You have saved me my betrothed!" Then he ran among the people to lead away the girl. Belshazzar ventured to speak.

"How now, Daniel?" ignoring Darius. "By Nergal, your wench has been the death of an African lion! Why here? You keep her locked at home, safe as a gold talent. I have never seen her."

"She was with Isaiah, her betrothed. In the crowd they were swept asunder. The king saw the rest."

Belshazzar was still raging.

"Yes, verily. A rare bull-lion sacrificed for a slip of a wench like her!" Then to the eunuchs: "Run, bring the lass to me. Rare treasure she must prove to make her more precious than the lion."

Darius saw a fresh cloud on the old Jew's face. In a moment Isaiah and the maid were before the king. Very young and fragile seemed the Jewess. The blood had not returned to the smooth brown cheeks. Her black hair was scattered in little curls, for veil and fillet had been torn away. She looked about with great, scared eyes, and all could see her tremble. She started to kneel before the king, but Belshazzar, regarding her, gave a mighty laugh.

"Good, by Istar! So this is your treasure, Daniel? Not the Egibi bankers possess a greater, you doubtless swear. Stand up, my maid. Bel never made those eyes to stare upon that dusty road. Closer. Look at me, and I vow I will forgive you the lion. There are more in the marshes, but only one daughter of Daniel!"

"Look up, child; his Majesty bids you," the old Hebrew was saying, but his face was very grave. Ruth raised her great eyes; her lips moved, as if in some answer, but no sound came. Belshazzar smiled down upon her from his car. Atossa was to be his queen, but when was a king of Babylon denied a maid that was pleasant to his eyes? He turned to Darius.

"Now, by every god, I thank you, Persian. I was about to curse, but your archery saved one beside whom Istar's self must flush in shame. Well are you named 'King of the Bow.'"

Then he gazed again upon the maid. "Mermaza," he commanded, "put the girl in a chariot, and take her to the palace harem. Give her dresses and jewels like the sun. Do you, Daniel, draw five talents from the treasury. Not enough? Ten then. Fair payment for a daughter—ha!"

Daniel was on his knees before the king. "Mercy! Hear me, my lord. If ever, by faithfulness serving you and your fathers, I gather some store of gratitude—"

Belshazzar cut him short. "Now does Anu, lord of the air, topple down heaven? What father says to a king, 'Mercy. Give back my daughter'? Oh, presumption! No more, or you forfeit the money."

"The money," groaned Daniel, "the price of my daughter? Kiss the earth, Ruth; and you, Isaiah, entreat the king to forbear!"

Belshazzar turned his back. "Fool," he cried, "the money is truly forfeit! Away with her, Mermaza. Great mercy I leave the Jew his life."

But Darius deliberately thrust himself before the king, and looked him in the face. "My lord," he said soberly, "if to any, the girl belongs to me. I saved her and restore her to her father."

"You beard me thus, Persian, barbarian!" broke forth Belshazzar, again in his wrath. The prince answered him very slowly:—

"Your Majesty, in me you see the 'eyes and ears' of Cyrus, lord of the Aryans. What if I report in Susa, 'On the day I delivered Atossa to Belshazzar, he, before her own eyes, showed his esteem for her by haling to his harem a maid chance sent him on the streets'? Would such a tale knit the alliance firmer?"

Avil-Marduk was beside the king in the chariot, and he whispered in the royal ear, "Risk nothing. Dismiss the maid; the eunuchs can watch for her and secure her quietly."

Belshazzar was again calm. His passion was swift; he subdued it more swiftly. "Son of Hystaspes," said he, with easy candour, "I am a man of sudden moods. The maid pleased me; but, by Istar, I did not think to insult the princess. Let the Jews go in peace, and to heal their hurts let the treasurer weigh to each a talent. The Jewess shall sleep safe as a goddess's image in the temple. I swear it, on the word of a king of Babylon. Enough, and now to the palace."

Darius was received with stately hospitality at the palace. He was told the arrangements made for Belshazzar's bride. The king would give her a great betrothal feast at the Hanging Gardens, but could not wed her for one year; for before marriage she must be taught the religious duties of a queen of Babylon. Darius paced the open terrace of the palace that evening. Below him and all about lay the city of the Chaldees, fair as a vision of heaven, with the white moon riding above the tower of Bel. But the beauty of the city brought no joy. Into the hands of what manner of man had Atossa fallen? The desire of Belshazzar to sacrifice the maiden for the beast, followed by the outburst of carnal passion—how unlike this king to Cyrus, whom the meanest Persian loved! At last, when it had grown very dark, Darius looked about him. No one was near. He lifted his hands toward the starry sky.

"Verily this Babylon is a city of wickedness, and most evil of all is its cruel king. But I am young. I am strong. Belshazzar shall not possess Atossa for one year. And in that year a brave man may do much—much. Help Thou me, Ahura-Mazda, Lord God of my fathers!"

CHAPTER III

Near the meeting of the great Nana-Sakipat Street with Ai-Bur-Schabu Street stood the banking-house of the "Sons of Egibi." The long bridge of floats across the river was close by, and in and out the portals of the wide river-gate poured a constant stream of veiled ladies, with their guardian eunuchs, intent on shopping, of donkey boys, carters, pedlers, and priests. Under the shade of the great stone bull guarding one side of the entrance, the district judge was sitting on his stool, listening to noisy litigants; from the brass founder's shop opposite rose the clang of hammers; and under his open booth descended a stairway to Nur-Samas's beer-house, by which many went down and few ascended, for it was hard to recollect one's cares while over the drinking-pots.

The Egibis' office, like all the other shops, was a room open to all comers, nearly level with the way, without door or window, but made cool by the green awning stretched across the street in front, and the shadow cast by the high houses opposite. In the office many young clerks were on their stools, each busily writing on the frames of damp clay in their laps with a wedge-headed stylus. Itti-Marduk, present head of this the greatest banking-house of Babylon, was a plainly dressed, quiet-speaking man; and only the great rubies in his earrings and the rare Arabian pomade on his hair told that he could hold up his head before any lord of Chaldea saving Belshazzar himself. At this moment he was entertaining no less a client than Avil-Marduk, the chief priest, who came in company with his boon companion, the priest Neriglissor, as did all the city at one or another time, to ask an advance from the omnipotent broker. As for Itti, he was angling his fish after his manner, keeping up a constant stream of polite small talk, sending out a lad to bring perfumed water to bathe his noble guests' feet, and yet making it plain all the while that current rates of interest were exceedingly heavy.

"Alas!" the worthy banker was bewailing, "that I must speak of shekels and manehs before friends, but what with heavy remittances I must send to agents in Erech, with the farmers all calling for funds to pay their help for the coming season, and a heavy loan to be placed by his Majesty to complete the fortifications of Borsippa, I have been put to straits to raise so much as a talent; and were you any other than yourself, my dear high priest, I fear I could do nothing for you."

"Yet I swear by Samas," protested the pontiff, with a wry face at the loan-contract before him, "you have enough in your caskets to build us poor priests of Bel a new *ziggurat*."

"A new *ziggurat*!" protested the banker; "am I like Ea, able to see all hidden riches? I declare to you that what with the rumour that the tribes in the southern marshes around Teredon are restless, money becomes as scarce as snow in midsummer. Ramman forbid that anything come of the report! It will wither all credit!" So at last, with many protests from Avil, the contract was signed, and stored away in a stout earthen jar, in the strong room of the cellar, where lay countless jugs of account books. And Itti, to make his guest forget that he had just bargained to pay "twelve shekels on the maneh,"[2] inquired genially if the recent taking of the omens had chanced to be fortunate. He was met by blank faces both from Avil and his chariot comrade, the toothless old "anointer of Bel," Neriglissor.

"The omens are direful," began the latter, in a horrified whisper.

"Hush!" admonished the chief priest, "a state secret. To breathe it on the streets would send corn to a famine price."

The banker had pricked up his ears. "I am not curious in matters of state; Marduk forbid! Yet if in confidence I were told anything—"

Neriglissor was only too ready to begin. "The Persians," he whispered, "the Persians! Barbarous dogs! Faugh! I sicken thinking of the strong Median nard the daughter of Cyrus smeared on her hair!"

Itti smiled benevolently. "What Persian can have the delicate taste of a Babylonian? Yet you have not told the omen."

Neriglissor's voice sank yet lower. "These Persians are friends to the Jews, that race of blasphemers. Each nation worships the same demon, though the Jews style him Jehovah, the Persians Ahura-Mazda. Long have the pious foreseen that unless these unbelievers were kept out of Babylon the gods would be angry. Yesterday this Atossa comes to Babylon to be his Majesty's queen. Thus we are about to strike hands with the foes of the gods, as if it were not enough to continue the old scoffer Daniel in office. And this morning follows the omen."

Itti was bending over that not a word might escape. Neriglissor continued, "As Iln-ciya, the chief prophet, and I stood by the temple gate, a band of street dogs, all unawares, strayed past, and entered the enclosure."

Itti started as he sat, forgot his manehs, and began to mutter an invocation to Ramman, while his lips twitched. "Impossible!" was all he could gasp.

"Too true," put in Avil, solemnly. "You know the ancient oracle," and he rolled out the formula:—

"'When dogs in a court of a temple meet,

The hosts of the city face swift defeat.'

We brought the news to the king. He is all anxiety. There will be a special council and consulting of the oracles. We trust, by laying extra burdens on these stubborn Jews, we can in some measure avert the wrath of heaven. Yet this is a fearful portent, just as his Majesty is about to marry a Persian."

Itti was still shaking his head, when an increased din rising from the street warned Avil that there would be no passing at present for his chariot.

"Way! way!" a squad of spearmen were bawling, forcing back the traffickers to either side. The banker and his guests stared forth curiously.

"Way! way!" the shout grew louder, and behind sounded a creaking and a rumbling. The chief priest glanced toward the gate.

"The new stone bull," commented he, "comes from Karkhemish. They landed it above the bridge; now they drag it to the old palace of Nabupolassar, which the king is repairing."

"Then the Jews," remarked Itti shrewdly, "are already being rewarded for their impiety. Has not the labour gang been taken from their nation?"

"You are right," said Avil, "they will fast learn that to keep clear of forced labour they must go to the *ziggurat* and the grove of Istar."

"Strange people," declared Itti, "so steadfast to their helpless god!"

"If Marduk gives me life," swore Avil, "I will bend their stiff necks. His Majesty promises the indulgence of former reigns shall end forever."

The rumbling in the streets drowned further words. Long before the bull came in sight appeared four long lines of panting men, naked save for loincloths, dusty, sullen. Each man tugged at a short cord, made fast in turn to one of the four heavy cables stretching far behind them. At times the march would come to dead halt; then every back would bend, and at a shout from the rear the hundreds would pull as one, and start forward with a jerk. The laggards were spurred on by the prick of the lances of the spearmen outside the lines, or felt the staffs of the overseers who walked between the cables. Young boys ran in and out with water jars, and now and then a weary wretch would drop from the line to gulp down a draught, and run back to his toil. So the long snake wound down the street, groaning, panting, cursing. Behind this thundered the bull. The stone monster was upon a boat-shaped sledge, itself the height of a man. Busy hands laid rollers before it. To steady its mass, men ran beside, holding taut the cords fixed to the tips of the huge wings. On the front of the sledge stood the guard's captain, bellowing orders through a speaking trumpet. The bull reared above him to thrice his height. Last of all came many toiling from behind, with heavy wooden levers.

"Ah, noble Avil," called the guard's captain, familiarly, "who would say the chief priest makes way for Igas-Ramman, captain of a fifty?"

And Avil, recognizing a friend, called back, "Beware, or I beg your head of the king! Make the Jews give full service."

"They shall, by Nabu!" And Igas trumpeted, "Faster now! Wings of eagles! Feet of hares, or your backs smart!"

The overseers' blows doubled, the bull swayed as it leaped forward, but suddenly Igas cursed. "Now, by the Maskim, foul genii of the deep, what is this? Down again, worthless ox!"

An old man had fallen from line. Overcome by weariness he lay on the stone slabs while the strokes of the overseers' staffs made him writhe. Rise he could not. Neriglissor recognized him.

"A Jew named Abiathar, a great blasphemer of Marduk. Ha! Smite again, again!"

Igas leaped into the throng, waving a terrific Ethiopian whip of rhinoceros hide. At the second blow blood reddened the flags. The Hebrew groaned, tried vainly to rise.

"Beast," raged Igas, swinging again, "you shall indeed be taught not to lag!"

The great whip whisked on high, but just as it fell, a heavy hand sent the captain sprawling. Young Isaiah stood above the prostrate Igas, his eyes burning with righteous wrath, his form erect.

"Coward! You will not strike twice a man of your own age!"

The spearmen stood blinking at Isaiah in sheer astonishment. Igas crawled to his feet; rage choked the curses in his throat, then flowed forth a torrent of imprecations. In his wrath he forgot even to call for help.

"Beetle!" howled he, bounding on Isaiah. But the Jew had caught the whip, lashed it across the guards captain's shoulders, and raised a smarting welt. Then at last all leaped on the intruder, but he laid about as seven, till a stroke of a cudgel dashed the whip from his grasp; he was carried off his feet, overpowered, and gripped fast. Around the motionless bull a tumultuous crowd was swelling, when a squad of red-robed "street-wardens" hastened up to arrest the peace-breakers.

"High treason against the king!" Igas was screeching. "His head off before sunset!" But the police rescued Isaiah from the spearmen, and their chief urged:—

"Softly, excellent captain, he must be tried before the judge."

"A Jew! A Jew!" shouted many. "Away with him! Strike! Kill!"

The multitude seemed growing riotous, and ready to attack the police, when a new band of runners commenced forcing a passage.

"Way! way! for the noble Persian Darius and the Vizier Bilsandan!" was the cry; but to the astonishment of those in the banking-house, they saw the young envoy leap from his chariot and plunge before his escort into the crowd. Dashing back the mob with sturdy blows from his scabbard, he was in an instant beside the Jew. For a moment few recognized him. Igas thrust at him with a lance, a quick thrust, yet more quickly had Darius unsheathed, and struck off the spear-head. "Treason! Rebellion! A plot!" shouted a hundred. The police endeavoured to arrest the new offender.

"Death to the Jews!" rang the yell, as many hands were outstretched. But the Persian had released Isaiah, and thrust a cudgel in his hands. His own sword shone very bright.

"Guard my back!" commanded he, and braced himself. The crowd cut him off from his escort.

Avil cried vainly across the deafening tumult.

"Hold, on your lives! Will you murder the Persian envoy?"

There was a rush, a struggle; those thrust against Darius shrank back howling, all save two, who had tasted his short sword.

In the respite following, Bilsandan had forced himself to the envoy's side. Mere sight of the vizier was enough to enforce quiet.

"Peace, dogs!" thundered Bilsandan. "Why this tumult?"

Darius had sheathed his sword, but looked about smiling. Joy to show these city folk the edge of Aryan steel!

"I struck only in self-defence," quoth he to the vizier. "You saw the cruelty of this scorpion. Isaiah deserves reward for avenging the old man. I will mention the evil deed of this captain to the king. We Persians hold that he who reveres not the gray head will still less reverence the crown."

Igas was falling on his knees before Darius. Well he knew Belshazzar would snuff out his life so cheaply to humour the envoy of Cyrus, if only Darius asked it. But the Persian laughed good-naturedly, forced him to swear he would pay old Abiathar two manehs, for salve to his stripes, and the king should hear nothing about it. As for Isaiah, spearmen and police were glad to leave him at liberty. They bore the two wounded away. Darius was about to return to the chariot in which Bilsandan had been driving him about the city, but gave Isaiah a last word. "By Mithra, I love you, Jew! You are like myself, swift as a thunderbolt, striking first and taking counsel later."

"Jehovah bless you again, my prince!" cried the other. "How may I repay? They would have taken my life."

So Darius was gone. The bull lumbered on its way. Isaiah alone remained to help home the wretched Abiathar. As he bargained with a carter to take the old man to his home on the Arachtu Canal, Avil-Marduk called from the banking-house: "Praise Bel, Hebrew, you are not on the way to execution! Be advised. I love men of your spirit. Enter our service at the *ziggurat*, and, by Istar, you may wear the goatskin in my place some day!"

Isaiah held up his head haughtily. "I would indeed enter the service of a god—not of Bel-Marduk, but of Jehovah. I am a Jew, my lord."

Avil smiled patronizingly. "Excellent youth, you are too wise to think I do not set your wish at true value. No offence, but where does Jehovah rule to-day? Fifty years long we have used the dishes from His temple at your village of Jerusalem, in our own worship of Bel-Marduk. Your god is helpless or forsakes you; no shame to forsake Him."

Isaiah bowed respectfully. "Your lordship, we gain little by debate," replied he.

"Nevertheless," quoth Avil, blandly, "I am grieved to see a young man of your fair parts throw his opportunities away. Be led by me; what do you owe Jehovah? Bel-Marduk will prove a more liberal patron. You are Jew only in name, your birth and breeding have been in this Babylon. To her gods you should owe your fealty. Believe me, I speak as a friend—"

Isaiah straightened himself haughtily.

"My Lord Avil, do not think Jehovah is like your Bel, the god of one city, of one nation. For from the east to the gates of the sun in the west is His government. And all the peoples are subject unto Him, though the most part know it not."

The high priest's lip curled a little scornfully. "Truly," flew his answer, "Jehovah displays His omnipotence in strange ways,—to let the one nation that affects to serve Him languish in captivity."

"I fear many words of mine will not make your lordship understand," replied Isaiah; and he bowed again and was gone. Those in the banking-house looked at one another.

"Sad that so promising a youth must cast himself away in fanatical devotion to his helpless god," commented Itti the banker. "Yet he only imitates his father, Shadrach, the late royal minister."

"Young as he is," responded Avil, "he is already a power amongst his countrymen. He has the reputation of being a prophet of their Jehovah, and many treat him with high respect. Nevertheless, if he is not better counselled soon, he will find his head in danger, unless the king stops his ears to my warnings."

Isaiah walked beside Abiathar as the cart rumbled homeward. The old Jew was all groans and moans.

"Ah, woe!" he was bewailing, "is this to be the reward of the Lord God for remembering Him, and keeping away from the *ziggurat*! Stripes and forced labour and insult! Speak as you will, good Isaiah, you who have the civil-minister to protect you from all harm; it is easy for you to toss out brave words. You are passing rich; we are poor, and all the stripes crack over our shoulders!"

"Hush!" admonished the younger Jew, severely; "my perils are great as yours, did you but know them. It is for our sins this trouble is visited upon us. Our fathers have forgotten Jehovah, and is He not now visiting their sins upon us, unto the third and fourth generation, even as says His Law?"

"I do not know," replied the other, moodily; "I only know that a little oil and fruit offered now and then to Sin or Samas would cure many aching backs!"

Isaiah did not answer him. In truth, there was very little to reply. He walked beside the wagon until Abiathar was safe at his little house by the Western Canal. Then he left him, and went in the bitterness of his spirit to the palace of Daniel, near the Gate of Beltis in the inner city.

Like all Babylonian gentlemen, the civil-minister had an extensive establishment, though the exterior was gloomy and windowless. When Isaiah had entered the narrow gate he found himself in a spacious court, surrounded by a two-story veranda, upborne on palm trunks. In the court were ferns, flowers, and a little fountain; an awning covered the opening toward the sky. In a farther corner maid-servants were pounding grain and sitting over their embroidery.

Isaiah entered unceremoniously; but just at the inner door of the farther side of the court he came on Daniel himself, dressed in his whitest robe, and surrounded by several servants, as if about to set forth in his chariot.

"My father!" And the younger Hebrew fell on his knees while the other's hand outstretched in blessing.

"The peace of Jehovah cover you, my son," declared the old man. Yet when Isaiah had risen, he was startled at the anxiety written on the other's face. He knew it was no light thing that could shake the civil-minister out of his wonted calm.

"As Jehovah lives," adjured the younger Jew, "what has befallen? Where are you going? You do not commonly ride abroad in the heat of the day."

"I have urgent need of going to Borsippa to see my good friend Imbi-Ilu, high priest of Nabu, on a private matter." The effort to speak lightly was so evident that Isaiah's fears were only doubled.

The minister turned to the others.

"Tell Absalom to hasten with harnessing the chariots," commanded Daniel. The servants took the hint and withdrew. Their master cast a searching glance about the courtyard, to make sure that no others were in easy earshot.

"Listen." His speech sank to a whisper. "I am in sore anxiety concerning the safety of Ruth."

"Of Ruth!" Isaiah's grave face grew dark as the thunder-cloud. "How? Who threatens?"

Daniel spoke yet lower. "This day I have received a message from friends in the palace, that the king still remembers her beauty, and desires her. His promise to Darius was a lie, to appease the envoy for the moment. I dare not doubt that some attempt will be made by Mermaza, or by others of his spawn, to carry away the girl at the first convenient opportunity. She must not sally abroad, however much she may desire it. I do not know how great is the immediate danger, but there is nought to be risked. On this account I am going to Borsippa without delay."

"Then as our God rewardeth evil for evil, so will I reward the king!" Isaiah had turned livid with his wrath. "I will slay Belshazzar with my own hand, and then let them kill me with slow tortures."

Daniel smiled despite his heavy heart.

"Small gain would that be to our people. The fury of the Babylonians would grow sixfold. If the yoke is hard to bear now, what then?"

"Yet will Belshazzar truly break his promise?" demanded Isaiah, plucking at the last straw of hope.

"Promise?" Daniel laughed grimly. "He will break ten thousand oaths, when they stand betwixt him and a passion. Avil-Marduk urges him each day to ruin me and mine, as a lesson to the rest of our people. The Jews are to be driven like sheep to the *ziggurat*, and forced to blaspheme Jehovah. Alas! When I think of the plight of our nation, the dangers of a few of us seem but as the first whisperings of a mighty storm! If no succour comes, Ruth and you and I are utterly undone; and our people will forget its God, as He in His just wrath seems to have forgotten them."

"And is there *no* hope?" groaned Isaiah in his despair.

Before Daniel could answer, a sweet girlish voice sounded, singing from the upper casement, over the court. The two men stood in silence.

"My beloved spake and said unto me,

'Rise up, my love, my fair one, and come away.

For lo, the winter is past, the rain is over and gone:

The flowers appear on the earth;

The time of the singing of birds is come,

And the voice of the turtle is heard in our land!'"

"It is the song of Ruth," said Daniel, as in dreamy melancholy. "She has waited you for long. Blessed is she; to her Jehovah thus far is kind. She does not know her danger. The 'Song of Songs' is ever in her mouth, in these days of her love. You must go to her."

"Let all Belshazzar's sword-hands take her from me!" was Isaiah's rash boast. But then he asked more calmly: "And why do you, my father, go to Borsippa? You have not told."

"To ask Imbi-Ilu if he will give sanctuary in the temple of Nabu to Ruth, if worst comes to worst. Bitter expedient!—a daughter of Judah sheltered in the house of idols! Such is the only shift."

"But Imbi could not guard her always, if the king's mind is fixed. And what of our nation, of the peril of great apostasy? Ah!" Isaiah lifted his hand toward heaven. "I am not wrong. I must kill Belshazzar; then if we die, we die not unavenged!"

Daniel quieted him with a touch.

"Do not anger God with unholy rashness. All is not yet lost. I have still my position as 'civil-minister,' and though the Babylonians may rage against our people, they reverence me still. My word and name are yet a power in Babylon. Even the king will hesitate to strike me too openly. And if the worst *does* come, let them know I have yet a weapon that may shake Belshazzar on his throne."

"What mean you? For Jehovah's sake, declare!"

Daniel smiled sadly at the impetuosity of the younger man.

"No, not now. Fifty years long have I served the kings of the Chaldees, and betrayed none of their secrets. I keep fealty as long as I may; yet the time for casting it off may be near at hand. The Lord grant I may not be driven thus to bay—"

"The chariot waits, my lord," interrupted a servant. And Daniel gathered his robe about him, to depart.

"Remain with Ruth until I return," was his last injunction; "the king will hardly wax so bold as to go to extremities to-day. But till Belshazzar lies dead, or Jehovah creates in him a new heart, we must not cease to guard her."

CHAPTER IV

The chariot of the "civil-minister" clattered away, and Isaiah stood for a long time in gloomy revery. Ever since Nabonidus had been thrust from power, the condition of the Hebrews had been growing steadily more miserable. Belshazzar was in all things guided by Avil-Marduk, and the high pontiff's rage against the Jehovah worship of the exiles was nothing new. Shadrach, Isaiah's father, had been a fellow-minister with Daniel, but the liberal sway of Nebuchadnezzar was long since past. Isaiah saw himself shut out of every office, so long as he clung to the God of his people. Amongst his fellow-Hebrews Isaiah had passed as a prophet; in moments of ecstasy he had poured forth burning words,—of encouragement to the faithful, of threatenings to the oppressor, of promised restoration to that dear Jerusalem he had seen only in his dreams. But at this moment the dreams seemed shadowy indeed. The events of the day had darkened him utterly; and, crowding upon Avil's scarce veiled threat, came the tidings of the king's unholy lusting after Ruth! The young man's heart was sickened. How could he sit with smiling face, and listen to his love, and her merry nothings? The task was seemingly impossible, when the sweet voice sounded again from the casement. "Ah! my wandering swallow, why linger? Up quickly! Say something to make me glad. I am exceeding vexed with my father."

Merry or sad, the young man waited no second bidding. He sped up the narrow stairway by the side of the court, and reached the upper veranda. Here a sort of balcony, overhanging the yard, had been walled with curtains of blue Egyptian stuffs, and behind had been set a tall loom, its frame half filled with a web of bright wools, where a brilliant rug was unfolding under skilful fingers. Two dark-eyed Arabian girls were aiding their mistress; but at sight of Isaiah, the red thread shook from her lap, and she flew twittering into his arms. Then like two birds they cooed together, their eyes talking faster than their lips; and at last—for all things lovely must find end—Isaiah was in his accustomed seat, a cushioned footstool beside the loom, and there he could sit and chatter while the broad web grew.

But Ruth was in no mood for small talk. Her little lips were wrinkled in a pout, the cast of her eye was sulky. And while she wrought over the loom, her fountain of wrath was emptied.

"Were I not an obedient daughter of Israel, I should say unholy things of my good father. Surely Jehovah forsakes us and suffers him to wax mad!"

"Daniel mad? He has the sagest head in all Babylon. Fie, little owlet!"

"Either he is mad or worse. There!" the red-thonged sandals over the small feet stamped angrily, "I will tell all, though it be a sin to revile a parent."

"Verily, for *you* to be wroth with your father must spring from no slight cause!" protested Isaiah, feebly attempting to smile.

"Is it not sufficient that I must be kept precious as a finch in his cage?—never suffered to go forth to any of the fêtes at the palace, veiled always, when I sally abroad, and guarded as if I were a prisoner about to make escape?"

"Old tales, Ruth,"—Isaiah strove to speak lightly; then more gravely, "Was the last time we sallied forth, and met the lion and the king, so joyous that you wish it repeated daily?"

He saw her shudder, and her mouth twitched, as he recalled that scene; but she was too thoroughly filled with wrath even to let that memory turn her.

"Not so—let my father send fifty servants about me, and wrap my face in twoscore veils! But now I am made utter prisoner. Yesterday I visited the bazaars with Gedeliah, our body-servant; and in the jeweller's shop of Binzurbasna by the Gate of Istar I saw an armlet that fitted my eye as water its cup. I had no money, but last night my father gave me more than the price. To-day Gedeliah starts at dawn with a letter to Kisch. Later I say, 'Father, I will take another servant and go and buy the armlet.' He makes all manner of objections to my going. 'Let the serving-man go; do you remain.' 'No,' answered I, 'only Gedeliah and I can tell which is the armlet; if I wait, it is sold.' I beseech exceedingly, whereupon he says, after his firm manner: 'Peace, Ruth; I know what is well for you. You shall not go to-day.' Then he summons his chariot, and departs to Borsippa. Have I no cause for anger?"

Isaiah did not reply immediately; and she returned to the charge. "Speak,—are you so jealous that no man may set eyes on the hem of my mantle? Speak!" And she snapped her bright eyes before his.

"Your father is a wise man," began Isaiah, cautiously; "assuredly he had reasons."

"Which clearly you agree in?" pressed she, sharply.

"I said not that; though, were he to tell, no doubt they would seem sufficient."

"He has not told them? What passed then so slyly, when you stood together?"

Isaiah had boasted that in a city where the clever liar was deemed the sage, he had been wont to speak truly; but he found himself close to equivocation.

"We spoke of the increasing power of Avil. Your father grows anxious."

"And was not *my* name mentioned once, twice?"

Ruth had turned from the loom, and was looking Isaiah in the face.

"You did wrong to eavesdrop," he faltered, nigh desperately, for falsehood tripped hardest off his tongue when those soft eyes were on him.

"No answer," she challenged, lowering her head till her curls almost brushed his cheek. "Speak! Why did you use my name?"

"You must have confidence in us," began Isaiah, putting on manly austerity, "to believe that whatever we said was only for your good."

A tart retort was tingling on her tongue, when a voice from the court interrupted. "Ho! Is the young master Isaiah above?"

It was the old porter's call; the other responded instantly.

"Since my Lord Daniel is away," went on the porter, "will my young master come down at once? His friend, the guardsman Zerubbabel, is here, and demands instant speech of weighty matters."

Isaiah was down the stairs by leaps. In the court he met a young man of about his own age, comely and erect, dressed in the short mantle of a soldier off duty.

"Where is my Lord Daniel?" was his quick demand; he was breathless with running.

"Has none told? Gone to Borsippa."

"Jehovah God have mercy!"

Isaiah caught his friend by the arm.

"Hold, Zerubbabel; gain breath, and speak to the point. Your wits are all scattered on the road behind!"

The guardsman took a deep breath.

"Be a man, Isaiah," he admonished, as if speaking sorely against his will; "I have a heavy piece of news for you."

"Touching Ruth?"

Zerubbabel nodded. "You have heard that the king had designs on her. Did you know Mermaza was to make an attempt on her this very night?"

His voice had risen, despite Isaiah's warning "Hush!" They heard a little cry on the balcony above—a louder scream. Isaiah clapped his hands to his face. "The Lord spare her now!—she has heard it!"

The next instant Ruth was beside them. She was trembling; her hand quivered in her lover's while he held it, yet it seemed as much in anger as in dread, though her face had blanched to the whiteness of a summer's cloud.

"Tell me all! All! Do you think me too weak to bear?" was her plea, turning her great eyes from the soldier to Isaiah and back again. "What danger waits?"

The young prophet's voice grew very calm.

"Beloved, blessing and bane come from the Lord God alike. He can do nothing ill. Let us listen to Zerubbabel."

The guardsman's speech came falteringly,—no joy to chase the gladness from those bright eyes.

"Daughter of Daniel, I know that your father reproaches me for having conformed to the Babylonish worship, and taken service on the royal guard; but, believe me, my heart is still faithful to Jehovah. At no small peril have I come here, to warn you. You, O Isaiah, have not been without an inkling; but did you know that Belshazzar has given his royal signet to Mermaza, chief of the eunuchs, commanding him—"

Before he could utter another word, a bitter cry had burst from Ruth: "Would God I had been unborn, or died while yet a speechless child, than win the love of Belshazzar. For the love of the king is tenfold more cruel than his hate. Slay me; slay now, rather than let the eunuchs lay hands on me!" So she cried in her sudden agony; and what might Isaiah say to comfort her? She could only feel the muscles of his arms grow hard as iron, as she leaned against his breast.

"Fear not," he answered, with that confidence born of a touch and a thrill that can make the weakling giant strong; "were Belshazzar seven times the king he is, he shall never do you harm."

"So be it!" quoth Zerubbabel, gravely, "yet the proof is close at hand. It is as I said. Mermaza has received an order, signed by the royal signet, authorizing him to take Ruth, the daughter of Daniel, when there may be 'convenient opportunity'—which is to say, when no disturbance will arise likely to hamper Avil-Marduk and his plots."

"How know you this?" demanded Isaiah, almost fiercely.

"One of the eunuchs, whose life Daniel had once begged of Nabonidus, told me. I more than fear that my visit to this house has been observed, and will be laid up against me."

"And what hinders the 'profoundly-to-be-reverenced' chief eunuch from coming this moment, with his Majesty's ring and order, and carrying away the maid perforce? Does not Belshazzar command all the sword-hands in Babylon?" pressed Isaiah, in cutting irony.

Zerubbabel smiled bitterly. "Even a king must know some restraints. He has passed his word to Darius, the Persian envoy, that the maid shall not be touched. What if Darius heard of the kidnapping! Would he trust Belshazzar's professions of friendship longer? And Daniel is popular with the city folk. Enter his house at mid-day, and let some outcry rise,—behold! there is a riot in the streets."

"Therefore the attempt will be made this evening, when all is quiet?"

Zerubbabel bowed gloomily. "You have said."

Isaiah shot one glance at the shadow cast by the tall "time-staff" set in the centre of the courtyard.

"It lacks three hours of sundown. There is yet time!" he cried.

But Ruth had suddenly steadied herself, and looked from one young man to the other. Her voice was very shrill.

"Who am I to make you rush into peril for my poor sake? If you hide me from the king, his fury will turn against you, and against my father. How can you save me? Go to Mermaza. Tell him he may take me when he wills. I can endure all rather than ruin those I love."

She stood before her lover with head erect, eyes flashing. The glory of a great sacrifice had sent the colour crimsoning through her cheeks. If beautiful before, how much more beautiful now, in the sight of her betrothed! Had she counted the cost of her word? No, doubtless; but for the moment she was the girl no more, but the strong woman ready to dare and to do all.

But Isaiah answered her with a sternness never shown by him to her till now: "Peace! You know not what you say. What profit is my life, with you sent to a living death in Belshazzar's impure clutch? There is but one thing left."

"Away! Leave me!" she implored, new agony chasing across her face. "Is it not enough that I should be victim? Those who cross Belshazzar's path are seekers for death."

"Peace!" repeated Isaiah, and not ungently he thrust his hand across her mouth. "Must the whole house hear us? You, Zerubbabel, indeed, begone. You can only add to your peril, not aid."

The guardsman hesitated. "If I can do aught—" he began.

"Avoid suspicion," commanded Isaiah; "if you learn of anything new plotted, forewarn. In so doing you prove truest friend."

"The Lord God keep you, dear lady," protested the guardsman, kissing her robe; "believe me, I am your and your father's friend, though men say I bow down to Bel-Marduk."

He had vanished; and Isaiah looked upon Ruth, and Ruth back to Isaiah. The peril had broken upon her so suddenly that she was yet numbed. She had not realized all she had to fear, and the ordeal awaiting. But if her lover realized, he proved his anguish by act, not word.

"Ruth," spoke he, "your father knew the king had not forgotten you, though that the deed was planned so soon was hid. He has ridden to Borsippa to see if Imbi-Ilu will shelter you at the temple of Nabu. If we await his return, it will be too late. The shadows are falling already. You must quit this house without delay."

"I am ready," she answered, but she spoke mechanically, not knowing what she said.

Old Simeon, the porter, had approached, his honest face all anxiety for his betters. "My mistress is in trouble? Zerubbabel brought ill news?" he ventured, not presuming more. But Isaiah ordered sharply:—

"Let the closed carriage be made ready at once."

"The closed carriage? For the mistress? My Lord Daniel commanded—" hesitated the worthy; but Isaiah's tone grew peremptory. "Daniel's commands weigh nothing now. Were he here, he would order the same. No questions; hasten."

The stern ring in the young man's voice ended all parley. Simeon shuffled away to rouse the stable grooms, and Isaiah turned once more to Ruth.

"Beloved, we must drive to Borsippa at once. Take what clothes you need, nothing else. No tarrying. Each instant is worth a talent."

"And this house? The room of my mother? The thousand things of my glad life—all left behind?"

The tears would come again. Ruth was weeping now—bitterly, but not from dread of Belshazzar. Events had raced too fast these last few moments to leave room for the greatest griefs or fears.

"Trust that Jehovah will send you back to them, in the fulness of His mercy. He is more pitiful than even Daniel your father."

She did as bidden; in the turmoil of emotions, at least some sorrows were spared her. The maid-servants stared at their mistress, as she flew about her well-loved chambers. The little bundle was soon ready,—so little! And so many girlish delights and trinkets all left behind. Isaiah's voice was summoning her. The carriage was waiting in the yard. Daniel had not taken his swift pair of black Arabs in the chariot, and for these Isaiah thanked his God!

Ruth darted one glance about the court—the well-known balcony, the drapery hiding the loom, the swallows flitting in and out of the eaves, a thousand dear and homely things, so familiar she had forgotten how much she loved them—one last sight; when could she see them again?

"The servants,—my friends,—I must say farewell," she pleaded; but Isaiah shook his head.

"You must leave with as little commotion as possible. The Most High grant we have not tarried too long!" He lifted her almost perforce, and thrust her upon the soft cushions inside the carriage. She heard him tying the door to the wicker body, to secure against sudden and unfriendly opening. The only light that came to her was from the little latticed window in the roof, through which she could see only sky. She heard Isaiah leap upon the driver's platform, in front, beside Abner, one of the stoutest and trustiest of her father's serving-men. The courtyard gate creaked open. The carriage rumbled forth. "Abner," sounded Isaiah's voice, "if ever you drove with speed, drive now. To Borsippa, to the temple of Nabu!"

The lash cracked; the restless horses shot away eagerly, the heavy carriage lumbering behind. Soon all around them buzzed the traffic of the streets. Onward, onward they drove, till Ruth ceased counting the time. Then at last the truth and her wretchedness fully dawned on her. She felt a weakness, a misery words may not express. She laid her head on the cushions and wept, as might a little girl.

CHAPTER V

If Bel-Marduk, "father of the gods," reigned supreme in his temple opposite the royal palace, he was not without rival. Older than the "Lofty House" of Bel rose the venerable *ziggurat* "*E-Zida*," the "Eternal House" of Nabu of Borsippa, "god of wisdom." Time was when Nabu had been the guardian god of all Babylonia, and his priests still refused to yield to the supplanting Bel more than a nominal concession of supremacy. Unlike the great city sanctuary, this temple in the quiet southern suburb sprang out of a great grove of nodding shade trees, girded about with pleasant gardens. A sluggish canal crept under the shadow of the terraces of the sacred tower, and mirrored the rambling brick buildings and leaf-hung walks of the temple college. For here at Borsippa was the most famous, as well as the oldest, university in all the fair land of the Chaldees. From time immemorial students had listened here to lectures on astrology, the science of omens, and the interpretation of dreams. Vainly had Avil-Marduk striven to raise his own temple-school to an equality with that of Borsippa. Were not these paths beside the canal hallowed by three thousand years of academic tradition? Had not every famous demon-caster, for more generations than could be told, learned his art under the shadow of this *ziggurat*? Then again, while Bel was fanatical, Nabu was tolerant. Avil moved heaven and earth to ruin the Hebrews, while Imbi-Ilu, pontiff of Borsippa, was Daniel's bosom friend, and his under priests openly declared that they hated Bel-Marduk quite as much as they did Jehovah. Of late the coldness between the two pontiffs had almost turned to open hostility; the king and court paid homage to Marduk, the city at large sent most of their gifts to Nabu. And within recent days Imbi-Ilu had more than once given offence even to the king by harbouring inside the temple precinct persons whose arrest had been urgently commanded; Belshazzar had fumed, and muttered threats, but Imbi was obdurate. There was the law,—graven on two stone tablets, by King Sargon I., a potentate three thousand years departed,—denouncing curses upon the body, goods, kinsfolk, and soul of the man or king who should dare to molest a suppliant that had once passed the boundary stones, which were set one furlong on every side of the enclosure of Nabu. The king had raged, but was helpless; not even the "son of Bel-Marduk," as he boasted himself, could abolish a privilege like that.

But on the afternoon in question, none would have dreamed that aught save studious repose brooded over quiet Borsippa. The lectures were ended. The boys in the lower school had flung away the tablets on which they had been copying the old dead language of the Akkadian classics.[3]

Teachers and pupils had wandered forth to enjoy the cool of the evening. From the crest of the great temple-tower drifted the chant of the litany to Nabu:—

"Lord of Borsippa,

Thy command is unchangeable like the firmanent.

In the high heavens thy commandment is supreme!"

So the chant had risen for four thousand years, each evening; so it would be repeated, unless all omens were profitless, for as many more. Dynasties might come and go,—the worship of Nabu endured forever!

Upon the housetop of one of the larger buildings, close by the gate of the wall enclosing the sacred precinct, two men in deep discussion were seated. The roof-tiles were covered with soft carpet, a yellow canopy stretched overhead, there were cushioned stools and divans—a cool and pleasant spot to lounge and rest.

But the two were not lounging; their talk had lasted long. The one, Daniel, had drawn his stool close beside the couch of the other, and was speaking earnestly.

"We have debated before, we debate again,—to little profit. You have been a true friend, Imbi-Ilu; the difference in our faith has never stood betwixt us. You have done what you could to abate the persecution of my unfortunate people,—in vain, but I thank you."

The high priest looked concernedly upon his friend. He was an eagle-visaged, majestic man, who bore his years lightly, and whose white locks sprang out all around his forehead, like the mane of a lion.

"It is as you say," he answered soberly, "yet I deserve no praise. Avil-Marduk urges on Belshazzar against the servants of Jehovah, as being the weakest of the gods opposed to the supremacy of Marduk. Soon he will try to crush Nabu himself. I have acted in self-protection. But this is old chaff; all the wheat was long since winnowed out of it."

"Well do I know that," replied the Hebrew, bitterly; "we are being pushed to bay, you Babylonians as well as I. Avil-Marduk has made the king entirely his tool; almost I think he seeks the throne himself, nought less."

Imbi nodded gloomily. "I believe you;" then, a shade more lightly, "but you, O Daniel, are under some greater constraint than distant anxiety for your people. By your own god, whom I much reverence, tell me truly, what brings you now to Borsippa? Since you saved my life, with those of the other wise men, because we could not reveal to Nebuchadnezzar his dream, have we not been sworn comrades, in good and in ill? Speak freely. Your wish?"

"Your friendship may be indeed tested," quoth the other, still soberly; "the king is none too much your friend to-day. If you grant my wish, he will neglect no occasion against you."

"By Nabu!" cried the pontiff, affecting carelessness he did not feel, "you interest me. Tell it out. But not yet." He snapped his fingers loudly; a white-robed servitor appeared. "This way, boy! Bring my Lord Daniel the oldest and coolest of the wine that came yesterday from Larsam, and a platter of honey cakes. He has driven far, and is weary." Then to Daniel, "No excuses. No sorrow is doubled by a cup from my own vineyard."

"Another time," remonstrated the minister. "I have not come hither to make merry; I must be back to Babylon with all haste."

"Not sleep in Borsippa? Your little goddess Ruth will not weep her sight away in your absence?"

"Ruth!" Daniel had started at the name; but, as if there were an omen in the word, there sounded a sudden rumbling and jarring in the brick-paved road outside the temple precinct, the noise of a heavy carriage at a headlong speed, the cracking of a whip, shoutings and cursings, all rising together. When before had a like din roused the peaceful suburb? Imbi sprang to the parapet and stared across in wonder.

"God of Borsippa," he swore, "have we a chariot charge!"

The clamour swept nearer, broken now by a yell of keenest pain, followed by a great shout from the younger priests and students watching from below.

"Nabu save him! The wheel has crossed his body!"

"Eunuchs! The king's eunuchs! They violate the sanctuary!" bawled many more, with a scamper of feet through the gateway.

"In Jehovah's name, what is this!" cried Daniel, leaping up beside Imbi; but the pontiff had just time to clutch at his friend, as he tottered almost in a swoon. The noise below grew sevenfold.

"Down! He has smitten Mermaza!"

Imbi was again at his post. A closed carriage had lumbered in at the gateway, the horses panting and steaming. The pontiff started in turn, when he saw a young man leaping from the driver's platform, still clutching tightly his long whip.

"Isaiah the son of Shadrach, and lifting Ruth the Jewess from the carriage! Why this tumult? Some fearful deed!"

The minister had recovered and stood at the pontiff's side. He was again self-possessed. "Let me know with what the Lord God has visited me," was all he said, and waited silently, as a breathless young priest rushed up to his superior, never so much as salaaming.

"Master! a frightful outrage. The royal eunuchs have pursued these fugitives past the boundary stones to our very gates. They attempted violence, and now clamour without, demanding their prey!"

Imbi turned very deliberately, took his white peaked tiara from the divan, and set it on his head.

"Gross sacrilege, indeed, Merdovah; impossible that his Majesty should authorize such violence!"

More priests and students were howling in the yard below: "Away with the eunuchs! To the canal with them! Avenge the insult!"

"Master," remonstrated the messenger, "except you quiet the temple folk, expect a riot. They are maddened and furious."

Imbi leaped upon the divan beside the balcony. "Below there, silence! What is this tumult?" The voice of the superior produced instant stillness.

"You there, Hasba, speak for all. Why is this carriage here, and these eunuchs?"

The priest addressed, a gaunt, athletic man, stepped forth from the crowd of fellows clustered around the gate.

"Why it is here, I know not, but I saw this,—the carriage approaching at topmost speed from Babylon, and many of the royal eunuchs pursuing on foot, crying loudly and calling to passers-by to aid. When they passed the boundary stone, the carriage slackened, as being in safety; and we looked to see the eunuchs halt. Not so,—they impiously followed after, and two snatched at the heads of the horses. Isaiah the Jew flogged them with his whip. The wheel passed over one; nor did my Lord Mermaza escape the mire. They are without the gate and still threatening."

"They may well threaten," spoke Daniel, hoarsely, at the pontiff's side, "for the king seeks Ruth for his harem. I came to Borsippa to ask sanctuary in her behalf. Be your god Jehovah or Nabu, fail not now!"

The civil-minister was very pale, but Imbi-Ilu flashed back proudly, "If I yield to Mermaza and his vermin, let the 'Eternal House' find other master." Then he turned again to those below. "This is no common sacrilege. Who is this crying so shrilly, 'Entrance'?"

"The master of the eunuchs himself. Shall we not buffet him to death?"

"Not so; admit him, but none other. Bring him here upon the housetop, with Ruth the Jewess, and Isaiah. Let them answer face to face before me."

In a moment a bevy of priests had ushered three persons before their superior: Isaiah, with flushed face and eyes that still darted fire, Ruth, whose cheeks were scarce less white than her dress, and the "very supreme" chief eunuch. The last was sadly lacking in dignity, for his purple-embroidered robe was rent and mud-splashed, and across his forehead spread the long stripe where the lash had marked him. As Ruth and he confronted one another, she shrank in dread behind her betrothed; but the scowls and muttered menaces of the priests about made even the venturesome eunuch cautious. There was an awkward silence before Imbi spoke.

"Well, my Lord Mermaza, has it slipped your mind that there is a certain law, old as the *ziggurat*, concerning the rights of sanctuary of the precinct of Nabu?"

Mermaza's perpetual smile had become a very forced grin indeed; he looked downward, without replying.

"And is it not also true," went on the other, haughtily, "that whosoever transgresses the right of the god incurs the wrath of all the host of heaven? He is 'devoted,' given to Namtar the plague-demon, and her fiends; his life forfeit, his soul cast into Sheol. Is it not thus, my lord?"

Mermaza had recovered enough wits to attempt an answer.

"Right, most reverend pontiff. But I seek no fugitive criminal. In performance of my duties I pursue one of his Majesty's runaway slaves, who can claim no right of sanctuary."

"A slave of the king? Where? We will never shelter such!" And Imbi stared about in well-affected astonishment.

Mermaza fumbled in his bosom, and produced a small clay cylinder, which he handed to Imbi, bestowing at the same moment a gleeful leer upon Ruth.

"His Majesty's own seal—read."

The pontiff read aloud deliberately:—

"*Belshazzar, 'King of Sumer and Akkad,' to Mermaza, 'Master of the Eunuchs':* You are commanded at the first convenient season to seize, and take to the royal harem, a certain maid, one Ruth, the daughter of Daniel the Hebrew. And hereof do not fail, on peril of your head."

Imbi examined the document the second time, and handed it back to the eunuch with a salaam of ironical reverence.

"Noble friend," quoth he, with mock politeness, "explain, I pray you. In what part of this warrant does his Majesty command you to set at naught the right of sanctuary, and commit gross sacrilege?"

But Mermaza, beneath whose veneer of urbanity lay a hasty and arrogant temper, answered with rising gorge:—

"This is no answer, priest; obey the king! Do you refuse to surrender the wench? Think well before you reply—the king's wrath—"

"Daniel," remarked Imbi, turning his back on the eunuch, "is it your desire that your daughter go to the palace?"

"By all you revere, by our bonds of friendship, no!" The Jew started to fall on his knees, imploring. But Imbi faced Mermaza, with a lordly gesture.

"Go back to the palace, and say that I will send Ruth the daughter of Daniel hence, only on her father's personal or written command. Low indeed is Nabu sunken if at barking of hounds of your litter he were to turn suppliants away!"

"The slave of the king—keep her at your peril!" threatened Mermaza, growing desperate, for his position was anything but enviable.

"A slave? When before in the royal harem? Where is the bill of sale from her father? Is she not freeborn?"

"She is a Jewess,—despiser of Nabu!" cried the eunuch, launching his last shaft. A yell of derision from all the priests answered him.

"Friend," answered Imbi, smoothly, "you are so dear a companion to Avil-Marduk and *he* reverences Nabu so exceedingly, that these words drop indeed fitly from your lips."

Mermaza swung about and faced Daniel and Isaiah.

"I see the pontiff is mad," he shouted, his thick cheeks reddening. "Do you Jews hear reason. For this resistance to the royal decree you shall both rot in the palace dungeons unless the girl is yielded, and that instantly."

Ruth had started forward, outstretching her hands.

"Not that, not that, O my father! Say you are willing. I will go."

But Imbi-Ilu sprang between the eunuch and the Hebrews.

"And I, high priest of Nabu of the 'Eternal House,' declare that only as you take oath with all the gods to witness, that Daniel and Isaiah shall be in nowise molested in this matter, will I consent to withhold a criminal charge against you of extreme impiety and deliberate sacrilege. The crime is notorious—twenty witnesses. Let Belshazzar himself save you, if I sow this tale of the outrage done the god, through Babylon."

There was a stern menace in the pontiff's voice that sent all Mermaza's bravado trickling out through his finger-tips. The unfriendly ring of faces about added nothing to his courage. Twice he faltered, while speech choked in his throat. His face was swollen with mortification at his blunder. "Will you swear, toad?" croaked Hasba, at his side; and Mermaza gasped out thickly, "I will swear."

"Good, then," was Imbi's dry comment; "but let us go down to the 'holy room' of the temple. There you shall lay your hands on the ark of the god, and take your oath. I spare no precaution, in taking a pledge of such as you."

The priests swept their victim down the stairs. The three Hebrews were left alone on the housetop, looking one upon another—at first in silence; then a great and grievous cry arose from Daniel:—

"Ah! Lord God of my fathers—must I, who have served Thee so long, see my one child brought to this!"

He opened his arms wide; and Ruth fled into them, there to be locked fast. It was a moment when Isaiah knew he might do and say nothing. He stared vacantly across the parapet, counting the herd of dun-brown sheep a countryman was driving past the temple gate. The sheep would be butchered to-morrow, but they shambled on with never a thought save for the little patches of grass that thrust through the chinks in the pavement. The sheep were happy, but he, Isaiah, the young man, whose heart was thrilled with high and holy things, with visions of the Great King and of His awful throne,—he was beyond words miserable! Darker, darker grew his thoughts; but the voice of Daniel recalled him.

"Isaiah, my weakness is passed. The Lord who saved your father and Meshach and Abed-nego from the flame of Nebuchadnezzar's furnace,— He is our refuge still. We must trust and bear. And not bear only. There is a deed for you to do this night. You have risked much to-day: will you face peril yet again?"

"You know I will walk through death at your least bidding, O my father!"

Daniel put Ruth gently away, and taking Isaiah by the arm, led him beyond her hearing.

"I told you before, I had one last weapon against Belshazzar; but scruples of loyalty restrained me. After *this*," with a weary smile, "all fealty truly ends. Hearken now to each word. You must be all resources to-night. You know the king gives a betrothal feast in the Hanging Gardens, in honour of the Persian princess. All the ministers and captains are invited saving myself—sure sign of the royal disfavour. You must contrive to enter the Gardens after the drinking has made the guards negligent, when you can shun discovery. After the wine has set the feast in confusion, seek out Darius the Persian envoy. God must aid you to have words with him alone. You must act to-night; for though Mermaza's oath may delay his revenge a little, none can tell when the stroke may fall, and we be helpless in prison or as fugitives. Tell Darius that I, Daniel, who know all the king's secrets, though they think it not, say that the treaty he makes with Belshazzar is a snare for the feet of Cyrus. The hand of Atossa was asked to lull him into security. Belshazzar negotiates with Amasis the Egyptian for a league against Persia, and Babylonish agents scatter sedition in Media and Carmania. Belshazzar is collecting troops and munitions. His bolt will fall as lightning from a smiling sky."

The younger Jew was startled indeed. "Jehovah Omnipotent! I did not dream this, that Belshazzar's and Avil's perfidy could sink so deep!"

Daniel laughed aloud at his simplicity.

"When you have my years, O Isaiah, you will have sounded the depths of many seas of guile, and never marvel. You are young and trustful. Alas, that you must grow wise! But go now, before Mermaza returns to the palace. Our persons are safe for the moment: and Ruth can find shelter so long as Imbi-Ilu is our friend. But for true deliverance, Cyrus's gratitude and the Persians' might,—the Persians who worship the one God like ourselves,—these are the only hopes."

Isaiah drove away from the temple that evening in a strange mingling of terror, yet of hopefulness. The warm touch of Ruth upon his cheek was still thrilling him, the sweetness of her kiss was on his lips. Was all lost while he was strong and free? And with the fate of his people and of those he loved resting upon him, where was the moment in which to dare to dream of failure? Darius had declared himself his friend; Darius, he felt, he scarce knew why, was already Belshazzar's foe. Why might not Jehovah raise up this prince as a second Moses, to lead His people out of their new and more grievous bondage?

CHAPTER VI

Nightfall—the light of a thousand flambeaux shivered over the great winged bulls guarding the palace gateways. The bulls formed the base of towers faced with brightly enamelled brick, and crowned with masts whence trailed the royal banners. In and out streamed the palace servants—eunuchs of the harem, cooks, grooms, chamberlains, guardsmen; sometimes a chariot thundered through at a gallop, bearing a nobleman to Belshazzar's banquet. As one peered inward from the gate, he could see the whole broad court of the king's house lit bright as day by cressets and bonfires. The pictured tiles on the inner walls displayed their lion-hunts, battles, processions, and sieges, so that he who regarded them closely could learn all the history of Babylon for a hundred years by a mere circuit of the court. But Khatin, the royal executioner, and two cronies, who sat drinking wine between the feet of a winged bull, had little heed to give to departed glories. Khatin was a stout muscular giant, with thick, black hair and beard shining with strong pomade and butter. His speech was gruff as the bay of a hound; and the two eunuchs, Nabua and Khanni, who divided with him the tankard of Armenian white wine, regarded him with awe, as being the person who might be the last to converse with them, in case his Majesty found them disagreeable.

"I tell you," declared the headsman, dipping his cup for the fifth time, "that Persian Darius is a pretty fellow. I dearly love a man of his spirit. You heard the story? The worthy Igas came near to scraping my close acquaintance. By Marduk! why was the envoy so tender-hearted as not to ask for his head?"

"Surely," ventured Nabua, "you have nothing against the captain. He only flogged a dirty Jew, and a second Jew interfered. But for Darius, this last, Isaiah they call him, would have been the one to speak with you."

Khatin gave a hoarse laugh. "Jews? They are mice. Small glory in beheading vermin. Give me men of spirit, my dear eunuch, men of parts, like Igas-Ramman. Ah! You cannot know the satisfaction of feeling the sword go through a stout, stiff neck."

"Ugh!" grunted the others, feeling their own heads none too firm on their shoulders; and Khanni began soothingly, "Now, by Istar, you would never do the last offices for a friend—for us, by example?"

The executioner burst into a braying chuckle. "Ah! my swallows, my lambs, the more I love a man, the more I love to be by at the end. My father-in-law, Sadu-Rabu, dear man, must needs turn robber; to this day I pride myself on my neatness. 'Beloved Sadu,' said I, 'be content; you have my best art for a smoother journey to the "Mountain of the World" than the late vizier.'"

"Ugh!" grunted the two again, very unhappy; and to turn the drift Khanni interposed, "But you began by praising the Persian?"

"Yes, a man of fine spirit—a very pretty neck—by Samas, an exceeding pretty neck! I wish I were in Susa, as Cyrus's executioner, just for the hope of testing it; there is small chance of Belshazzar needing me to attend to an envoy."

"They say," answered Nabua, "Cyrus has little use for his headsmen. The Persians all love him; they keep the laws, and there are no executions for days together."

"Then, by Allat, queen of Hades," cried Khatin, in disgust, "Cyrus is no king! Hark you! Some day I will plot treason and wear the royal cap myself. Then how many ministers will I have? Just one—an honest headsman. A king and an executioner—the one to begin, the other to finish—these are governors enough for the wide world."

But as Khatin was running on with more wisdom, scarlet-robed torch-bearers began pouring through the gate, with the cry, "The knee! the knee! The king, the daughter of Cyrus, and the Persian envoy!"

The executioner and the eunuchs fell on their knees, to make obeisance. A vast host of guardsmen, priests, and pages came first; and Khatin asked Khanni, "They go to the Hanging Gardens?"

"Yes; the betrothal feast for Atossa will be held there. But they are late. Something has delayed the chief eunuch, and all has waited for him."

"Yet they come at last. See his Majesty and the Persians."

The royal party advanced, hidden by a moving hedge of steel-clad guardsmen and the shadows of fifty torches. Belshazzar was in his state, the jewelled embroideries on his robes worth the plunder of six cities. At his side in the chariot stood Darius, no longer in native dress, but in the splendid Median blue caftan. Men whispered that the Persian looked none too merry, though he seemed to be laughing at some jest from the king. Directly behind the car came a litter—all gold relief work and ivory—borne by eight of the Chaldee nobles, wherein rode Atossa and Mermaza, chief eunuch. When the torchlight flashed on her fair hair and the rose and white of her face, there was a loud shout of admiration from great and small, "A goddess! Istar come to earth! The 'Great Lady' is amongst us!"

Whereupon Atossa leaned from the litter, crying in her sweet, foreign Chaldee, "The Most High bless you, good people, for your praise!" At which there were more cheerings. But Atossa had sunk back on the muslin pillows, and closed her eyes to the torch-glare.

They passed down the inclined plane leading from the palace terrace; all about, outside of the red circle of the flambeaux, stretched the dim masses of the foliage of the "paradise,"—the wide park around the king's house. Then the company came again to a rising way, and a word from Mermaza shook Atossa from her revery.

"Look!" Atossa saw before her, in the faint gloaming, the columned halls of a far-reaching temple, as it were—massive pillars curiously carved and banded, which stretched away along long colonnades, yoked together by heavy vaulting and arches. Marvel enough this would have been, even in Babylon, city of marvels, for these galleries covered a prodigious area; but they were only the beginning of the wonder. Above them, springing from their roof, was a second system of like columns, and arched above this, a third; and above this, so high that the eye grew weary of staring upward, rare Indian palms and stately cedars of Lebanon were spread against a sky dyed red by a hundred great bonfires.

"Do we mount to heaven?" cried the princess.

And Mermaza answered, smiling, "Ah, my lady, I think the 'Mansion of Ea' will be scarce fairer than the Hanging Gardens."

The king had left his chariot, to ascend on foot; but the litter went straight up an easy stairway—higher, higher, till it seemed the climbing would never end. Mermaza told how luxurious chambers were hid in the masses of the lower colonnades; and how a hydraulic engine was pumping unceasingly, raising water from the Euphrates. Then, when at last the crest was reached, suddenly the stars were blotted out by the flaring of innumerable fresh cressets, till the avenues of trees and the almost virgin laurel bowers and fern-brakes glowed as if touched by the dawning.

They had arrived, it seemed to Atossa, upon a broad mountain summit, thickly overgrown with trees, but with here and there a clearing. In and out the trees were flitting white-robed figures, ghost fashion. Scattered about where the torches glimmered brightest, she could see the guests of the king, the nobles of the Chaldees, the chiefs of the priesthoods, their wives, and harem women, all in their gayest robes, crowned with flowers and myrtle wreaths. Out of the shadows of the groves drifted music, now soft and sensuous, now swift and martial, and delicate voices lifted up their song.

But the litter moved onward, through all these leafy ways, until it halted in the open air, at a space on the side of the gardens overlooking the river.

On north, south, and west the woods closed in, dense as the primeval forest: but here all the ground was carpeted with sweet grasses, and there was a clear view eastward over the wide stretch of the city, where the shimmer of its lights answered the twinkling stars on high. There were bowers of wreathed blossoms, ivy, and tamarisk; under these were spread many small tables loaded with food and drink; and behind each table waited a eunuch, dark, silent, statue-like, in gaudy livery.

The king had gone on foot before the litter; now he halted in the centre of this sky-canopied hall at the tallest of the bowers, and they set Atossa down beside him.

"Behold," spoke Belshazzar; "look on these gardens, the like of which is nowhere else in the world. They are given to you. This shall be your feast. These eunuchs are your slaves. We shall all eat of your bounty."

"The king is kind," said the Persian, meekly. "What have I done that he vouchsafes such favour?"

Belshazzar laughed before them all.

"Done? Who demands of Istar anything save the brightness from her eyes and honey from her lips?"

"True," cried fifty at once; "there is no lady like Atossa, like Atossa, daughter of Cyrus."

Then Mermaza ceremoniously handed his mistress to the high seat beside the two couches prepared for the king and Darius.

Now, in the feast that followed, Belshazzar bore himself as if all the world's joy were summed up in that one night; he drank, laughed, jested, and went to no small lengths to make Darius as merry as he. But though the prince paid laughter for laughter, and played his part in the game of repartee, he never forgot that close by sat one for whose sake he would have braved the might of Belshazzar and all the host of the Chaldees. And Atossa laughed with her lips, but could not with her eyes. The Persians dared not glance at one another. How much better if Darius had never come on the embassy! It would now take so long to forget!

During the feast the court poet came before Atossa, with a great orchestra of harpers and dulcimer players. The poet sang a marvellous song, full of all the flowery flatteries of the East, praising the princess:—

"O light of heaven who hast come down to dwell among men,

Thou art exalted in strength!

Mighty art thou as a hyena hunting the young lamb!

Mighty art thou as a restless lion!

Thou art Istar, maiden of the sky!

Thou art Istar, consort of the very Sun!"

So the stately poem ran, and Atossa gave its author her thanks and a bracelet unclasped from her own white wrist. But Mermaza, who served her, noticed that she ate little of all the venison and fresh-caught barbel, of the pomegranates and grapes. And he shrewdly observed that Darius did scarcely better. At last the viands were borne away. Belshazzar turned to Mermaza. "Let them bring the drinking bowls," he commanded.

"Yes, my king," was the answer; "and shall the sacred vessels of the gods of the nations conquered by my lord's predecessors be filled, that we may drink to the health of the princess and the glory of Bel-Marduk?"

"Bring, then, those from the sack of Nineveh, the spoils from the victory over Pharaoh Necho, and from the temple at Jerusalem."

But Atossa touched the king's hand. "May my lord's handmaid speak?"

"Yes," swore he, "though you ask the head of the chief prince of Babylon."

"Then do not bring the vessels sacred to the Jewish Jehovah. For though under different names, Persians and Jews alike worship one God."

Avil-Marduk, close by, was frowning; but Belshazzar answered graciously: "Is this not your own feast? Let Jehovah's vessels lie in their coffers."

So the eunuchs set on the tables huge bowls of chased silver, and into these emptied many wine-jars. A sweet odour was wafted by the night breeze from the perfumed paste dissolving in the liquor. Soon the cups began to go about, and the Babylonian nobles roared their pledges,—to Belshazzar; to his betrothed; to Cyrus, their new ally; above all, to Bel-Marduk, guardian of Babylon, "god of gods, and lord of lords, through whose might their city had waxed great for a thousand years." Belshazzar drank deeply; Darius only touched his goblet; Atossa did not touch it at all.

"Ha, son of Hystaspes!" cried the king, his spirits rising with the wine that was flushing his temples. "You Persians have a custom to take counsel when drunken. Strong wine is a gift from your god, yet they wait to fill your second goblet."

Darius drained his cup, and handed it to the eunuch behind him.

"True, your Majesty; but the spirit of the wine is not to be invoked lightly. On what take counsel? War? We sealed the treaty of peace to-day."

"Yet wine is a gift from Nabu, lord of the wise. Woe to the despiser! Come, evening wanes; they call the third hour of the night from Bel's *ziggurat*. One thing is left."

Belshazzar rose from his couch. There was a great crash of music. The drinkers were silent instantly. The king stepped beside Atossa.

"Look, lords of the Chaldees!" rang his voice. "This hour I proclaim Atossa, the daughter of Cyrus, my affianced wife. One year from this hour shall be my bridal feast. Behold the sovereign lady of the land of Akkad!"

He lifted the blue and white mitre from his head and placed it on the Persian's golden hair. A great shout reëchoed, making the dying torches shimmer.

"The queen! The queen! Hail, all hail, Atossa!"

Darius rose also. No Babylonian knew what the words cost him. He raised his goblet:—

"To Belshazzar, son of Cyrus. May Ahura grant him and his house prosperity for ten thousand years!"

Another shout. Avil-Marduk, leading the rest, leaped to his feet, crying:—

"To the favour of Sin, of Samas, of Marduk upon the house of Cyrus, and upon the noble Prince Darius!"

The pledge was drunk amid furious cheering and the clatter of wine-cups; and the king shouted, last of all:—

"To the peace betwixt Persia and Babylon, may it be firm forever!"

More applause. Mermaza was bowing before Atossa:—

"Dread lady, the feast is at an end. All the women will return now to the palace; but, after our custom, the king's nobles will sit over their wine as long as they desire."

Darius had not spoken to Atossa during the entire evening. But he knew that the end had come, and could not see her go without one word.

"My lord," said he to Belshazzar, "I must say farewell to the Queen of the Chaldees. Henceforth she is Babylonian, not Persian. Into your hands I commit her. Yet, with your permission, I will speak with her—for the last time, before she enters your harem."

"Say what you will," came the careless answer.

Darius stood beside the princess's chair. It was only for an instant. Why did his voice sound so harsh and metallic? Why did Atossa seem to fear to look him in the face?

"My lady," said he, "I am at the end of my commission concerning you. I shall be in Babylon for some time upon your father's business. But we shall see each other no more. Farewell; may Ahura the All-merciful grant you peace and every joy. And before all, may you learn to forget the name 'Darius.'"

It was not what he had intended to say; he had thought on these words of parting since the feast began. Why was it his tongue would not move obedient to his will?

Atossa raised her head, gave him one look out of those blue Persian eyes—so blue! Was Mithra's light-robed azure fairer sight than they?

"And may you forget there was a maid named Atossa, who found all Paradise in sight of you. You are right. Time will be kind. Farewell."

That was all she said. They had spoken in their own native Persian, which the rest could not understand. And if the sly Mermaza had thoughts in secret, while he watched them, what did Darius care?

Then they took her away in the litter, after Darius had knelt and kissed the hem of her dress. He found himself beside the king, but ceremony was at an end. Noblemen were wandering from table to table, bawling to the yawning eunuchs for more wine. Avil-Marduk came to the king and entered into a familiar conversation on some matter of repairing the temple at Uruk. Seeing that nothing more was expected of him, Darius craved the royal permission, readily granted, to wander about the gardens.

Only a few steps carried him under the shadow of the woods. The cries of the revellers drifted through the thickets; a pale moon was hanging in the sky; there was an uncertain light on the carpet of moss and turf under the great trees. He almost thought himself, except for the shouting, in the heart of an untrodden wood. He wandered on aimlessly, half in a dream. How beautiful Atossa had been that night! He knew that the pain in her heart was as great as that in his—and his, how great! Would Belshazzar treat her honourably, cherish her as "first queen" in his harem, after the immediate need for propitiating the all-powerful Cyrus had passed? The king had impressed him more favourably that night than ever before; he had shown himself affable and generous. Doubtless his flaring passion for the Jewish Ruth had long since vanished; but what if his desires and impulses always mastered him thus easily?

Darius wandered onward, looking within, not without, until he was roused by stumbling against a brick parapet that marked the outer wall of the gardens. He sank upon the trunk of a fallen tree—for this strange forest had been suffered to grow nigh wild since its creation. The noise of the drinkers seemed to come to him from a great way off. Despite the fact that he had touched little wine, he felt his head becoming heavy. Bred as he was to the life of a Persian cavalryman, able to pillow upon the hardest steppe, the prince was close to falling asleep and slumbering soundly. He was drifting into semiconsciousness; the shouts, the torchlights, were alike fading away. A moment more and he might have slept till daybreak, if not searched for, when a sound of crackling underbrush startled him.

"A deer!" his first thought, the hunter's instinct foremost, and his hand felt mechanically for an absent sword. In an instant he recognized human voices—three forms approaching through the darkness. "Drinkers," he argued; "they leave the rest to enjoy a bowl in secret." And he arose noiselessly, as one of his training could, not desiring to interrupt such a party. Suddenly a familiar voice sounded—Belshazzar's.

"Darius? Where is he?"

And the voice of Mermaza replied, "Almost I can swear he was in the party that went to the chariots for the palace."

"More likely asleep under the tables," came from a third, clearly Avil-Marduk.

"Not there," commented the eunuch; "he was barely civil in his drinking."

"No matter if he is not here," answered Belshazzar. "Faugh! How much longer must I juggle with this marvellous envoy? By Nergal! his only sane talk is of hunting. I grant that he is a fair archer."

"Not comparable with my lord," flattered Mermaza.

"Most headlong and unprincely," added Avil. "Could the king have but seen him this morning rush into strife as a dog after a carcass."

"Hist!" cautioned the king; "what stirs in the thicket?"

Mermaza peered into the dark. As Darius stood, he could have touched the eunuch; but he remained motionless, and Avil-Marduk reassured: "Only a harmless snake. We are more alone here than in the palace, where every wall has ears."

Belshazzar groped his way to the log Darius had just quitted and seated himself. The others dutifully remained standing.

"By Samas!" began the king, as if rejoiced to feel himself free to speak, "we have thus far played the game out well. Marduk grant the sky may remain calm! What do they say in the city concerning Nabonidus, my father?"

Avil laughed softly. "Let the king's heart be enlarged. My underlings tell me the people say, 'Though the public records still run in the good Nabonidus's name, he is grievously stricken by the "madness-demon"; and praised be Istar who sends the noble Belshazzar to replace him!'"

"If the tale spreads that Nabonidus is in sound health, shut up in Tema, what then?"

"Many things, my lord,—revolt, mutiny in the army; but nothing shall leak. In a year you will be firmly set upon the throne and can mock at all rumours. Only I fear the two men we have looked askance at for so long, Imbi-Ilu and Daniel."

"Daniel!" exclaimed the king, as if struck by a sudden suggestion. "I had forgotten about his wench. She is at the harem, of course, Mermaza,—you shall bring her to me in the morning."

There was a long and very awkward interval before the eunuch found courage to stammer:—

"Pardon, River of Compassion,—I, the least of your slaves—"

"She *is not* at the harem?" demanded the king, threateningly.

What followed, Darius did not well comprehend, thanks to the darkness, and the mingling of Mermaza's snifflings with Belshazzar's curses and oaths. The Persian imagined the eunuch had fallen upon his knees, and was almost pleading for his head. It sufficed that substantially the full story of the fruitless pursuit of the Jewess, and the defiance of Imbi-Ilu, was gasped out at last. When it was finished, Belshazzar swore madly.

"Now as Marduk lives, I will have the life of Daniel by another day, and pluck his daughter—"

"Peace, your Majesty," interposed Avil, abruptly. "Will you raise all Babylon in an uproar? Believe me, Daniel is a power, even as against you, my king. Men may think him old, honest, unsuspecting; but I know better.

He is rich, like all his accursed race. The city folk worship him. Imbi-Ilu can rally half the priesthoods, as many as are jealous of Bel-Marduk, in his behalf. And again beware; for raise a wind that will blow into the Persian envoy's ears that you are seeking the maid, and when will he trust oath of yours again? I pray all the gods he hear nothing of Mermaza's rash blunder this day."

"The envoy!" grunted Belshazzar. "What does he see and know while in Babylon? No bat is blinder to all save his sport."

"The king is mistaken," admonished Avil, smoothly, "if he thinks Darius utterly witless. I have watched him, and I boast to be a judge of men. When not in liquor, he is deep and crafty beyond appearance. Do nothing to offend him till the proper time; and as for the Jew's daughter, let the king wait. Mermaza can find many another as likely maid, sold in the market for twenty shekels."

"No, by Samas!" asserted Belshazzar, testily. "I wish for no fowls out of that flock. Whatsoever I once set my heart on, that will I possess, though all the plague-demon's sprites rage round me. I have sworn to gain the girl, and were she ten times less comely than she is, no power of man shall say to the king of Babylon 'nay.'"

Avil coughed, it seemed derisively, and spoke in an authoritative tone wondrously disrespectful to a crowned monarch:—

"Lord, we have many things to think of before wasting time or sleep on a slip of a girl. When the father is snug in the palace prison, we can give thought to the child. Yet give me time, your Majesty, and I will weave a net for Daniel, and his daughter, too; but make no new attempt on her for the present. Again I repeat, nothing to offend the Persian."

"Now, by Allat's fiends!" cursed Belshazzar, "must it be the Persian, always the Persian? I grow weary dissembling; yet I do it well?"

"Excellently well," soothed Avil, who felt he might be stepping too far. "But consider once more: touch Daniel before there is proper occasion, or outrage the envoy, and abroad we have war with Cyrus, and at home all Babylon buzzing about the palace in revolt. Gently, my king, gently! Remember that your government is not two months old."

"Daniel the Jew!" repeated Belshazzar; "the Jew! I do not know why I hate that race so utterly. They are a stiff-necked people, sticking to their Jehovah-worship like flies at the mouth of a wine-jar. And the Persians are like them. Oh, that they all had one neck, that Khatin might cut it!"

"Let the king's liver be at peace," began Mermaza, comforting; but he took a step backward. Darius, behind a shrub, had been unable to stir hand

- 53 -

or foot from the beginning of the conversation, for the least sound would have betrayed. His cheeks had flushed hot when he heard his own name spoken; he had swelled with utter wrath when he knew that the pledge touching Ruth had been given only to be conveniently broken. Mermaza's arm swung at a careless gesture, and brushed the Persian's face. A shout, and Avil and Belshazzar had leaped upon the eavesdropper before he could escape in the dark.

"Conspirators! Assassins!" Avil-Marduk was howling. "Help, guards! The king is beset!"

But the royal wine had laid half the attendants low with unseen arrows, and the wits of the rest moved very slowly. There were answering cries from the distance, torches tossing, commands thundered; but it was nothing easy to find one's way in the wood. Avil had gripped the Persian round the throat, so that for an instant he gave not one gurgle; but when Darius once put forth his strength, the three found they had bayed a lion indeed. With his left fist he smote over Mermaza, so that the eunuch went down with a groan. The chief priest nipped fast, but the Persian tore away his fingers, plucked him round the girdle, and flung him sprawling. The king remained. Darius's first impulse was to cry aloud, but thoughts raced fast at that moment. To betray his identity might mean ruin for kingdoms. For an instant prince and monarch grappled. Belshazzar's fingers closed like talons of steel, but Darius had not been vainly trained to wrestle. Twice he lifted Belshazzar, and the king clung to the ground; the third time, just as Avil-Marduk was staggering to his feet, Belshazzar's foothold spun from beneath him, and he fell heavily upon the greensward. There were shouts now, torches coming nearer.

Darius could see them flashing on bright steel.

"Murderers!" bawled Avil. "The king is slain!"

Darius took a great bound into the thicket, a second, a third; then ran swiftly as a cat, and as silently, onward in the dark. His long Median cloak caught on a thorn bush and was whisked from his shoulders before he realized it. To recover it in the gloom and danger was impossible. "Ahura grant," ran his prayer, "none may find it and recognize!" Many of the drinkers had staggered from their wine and were wandering about, shouting, "Murder! Save the king!" but their pursuit was aimless. Yet he saw men staring at him as he ran back toward the banqueting area. Who was this at the royal feast without a courtly garment? None recognized him as yet, but he knew that his condition, if he remained, must excite speedy comment. He was a stranger to the place, and wandered vainly about, seeking the exit, and only running on new groups of frightened eunuchs and tipsy guardsmen. His position was becoming serious, when of a sudden he was startled by a hand plucking at his elbow.

As he started, a familiar voice sounded in his ear:—

"My lord, do you not know me? Your servant, Isaiah the Jew. My lord is in trouble. What may I do for you?"

The prince wasted no words. "In Ahura's name, lead me down from these gardens and away from all these people before I am recognized."

"Willingly," came the answer. "I know this place as well by starlight as at noonday. We are near the private staircase by the northern wall of the gardens." And Isaiah led away into a winding path between dark shrubbery. In a moment they were at the head of a long, narrow stairway that wound downward and was lost in the gloom below. There were two spearmen on guard at the upper landing, but both had long since invoked the wine-god over-piously, and were stretched prone and helpless. Isaiah gave them only a sniff of contempt. He plucked a flickering flambeau from the wall, and guided the Persian downward—a weird and uncanny descent. Above there were shouts and commands; and before they had put twenty stairs betwixt them and the landing, there came a cry from over their heads.

"Guard this exit! These swine are drunken; the assassins may have fled this way!"

"Speed, my lord," admonished Isaiah in a whisper. The sound of many feet following made them descend by bounds. Well it was that their pursuers were deep in their cups, and they themselves were sober. At the foot of the stairs there were two more guards, each as prone and senseless as their fellows on high.

"The danger is at an end, my prince," declared Isaiah; "they can suspect nothing now."

He led the Persian by a second dark circuit under the colonnades of the lowest stage of the gardens to where they had left the carriages at the beginning of the feast. Here none met them, though there was still much din from the gardens. Darius told himself that if the king of Babylon and his lords often feasted thus, not fifty sword-hands would be found sober if an enemy attacked the palace on such a night. They found no chariots waiting to bear the royal guests back to the palace. And Isaiah remarked, with a shrug of the shoulders:—

"None expect them, my lord. Good Babylonians drink all night."

"All the better. Guide me back to the palace in secret."

So the two walked back together, and a man need not be wise to imagine what the Persian told the Jew, and the Jew told the Persian.

At the great gate of the palace they met more drunken guards, and Isaiah conducted Darius to his own chambers, where at last they found the Persians of the prince's suite moderately sober.

"Let us pray the one God, my friend," were Darius's words at parting, "the one God we both fear, for strength and wisdom beyond that of man. A great work lies before us, and by His help we will bring low the 'Lie' whose seat is this great Babylon!"

CHAPTER VII

As the afternoon waned, Nur-Samas's beer-house buzzed louder and louder, until a stranger might have deemed it one vast beehive. The jolly liquor and the bouncing serving-maids about Sadasu, the hostess, were twin lures that stole the stamped silver out of the pouches of the most wary. The room was large, cool, and dark. Stools were scattered about in little groups, every seat occupied with its toper. In the hands of each was a sizable earthen jug that was replenished by the girls as often as its holder snapped his fingers or clapped his hands. Everybody was talking at once, with little heed whether his neighbour was also talking or listening. All were trying to barter broad jests or roaring at them, though scarce a man or woman there but was too tipsy to tell a straight story or understand the point of what was told them.

When Khatin, the executioner, went down the stairway to enjoy his afternoon tankard, he found Gudea, the lean "demon-ejector," and Binit, his angular wife, who acted as hired wailer at funerals, both with their noses deep in their cups, and they only lifted them when Khatin drew his stool close by theirs, and began to tell of the mysterious attack that had been made on the king's own person at the great feast.

"A fearful atrocity!" the headsman was bewailing; "and the worst of it all is that no one has yet been laid by the heels and brought to me for it. Only two heads sheared to-day—wretched eunuchs who fell out with the queen-mother Tavat-Hasina. I grow sluggish for lack of work."

"Poor Khatin!" commiserated Binit. "Yet sympathize with Gudea; for two days he has not cast out a single 'sickness-demon,' and I have only wailed at one funeral, that of the rich old goat Isnil, who died of sheer age. The city grows impious and healthy. Men give up calling in an honest wizard when sick, and trust to roots and herbs and those horrible Egyptian doctors. The gods must grow dreadfully angry. The Jews still refuse to worship Bel and Nabu, despite the forced labour, and this makes heaven yet more furious. Alas! Such evil times!"

Khatin raised his head, with a chuckle.

"Now by all the host of heaven!" professed he, "I think the gods must get on excellently well, even if a few less shekels are wasted on such worthy servants as you, my dear Binit and Gudea. They *do* say that even if the gods grow furious, when one really longs to be rid of a sickness, it is safer to trust the Egyptian doctors than the most noted wizard in all Babylon."

"Khatin," admonished Gudea, rising in his dignity, "you call yourself my friend; understand that if you call down the wrath of the gods by your blasphemies, you need expect no help from me to avert their rage."

"No offence, brother," responded the headsman, as soothingly as he knew how. "Here, girl, fill the noble exorcist's jug again, and put it on my reckoning. A long pull now,—to the confusion of every Jew and traducer of the gods! Ha! What a happy life this would be, if it were all one round of quaffing palm-wine."

"You are very generous," remarked Gudea, appeased. "I swear these last skins Nur-Samas had sent up from Sirgulla are delightfully heady. My crown already begins to go round like a chariot wheel. You are an excellent man, my lovely Khatin, a most excellent man! By Marduk, I love you!" He had pulled his stool beside that of Khatin, put his arm around the executioner, and rocked to and fro, displaying his affection.

Khatin likewise, feeling the liquor loosening his tongue, began to grow confidential.

"Hist!" admonished he, "I am in a great way to be consoled. Do you know there is a rumour around the palace, about Daniel—"

"Daniel the 'civil-minister,' the great Jew?" demanded Binit, jerking her nose out of her jug.

"The very same," grunted Khatin, chuckling again; "it is reported that Avil-Marduk—"

Before he could finish the sentence, which all around had stopped drinking and talking that they might hear, a call came down the stairway from the street entrance.

"Where is Gudea the exorcist?" The wizard rose, not too tipsy to answer:—

"I am he. Who are you? What do you wish?"

"I am Joram, son of Saruch, the rope merchant," came the reply. "My father is again torn by convulsions. Terrible demons are rending him. Hasten! Come and cast them out."

Gudea put on a professional tone at once.

"Take comfort, excellent youth; you command my best skill. Yet my time is valuable; in justice to my wife I must ask five shekels."

"Say ten, if only the demons never return."

"Will you come also, my Khatin?" said Gudea, adjusting his long robes. "You shall see my spells accomplish that of which no Egyptian dreams. And you, wife, hasten home, bring the incense pots, aromatic herbs, cloves, garlic, the wool of a young sheep, and some raw serpent's flesh. We shall need a powerful exorcism." And with that Binit went her way, while Khatin followed his friend into the yet busy street.

The young man who had summoned them bore indeed a Jewish name; but, as Gudea explained, he and his father Saruch were men of true worldly wisdom. If they still prayed to Jehovah, they had long since cast off their native bigotry; they brought offerings to the temples, and knew that in times of illness one must run for the wizard. As idlers recognized Gudea, and the whisper spread that he was headed for Saruch's house, a great crowd followed, for there were few better sights than a skilful incantation. So, with a long train of pedlers, donkey-boys, guardsmen off duty, and their kind, the exorcist came to the dwelling of the rich Jew, beside the quays. The courtyard was open, and soon thronging, but Gudea ostentatiously bade the servants to clear a space and bring forth their master. The convulsions were over for the moment. They laid Saruch, ghastly pale, and scarce conscious, on the cushions in the sunlight of the court. Gudea knelt, blew in his nostrils and ears, and rose with a long face. To the anxious wife and son he announced solemnly:—

"Good people, you have indeed done well to summon me. Nothing less than the 'Maskim,' the 'seven arch-fiends of the deep,' have entered into the worthy Saruch." Whereupon all the jostling crowd began to shrink and shiver, though none cried aloud lest the demons quit Saruch and slip down their gaping mouths. But Gudea reassured them pompously. "Be not afraid, excellent friends. The demons are still in Saruch, but I have muttered an infallible spell to control them as they pass out. They will enter no other." The crowd pressed again nearer.

"Alas, noble wizard," began the wife, weeping, "can even *your* skill eject the 'Maskim'?" Gudea drew himself up, offended.

"Were I another exorcist, perchance you might doubt rightly. But am I not the most notable conjurer in Babylon? Fear nothing; you shall yet see Saruch walking before you, well and happy."

"Nevertheless," muttered Khatin, impiously, "it were no harm to call an Egyptian." But Binit had bustled in with divers bundles, on which all cast awesome glances. Gudea unpacked; took sundry earthen pots, filled them with spices, struck fire, and presently from them drifted a thick aromatic smoke, that blew in Saruch's face and set him coughing.

"Back, all of you. Adore the gods!" commanded the wizard. "I will now commence the never failing exorcism of the Maskim."

There was not a whisper, while the conjurer began casting bits of wool, hair, dried flowers, and beans into the fire, each time repeating loudly:—

"Even as the bean is cast in the fire,

Even as the fire consumes the bean;

So may Marduk, chieftain of the gods,

Drive the demons and their spell from Saruch!"

At first Gudea stood still; then, laying off his shoes and rubbing his hands,—token of purification,—he commenced the sacred dance about the sufferer. In the first rounds he moved slowly, his white garments swelling and falling as he turned, while his watchful wife fed the fire with scraps of dry flesh, spices, and splinters of magic woods. Gudea recited incantation after incantation, calling on Marduk, Istar, Ea, and every other god to aid in driving the "seven fiends" out of Saruch's throat. He continued, until suddenly the sick man began to quiver and foam at the mouth.

"The convulsion again!" moaned the sufferer's wife, starting forward. "Alas! my Saruch!"

"Peace, woman!" thundered Gudea, "will you break the spell? No danger, the fiends are risen in his neck. They struggle against coming forth, but I compel them." The sufferer almost rose from his cushions; his face was black, his eyes bloodshot.

"Glory to Marduk!" howled Gudea, "the spell works. The Maskim depart. Now, wife." Binit leaped to her feet with a screech that sent all the sparrows scurrying from the eaves. Seven times she screamed, until every ear was tingling, and all the time Gudea danced faster, faster, in a narrow circle about Saruch.

"Come out of him! Come out of him! Away, away!" he yelled at each interval in the screeching. The sick man was tottering to his feet.

"Glory to Marduk!" bawled Gudea again, "the fiends are mastered. The final spell now, the infallible incantation."

And every breath was bated while he chanted, still dancing, the age-honoured song of the "Maskim":—

"Seven are they, they are seven!

In the deeps below they are seven;

In the crest of heaven they are seven;

In the low abyss were reared the seven;

Man or woman are none of the seven;

Whirlwinds baneful are all the seven;

Wife or child have none of the seven;

Mercy or kindness have none of the seven;

Prayers and tears hear none of the seven;

Eager for mischief are all the seven;

Sky-spirit conjure away the seven!

Earth-spirit conjure away the seven!"

A final howl from Binit. Saruch's answer was a groan of mortal pain; he reeled, fell.

But the wife and son had rushed to the old Jew, and a fearful cry burst from the woman:—

"Dead! dead!" When she lifted the head, it fell back lifeless. Almost at the same moment the crowd was thrust aside by a heavy hand, and all saw the stalwart form of Isaiah striding toward Gudea, and at the Hebrew's heels a dignified, dark-skinned man, in a spotless white robe.

"Urtasen, the great Egyptian doctor," whispered one fellow to another.

Gudea was standing panting, gazing upon the dead, the widow, and Joram. His jaw was dropped, his eye vacant. Even his own effrontery had failed him. Isaiah plucked him roughly by the robe.

"Make your feet wings, or I will aid you," he commanded. "You have truly raised the 'Maskim' now."

The wizard recovered his tongue.

"Isaiah plucked him roughly by the robe.

"'Make your feet wings, or I will aid you.'"

"Dead?" cried he, incredulously; "he is but in a trance. He sleeps; he will awake in quiet. The demons tore him grievously in departing, but he is not dead."

Urtasen had knelt by the body, examining. Now he looked upward.

"Saruch had an incurable disease. Thoth, the wisest god, could have scarce saved him in the end. But this smoke and bellowing brought on a last convulsion. With treatment he could have lived many years. Now he will wake only at the call of Osiris."

The widow and Joram had leaped upon Gudea.

"Imposter! Juggler!" screamed the Jewess; "*you* boast to cure? Call my husband's spirit back from Sheol, if you may."

In their rage they would have wrung the wizard's neck. Isaiah interposed. "You alone are to blame, Joram—you, false Jew, who have forsaken the faith of your fathers! Jehovah justly requites you. How long have you forgotten our law forbidding dealings with wizards and necromancers? I heard the rumour of Saruch's state, and hastened hither with Urtasen to forestall this viper,"—with a glance toward Gudea,—"but the Most High ordained that I should come late, and you all be dealt with after your sins."

"No more! On my father's soul, no more!" Joram was moaning, while his tears came fast.

"You do well to weep," was the stern retort; "but I have said enough. Now let these servants of the very fiends depart."

Gudea had recovered his composure.

"Luckless people," began he, "it was none other than the counter spells muttered by this Isaiah which ruined my incantation and gave victory to the demons. I accuse him of black magic and murder."

But Gudea had lost all favour with the crowd. A guffaw answered him.

"Ha, scoundrel!" yelled twenty, "do not cover your mummery!" And Khatin added, "Verily, friend, if any murderer needs speech with me, his name is Gudea."

"Out with him!" roared all the onlookers, putting forth rough hands on Binit and her husband.

"No tumult; respect the dead!" implored Isaiah.

"And my ten shekels?" howled Gudea, struggling in the clutch of ten men.

"Let the crows weigh them out to you," groaned Joram, in his agony.

"And may I not engage to wail at the funeral?" pleaded Binit, never setting safety before business.

"Screech at your own," admonished many at once.

Khatin joined the rest in thrusting the necromancers very ungently into the street.

"Good people," said Isaiah to those yet in the court, "this is the house of death. Let all who are needless here go their ways."

"You shall repent this!" belched Gudea, as they haled him away, but none heeded him.

The servants drove the rabble from the court. The portals clanged; the household was left to its grief. Khatin was laughing like a jackass.

"Ah, my wise raven! Ah, my sweetly chirping sparrow! How amiably the demons obey you! Pity they took Saruch's soul with them when they flitted forth."

"The Jew! the Jew and his sorceries!" groaned the wizard.

The roar of the bystanders drowned his protest. Since most had with them a heavy freight of palm-wine, they might have dipped him in the Euphrates; but at this moment a squad of police charged down the street and dispersed them. Gudea, Binit, and Khatin found themselves thrust into a side alley.

"By Nergal! my pot at Nur-Samas's turns sour," cried the headsman, "yet not so sour as your smile just now, dearest brother. That Isaiah is a pretty fellow also, if he is a Jew! A fine neck! Pity I missed him the other day." He turned on his heel. For a moment Binit's tongue flew so fast that she soon stopped for want of breath.

"Our conjuring vessels, the herbs, spices, charms, amulets—all lost. Sheerest theft! Go to the magistrate. Seize Joram, Isaiah, the widow, the—"

"Silence!" commanded her husband. "All this talked in a crowded court? Bel forefend! I could never exorcise another demon for a year. You are a fool!"

"But did I not screech beautifully?"

"Sweetly as the king's musicians, my dear one. But how shall we be avenged on this Isaiah? All Babylon will hear of this. Woe, woe!"

"Avil-Marduk?" suggested she.

"I do not understand you, wife," quoth the wizard, his wits still shaken by the rude events of the hour.

"Are you become senseless as a sick sheep?" cried she, scornfully. "What was Khatin about to say at the beer-house? You know the chief priest would love nothing so much as some ground for new accusations against the Jews. Go to him boldly. Accuse Isaiah of murder by means of sorceries. Say he hated Saruch because he adored our gods of Babylon. The moment your spell begins to work, the sick man falls dead. Isaiah appears the next instant. Clearest proof! If Avil-Marduk can be persuaded to make your cause his own, an accusation supported by him will be true as an oracle; though all the city might mock if you brought the charge alone."

The wizard's eyes were shining with relief and glee, as the inspiration came to him.

"Ah! my Binit," cried he, merrily, "happy the day when Istar made you my wife! Not Ea himself could counsel more craftily."

So it befell that the wizard wended his way in the cool of the evening northward to the precinct of Bel-Marduk, guardian god of Babylon.

The temple of Bel was far more than a shrine perched on the crest of a *ziggurat*. Its walls, outbuildings, and priests' houses covered many "large acres." It occupied a site with the river on the west, the great "Eastern Canal" to north, and on south and east there was ready entrance through the towering gateways, guarded, like the king's palace, by stone lions and winged bulls. Here sleepy priests on watch gave not a glance to the exorcist as he entered. Once past, he found himself in a broad court girdled by a façade of lofty pillars glittering with silver plating and brilliant enamel, and behind the columns all the walls shone with brightly glazed bricks. Burnished bronze glistered on the doors of the many rooms, and Gudea could just see the sheen of jewels inside the "dark room," the great sanctuary at the end of the court, where was guarded the ark of Bel, of which the portal chanced to be open.

Through a noisy crowd of priests, priests' wives, children, and visitors, Gudea wormed his way to the west side of the court, till almost under the shadow of the towering *ziggurat*. Here he was halted by a serving-man guarding a private doorway.

"Hold, friend! Your business."

Gudea made a lowly salaam.

"Excellent sir, be so gracious as to tell whether the high priest, Avil-Marduk, my lord never-to-be-too-much-praised, is willing to listen to one of his slaves who craves his compassion."

The sentinel put his hands on his hips.

"Now, by Bel himself, are you a peasant just from the country? Does Avil have evenings to squander on fish of your spawn? Shall I call the dogs?"

But Gudea knew his game. Down went his hand into a little bag. Up came a silver quarter shekel.

"Not so roughly. I am an honest citizen, as expert a wizard as you will find from Sippar to Erech. If at any time you have need of exorcising a demon—" here the silver changed hands, and the other replied, three shades more affably:—

"Assuredly the chief priest's time is not for all. Still, I will endeavour—"

"Tell him Gudea, the exorcist, desires speech as to certain plottings of one Isaiah, betrothed to the daughter of the civil-minister, Daniel."

The other vanished and returned speedily. "The high priest will speak with you," he announced.

Gudea was led down many darkened hallways, until he entered a small, cool room, where a few lamps already twinkled, where the footfalls fell dead on heavy carpets, and all the walls were bright with blue and white tiles picturing the long-famed combat of Bel and the Dragon. There was very little furniture in the room—a few armless stools, a low table covered with writing tablets. At the extreme end stood a high arm-chair, whereon sat Avil-Marduk himself, for the moment idling over a cup of wine. Old Neriglissor, who had been invited to keep his superior company, sat at the right, on a chair much lower; at the left squatted a negro boy, watching the moment to rise and refill the cups.

Avil-Marduk vouched no sign of recognition until Gudea had come and knelt before the high seat. Then the pontiff raised his eyes.

"You say you are Gudea the exorcist?"

"Yes, noble lord," and the wizard still knelt.

"Stand up, then. State your errand. You have something against Isaiah the Jew?"

Gudea bowed; it was not well to risk long speeches with the great. Avil demanded again:—

"Well, do not waste any time. What is the complaint?"

"Lord," came the reply, "he commits murder."

"Murder?" Avil raised his eyebrows. Neriglissor laid down his well-beloved wine-cup. "But why come to me? Am I the judge? Who is dead?"

"Saruch, the rich rope merchant, by birth a Jew, a most pious servant of the gods, especially of Bel-Marduk."

"Ah, woe!" began Neriglissor; "he gave five skins to us at the last feast. Excellent wine! Cruel murder!"

"And how has this worthy servant of Bel been butchered by Isaiah?" quoth Avil, sternly. "Is justice denied? Where is the magistrate? Can assassins stalk scatheless in our very streets?"

"Alas, lord! Isaiah is worse than those who slay with dagger. What armour can repel the evil eye, the secret incantation?"

"Ah!" Avil dropped his jaw. Gudea felt uneasily that the high priest was very close to a smile. "Well, how did Saruch die?"

Whereupon Gudea launched into a long and tearful narrative of his unlucky exorcism, and how, just as the "Maskim" were mounted to Saruch's throat, Isaiah appeared, and behold! the sufferer was dead. Gudea had seldom seen or heard of a crueller taking off; and, what was worse, it would be vast encouragement to those stubborn Jews to continue to worship their foul demon, Jehovah.

"You bring a sad tale, my friend," patronized Avil, when the wizard was ended. "It is too true that in these days, when faith in the gods is failing and so many noble *ziggurats* are sinking in ruins, your noble art is threatened by these pestilential Egyptians. Your tale is but too common. But this Isaiah is no ordinary scoffer. His connection with the civil-minister makes him trebly dangerous."

"True, lord; and if a blasphemer like him is seen to go harmless, where will be any piety in Babylon? Men serve the gods through fear only. They say, 'If we do not, trouble hastens.' When one mocks, yet prospers, the rest all follow after. The very priests of Bel will starve."

"Oh, such days of impiety!" groaned Neriglissor. "Religion withers like an unwatered palm. When I was a lad, no man dared buy a kid on an 'unfortunate day'; now—"

Avil cut him short.

"You do well to be anxious for the gods, my Gudea; but I have other reasons for wishing the end of these Jews. Not of Isaiah so much as of the civil-minister."

Avil turned to the squatting cup-bearer, and at a motion toward the door the servant salaamed and vanished. The chief priest's eye suddenly fixed itself on Gudea, and seemed to go through him like a sharp sword.

"Now, fellow," and Avil's tone was low, but piercing as his gaze, "are you a rascal of discretion? Can you lie piously? Can you lift your hands, bidding Marduk and Samas strike dead if you are perjuring? Have you the nose of a dog, the teeth of a cat, and the stealth of an adder?"

The wizard hung down his head. The priest, with a single blow, crushed a fly that lit on his palm and snapped:—

"Understand, you are clay in my fingers. At my will I dash you out as this fly. Silence now, or your wagging tongue wags your head off also."

"Ah, lord," answered Gudea, "Bel forbid I should whisper one secret—"

Avil sprang to his feet and paced the room.

"Hark, you knave! I see through you as through Phœnician glass. You will mortgage your soul for ten shekels,—say five rather. If I take oath from you, it will bind while your interest holds, no longer."

"Alas, your Excellency, enemies blast my character."

Neriglissor raised a great laugh, crying:—

"An exorcist of honesty! Hear, Heavens! Behold, Earth! Wonder of wonders!"

But Avil-Marduk ceased pacing.

"My dear wizard," said he, in his oiliest manner, "I am infinitely delighted to have a man of your liver seek me to-night." His voice fell to a confidential pitch. "Great things are afoot. If certain events befall,"—he hesitated,—"Daniel will become a most undesirable man to remain in high office."

"Ah!" Gudea dropped his jaw in turn. Avil ran on:—

"If Daniel were found to have resorted to magic to work harm to Saruch, whom he hated for leaving Jehovah; if many witnesses were found who could swear 'thus and thus the civil-minister slew Saruch with sorceries'; I say, if such testimony were brought against Daniel, it would be most ruinous to his popularity. He might even be brought to pass words with Khatin."

"To suborn witnesses is costly," hinted Gudea, rising to the bait.

"Suborn?" cried Avil. "I did not speak the word. I say, '*If* the evidence were found.'" And then, turning suddenly, his tone lost all smoothness. "I will give you three manehs this night. If one month from to-day Daniel (Isaiah matters nothing) lies in the palace dungeon, I will weigh you two talents. If not—" The exorcist was very uneasy, while Avil's eyes burned through him. "If not, if you play me false, if you fail, I will blow you out as a lamp! A nod from me to the vizier suffices."

Two talents were life riches, but the wizard's heart was thumping when he answered, "Lord, lord, I am a poor man, my skill is small. Some other—"

Avil cut him short again:—

"No grunting now, pig! After telling you this, did you expect me to say: 'Go in peace. Tell the story to all Nana Street'? You shall do as bidden. When the evidence is ready, silent as a tomb you come to me, and I use you and your witnesses in my own time and way."

"And if I fail?" began Gudea.

"Then, by the king's life, you fail only once! No goad to a man's wits like saying, 'Do this, or visit Allat, Queen of the Dead.'"

Avil-Marduk recalled his servant, and had the three manehs wrapped in a napkin given to Gudea. With many protestations and excuses the wizard took his farewell.

"You risk all on this juggler," declared Neriglissor when the fellow was gone. But the chief priest shook his head.

"I know him by rumour to be one of the cleverest rats in Babylon. He will have enough real bricks to build his tale with and make it credible. I have him utterly in my power. Should he confess all to Daniel, who would believe him against my denial? He will not fail."

The "anointer" cast a shrewd glance at his superior.

"You are a man of many devices. When did it enter your head to make use of this exorcist?"

"The moment he opened his business. I had been casting about for many days for a chance like this against Daniel, and was at my wit's end."

"Therefore, if we were not priests, we should say, 'Bel has wondrously favoured us'; but since we are priests, we will preserve our thanksgivings—"

"To ourselves," interposed Avil, dryly; "and now to the other part of my business. You must ride with me to the palace. The king will hold council again."

Neriglissor grew even more insinuating.

"My dear lord, *was* that cloak, found in the shrubbery after the assault on his Majesty, the garment of the Persian envoy?"

But Avil only gave a great shrug with his shoulders. "My very good friend," answered he, "there are some things which if whispered to a gnat would put even my throat in peril. But I can tell you this: the subject of our debate this day might prove wondrously entertaining, if overheard by the 'exceedingly noble' Prince Darius."

CHAPTER VIII

Atossa awoke the morning after the feast with the same aching heart she had carried for more than one weary night and day. She had probably spoken with Darius for the last time. He had sat beside Belshazzar, and all through the feast she had been arraying the two men against each other,—and the All-Seeing knew who found favour in her partial eyes! But the deed was done, and no human chance promised to mend it. Already Pharnaces, the subordinate envoy, had started for Susa to inform Cyrus of the splendour of his prospective son-in-law. For one year Belshazzar could not actually take Atossa as his bride, but she was none the less the inmate of his harem. Life had hitherto been very lovely to the Persian; the turn of destiny that sent her to this gilded bondage had darkened her life utterly. Love lost, kindred lost, home lost,—and only half-known pains before! Small need to say further; enough that, as Atossa looked forth upon the city that day, she saw not one friendly object that made her sense of loss less keen.

Early had come Avil-Marduk to instruct in the mysteries of the Babylonish religion. The high priest, from whose tongue smooth words flowed as readily as oil from the oil-jar, exerted himself to entertain her by recitations of the ancient poems,—how the hero Gilgamesh was sought in love by Istar, and having dared to repulse her, was smitten with leprosy; and how he journeyed to Khasisadra, the Old Man of the Sea, and by him was healed. Avil flattered himself that he declaimed uncommonly well, and had amused his pupil not a little. He did not hear the ill wishes sped after him, when he salaamed himself out of her presence.

Later Atossa was taken to a wing of the palace, where in solitary state ruled Tavat-Hasina, daughter of Nebuchadnezzar, and queen of the deposed Nabonidus. There could be little friendship between the royal ladies. Tavat's political power as queen-mother was still considerable; but she saw in Atossa the rival who would in time strip her of the vestiges of authority, and greeted the other with studied coldness. And Atossa saw merely an elderly woman, tricked out with wig and Egyptian rouges, fleshy through her inactive life, supercilious and querulous because of ennui. Their interview was as brief as the punctilious chamberlains would allow.

The rest of the day was Atossa's own; the king had promised to visit her, but she had small grief when affairs of council prevented. As the first cool airs of the afternoon began to creep over the place, she was pacing the roof of the harem, thoroughly out of temper with herself and all the world. And truth to tell, the Babylonish maids and eunuchs set to wait on her whispered to themselves that the new queen was no more gently disposed than her kingly consort, and it would be only the favour of the gods that could keep them out of Khatin's clutch, if she was always so unreasonable.

Therefore Atossa without difficulty scared them from her presence, and had the harem roof to herself. A delightful place, she would have said in other moods: lifted up above all the earth,—only the *ziggurats* higher. The city lay spread below; she could trace the great Euphrates north and south, until it faded to a darkling thread upon the horizon. The roof tiles had been strewn with white sand and gravel; there were seats, divans, flowering shrubs, and tropical plants in huge earthen vases,—a second hanging garden, scarcely less.

Atossa had thrice paced the length of the long walk, when her eye caught a face timidly upraised from the entrance. She spoke at once,

"Come up, Masistes; I did not command *you* to stay away."

A gray old eunuch shuffled up the stairs, and knelt and fawned around her feet. The face of Atossa had softened as she smiled down on him, though her smile was still bitter.

"Ah! Dear old playfellow, rise up! Have I not been your fosterling since first I could walk? When at Susa or Ecbatana have I passed one day without you close by to scold and grumble over me? And now that all other friends are gone, you alone are left; and I have learned to love none too many new faces here, to wish to keep you quite afar."

The honest fellow thrust his arm within hers,—a familiarity born of lifelong comradeship.

"Ah! Little mistress, you do not right in crying down this wondrous city. Surely, there is naught else like it under heaven!"

"Masistes," said Atossa, looking upon him half playfully, half in anger, "I must have you whipped. Since coming hither you have learned to lie."

"I lie?" he lifted his hands in dismay. "Ahura, Lord of Truth, forefend!"

"Nevertheless," she answered, laughing now, "you speak falsely, praising Babylon. From the bottom of your soul you hate it. How do I learn this? Because I know when you are indifferent to a thing, you are silent; you like it, when you begin to mutter against it under breath; but if you love it exceeding well,—there is nothing you may say of it too ill! But I am open, and I say to you,—and to any who wills to hear,—this city is the abode of *dævas*: *dævas* are all its lords, its priests, its people; and Angra-Mainyu, archfiend, is little fiercer than its king."

"Alas! lady, such speeches make no winds pipe sweeter!"

"Not sweeter? I only know that except I empty my heart to some one, it will burst; and I think no Egyptian doctor could heal that with all his cordials!"

"Come, little mistress, in five years Babylon will have become dearer to you than Susa. What is strange, we hate."

"So has said Darius; but I would answer this: When Belshazzar can love a maid above a lion, I will try to think otherwise."

"But at the Gardens last night was he not all courtesy and compliment? Doubtless his manners are not those of your august father—"

"Silence!" she commanded, truly wrathful now, "speak not of Belshazzar and of Cyrus in one breath! Where is the king worthy to sit beside my father? I say nothing of his power,—but of his tenderness, his mercy. And Belshazzar,"—some force seemed tugging the name across her teeth,—"no doubt he can speak glozing words; but his heart is dark, and under the softest of his speeches you can hear the muzzled roarings of the lion."

The good eunuch began to whimper in sympathy, a great tear on each cheek.

"Alas! lady, all is as you say. Yet you will not curse Cyrus who sent you?"

Atossa's eyes were dry; she held her head up proudly.

"No, I may not curse. I am born a king's daughter,—and therefore a slave,—a slave to the welfare of my people. Better that I should dash my wings and beat out my little life against the bars of this cage, than that thousands of our Aryan sword-hands pour out their blood in war with Babylon. I am but a maid; but I am wise enough to know this,—king's child and peasant have alike one heart, and in it the same pains. Happy for the world, if the grief of the first may spare grief to the thousand others!"

"The world says, 'Let the thousand suffer, that the one may laugh.'"

Atossa threw back her head again. "Yes—so Belshazzar would say, but not Cyrus; therefore, my father is a great king, and Ahura prospers him."

"Peace, little mistress," exhorted the faithful fellow, tenderly; "let us say no more. Verily, your heart is emptied now!"

They paced side by side, measuring the ample circuit of the harem roof, each striving desperately to talk on indifferent matters. Presently they were both startled by a slight scuffling as of feet, in one of the small courts at the farther extremity of the walk. They leaned across the parapet, but the court seemed unoccupied save for a dozen white doves who were plashing in a little fountain, prinking their feathers, and admiring themselves in the rippling water. Atossa tossed a bit of loose mortar downward into the fountain. There was one whir of wings, and the doves returned to their stations. She was turning away, when, as if in answer to her missile, a tiny brick was flung upon the parapet beside her. She looked across—the court was still empty, but the brick was covered with writing. She read these words:—

"If the Lady Atossa is alone upon the roof of the harem, or with those she may trust to the uttermost, let her throw back this letter, as sign that I may mount to her. Some danger must be faced, for the danger of Prince Darius is yet greater."

Atossa knew perfectly well that the stranger who penetrated the harem of the king ran the risk of being sawn asunder. The consequences to herself of a stolen interview might be more than disagreeable. But the princess was in no mood for prudent counsels. Masistes had naught but fears. "What danger could lurk for the sacred person of the envoy? An insolent interloper! Summon help, and give alarm at once."

She would have nothing of his caution. None could overlook the harem roof. The others had been bidden to keep below stairs; a shout could bring aid if there was the least need. "Danger to Darius" whispered by a flitting breeze would have made her open to far more desperate recourses. With a heavy heart Masistes saw her fling the brick down beside the fountain.

A moment of waiting, and forth from the shadow of the wall, directly under Atossa's station, appeared a young man, with a companion in the armour of a guardsman. The first stranger, without word or hesitancy, swung himself upon the thick-stemmed vine that twisted upward to the parapet from the court below,—no easy feat; but he clambered upward with an agility worthy of Darius himself, and landed beside the lady almost before she realized he had commenced ascending. Once mounted, he shot about a single glance in search of some unfriendly eye, then stared abruptly upon Masistes.

"Is this eunuch trustworthy?" he demanded, with no courtlier greeting.

"He will die for me; is that sufficient?" answered Atossa, still wondering, and almost off her guard.

"So the Lord God grant!" The newcomer glided behind a wide tamarisk bush that cut off view from any mounting the stairs. "And the others below are quiet?" he pressed.

"They will only come when I summon them."

He leaned across the parapet, saying something softly to his companion. Atossa did not know the language, but imagined it Hebrew. When he turned to her again, she saw he was a powerful, handsome young man, with a manner of speech not unlike that of Darius.

"Lady," said he in Chaldee, "doubtless you know me not. You were in the closed carriage when his Highness the prince saved Ruth, my betrothed, from the king's lion. Prince Darius deigns to call himself my friend; last night in some slight measure I repaid the debt I owe. To-day I strive to pay more, but I need your aid."

"Good sir," spoke Atossa, her dignity rising, and cautious at last, "he who is Prince Darius's friend is mine; but I know neither your name nor race. At best your errand here is a strange one."

The young man took one step nearer Atossa.

"Lady, are you so fond, concerning Belshazzar, that you seek many tokens to vouch for him who declares himself the foe of the king and the well-wisher of Darius?"

Atossa became yet haughtier. "Belshazzar is my betrothed husband. Will you revile him to my face? Am I not mistress in this palace?"

A nod from her would have sent Masistes to summon help; but without premonition the newcomer held out his finger, showing a ring—on the beryl seal a swordsman was stabbing a lioness.

"When last did your Highness see this?" he demanded, very quietly.

"It was on Darius's finger at the feast last night." And even Masistes, as he looked, stifled the cry that was on his tongue.

"Know, O Lady Atossa," went on the stranger, "that Darius, son of Hystaspes, gave me this ring, after the feast, in token of sure and abiding friendship. Will you hear me now, wherefore I would speak with you?"

"I will hear," answered she, almost faintly, and there was no colour in her cheek. But as she spoke a voice sounded from the hall below, and the young man shrank behind his tamarisk.

"Gracious princess, condescend to honour your slaves by coming down to the luncheon, which is ready."

Atossa sprang to the stairway.

"Have I not bidden you magpies keep silence? Do I not know when I hunger? Begone, or—"

Retreating footsteps told that the menials had not waited for her threat. She turned to the stranger, and faced him fairly.

"Sir," she said directly, "I will believe you are Darius's friend. Say on."

Now what Isaiah told of the adventure of Darius with the king in the Hanging Gardens we will not here repeat. When he had finished, when Atossa knew the height and the depth of the Babylonians' guile, the Jew looked for a scene of terrible agony. He did not know the royal strength of the daughter of Cyrus. Her white cheeks grew yet whiter, but her only answer was, "Yet though I know all this, what profit? Am I not prisoner here? I shall see Darius again, at a time only Ahura the Merciful knoweth. By your own mouth the prince is safe and free."

"He is free, but not safe."

"Not safe? Belshazzar will put forth his hands against the sacred person of an envoy? I cannot believe this guile,—I will not!" Atossa flushed as in the anger of despair. "The king may swear a thousand oaths, as you say, and keep none; but to murder an ambassador were a deed which Marduk and Ramman, his own foul gods, would reward with swift vengeance!"

"Lady," said the Hebrew, gently, "whether Marduk and Ramman may requite or not, Avil-Marduk is the physician who can mingle drugs to soothe the king's conscience. Since morning those who brought me the earlier warnings have borne me this: The king and his council have pondered long over the ownership of the Median cloak torn from the shoulders of the wrestler in the gardens. They have suspicions,—suspicions only; but if they seem well grounded, Avil and Belshazzar are not prone to stickle at trifles with such a stake."

"Jew," Atossa spoke slowly and calmly, "tell me, in what way is the prince to be attacked? Answer truly, as we Persians and your people call on one truth-loving God."

Isaiah's answer was given in so low a tone that Masistes heard none of it. When he finished, Atossa asked aloud.

"And why do you not go to the prince yourself? Why bring all this to me?"

Isaiah smiled bitterly. "Already a net of spies is spread around Darius. This morning I found I was more than suspected. An attempt to meet the prince would have been the signal for my arrest. But Zerubbabel, my good friend, stood sentry at the harem gate, and suffered me to pass. He guards below. The harem is accounted so inviolable, that in mere security it is less watched. Though you may not see Darius, have you no Persian servant who can be trusted to warn? Who dreams that you are to be guarded against?"

"Behold the messenger!" interposed Atossa, turning half playfully to Masistes.

Before Isaiah could answer there were steps again on the staircase, and there thrust itself into view of the fulsome smile of Mermaza.

"Samas pity me!" smirked that notable, "the 'supereminently admirable' lady alone on the harem roof with only two under-eunuchs for company! Verily, she may well cry out against the palace that supplies no more agreeable companionship!"

"Two eunuchs?" answered she, facing him with cold dignity, and moving directly before the tamarisk,—"two? I trust I grow blind, for by all gods, Persian and Babylonish, if there is another of that breed here, saving Masistes, he comes against my express command. And I will teach these well-fed underlings of yours that Cyrus's daughter may fall in love with their heads!"

Mermaza cast his eyes about, winked, and replied suavely, that "he had thought he saw the forms of two persons near her, but was deceived. Only Masistes was present. The 'blindness-demon' had begun to plague his sight. Only he fell at his lady's incomparably beautiful feet, and besought that she would not forbid him her presence."

Atossa moved slowly away from the tamarisk, keeping herself carefully betwixt it and Mermaza. "My excellent sir," quoth she, taking care never to lose the chamberlain's eye, "I am most delighted to have you here. Masistes has been telling a wondrous tale. This morning he was crossing a court, when behold! his hair rose in cold fright, for a groom was leading a great lion past him, by no stouter tether than a hound's leash; yet the beast seemed gentle as a little dog. Surely, the cowardly rascal was merely affrighted by some monstrous mastiff?"

Atossa saw the worthy dart one sidling glance of keenest scrutiny upon her, but she endured it.

"My sweet mistress," said Mermaza, speaking more halting than was his wont, "Masistes brings only truth. You have not seen, then, the king's tame lions?"

"Assuredly not." Atossa led the chamberlain to the opposite parapet, and gazed across, seemingly enraptured by the panorama of the city. In his anxiety to seem interested he never looked behind, where her keener ears detected the crackling branches as of one descending.

"Then," smiled he, "we have a new wonder to show you. As soon as the king returns from the hunt we will bring the lions into the harem; you will find them harmless as cats, and vastly more entertaining."

"Why not to-morrow? Does the king use them for hunting?"

"They are better than hounds. To-morrow his Majesty takes our dear friend the 'worshipful' envoy to his game preserves. The gods grant," he continued piously, "that no wild beast harm the prince! 'Prudence,' I fear, is not a Persian word. He is all rashness."

Atossa deliberately led him back to the other end of the walk. The refuge behind the tamarisk was empty, and so was the little court below.

"I have strolled here long," asserted she suddenly; "even the view of the city grows wearisome. Let me go down to the luncheon."

Mermaza was not pleased to have her end the promenade, yet perforce consented. But when Atossa's petulance had chased the frightened maids from her chamber, it was to have a moment alone with Masistes, and to put in his hand a written slip of papyrus.

Later in the evening he was back, and a nod told her that the message had been safely delivered. But Atossa slept little that night. Once the eunuch who kept her door thought he heard some one within speaking, and entered unbidden lest there be an intruder. His mistress did not see him, for she was kneeling beside her bed, and praying softly in her Persian tongue. Before the fellow tiptoed away he noticed that ever and anon she would shake with sobbing.

"Marvel," he grunted to himself, "the 'Lady of Sumer and Akkad' is weeping! What can such as *she* have to move to tears?"

CHAPTER IX

Darius the envoy had been assigned a spacious suite of rooms in the old palace of Nebuchadnezzar; he had his own guards, his own retinue of Persian body-servants. The prince's private chamber was a high vaulted room, elegantly tiled, with little windows pierced in the arching roof. During the heat of the day the serving lads sprinkled the brick floor with water, and, as this evaporated, there arose a cool and refreshing vapour. All that afternoon the prince had kept to his chamber, and appeared to be in even less of a merry mood than had been his wont lately. Boges, who kept the door, was whispering toAriæus the chamberlain that their master must have been mightily disturbed over the murderous attack on the king during the feast in the Gardens.

"As Ahura lives!" protested the worthy, "there is somewhat on his lordship's mind. He has kept company with his writing tablets all day."

And it was indeed so; for though the scribe's art was not commonly among the accomplishments of an Aryan nobleman, Darius had long since mastered it, and now for a long time he had sat with his clay frame in his lap and his stylus in hand. Boges had ventured once the question:—

"And does my prince require me to send Artabanus to copy down the despatches to Susa?"

"I do not," came the answer, so curt that Boges risked nothing more.

Presently Darius rose from his stool, and turned to the doorkeeper.

"The time grows late," said he; "the city gates will soon be shut. Yet no messenger has come from Cyrus? from Susa?"

"None, master; we have heard that the Elamite mountain tribes are restless and stop couriers."

"Couriers of Cyrus? Do they so desire to be made jackal's meat that they must stop the Great King's despatches? No, no, Boges—the Elamites are not the delayers."

"Who if not they, lord?"

"I do not know," was the answer, in a tone that made the servant sure his superior had lively suspicions.

"And will my lord dress for the supper Bilsandan the vizier gives to-night?" askedAriæus the chamberlain, smoothly.

"Another feast! Angra-Mainyu, arch fiend, confound them!" fumed Darius; "these Babylonians boast many gods. In truth they have but two—the mouth and the belly. Praised be Mithra, the king goes hunting to-morrow, which will give some respite!"

But just as the prince was about to letAriæus lead him away to the bath, his eye lit on a newcomer among the knot of attendants by the door. His tone changed to that of good-natured banter, for he saw his favourite body-servant, a sharp-tongued, keen-witted Persian of about his own age.

"Ha, Ariathes! So you have been roaming about the city once more. Tell me, is there one beer-house in all Babylon you left unvisited? Where did you find the most heady liquor?"

"My lord wrongs his slave," quoth the fellow, demurely. "See! I am quite sober."

"By Ahura, that is true. Surely the throne of Cyrus must totter, now a marvel like this can befall!"

"My prince," answered Ariathes, very respectfully, "I have heard something that made me in no mood for palm-wine. And I think my lord should hear it also." There was something in the rascal's eye that made Darius bid all the others stand back, while he led Ariathes to the upper end of the chamber, after drawing close the door-curtain.

"Well, fellow," began he lightly, "your tales are commonly of witching black eyes and the bottoms of deep wine pots. What now—a strapping lass slapped you?" But Ariathes did not smile at the sally.

"My lord," he said, "I have quite another story. Does the prince remember Igas-Ramman, the captain who flogged the old Jew?"

"Assuredly. I curse myself I did not require his head."

"I have hatched a great friendship with him. He has been taking me about the city. To-day we went to the temple and grove of Istar, and the girls who serve the goddess brought wine enough to make us stagger till the great day. But it was too sweet for me, and I took little; though Igas would never cease pulling at his beaker. At last, when he seemed well filled, he led me to the summit of the great temple tower to have a sight of the wide city. The tower stands by the northern wall, where Ai-bur-shabou Street passes through the Gate of Istar, close by the canal. There is a marvellous view to all sides; but what made me wonder most was the sight of many squadrons of horsemen drilling in the open country before the Gate of Bel—ten thousand lances, to my thinking."

"Ha!" and Darius's jaw dropped involuntarily.

"My lord is interested? Shall I go on?"

"Yes, by every archangel!"

"I said to Igas, 'Brother, what are all these horsemen? Your king is at peace. To maintain so many cavalry will make his treasury as empty as a leaky water-skin.' Thereupon he began to laugh, then, clapping his hand across my eyes, he cried, 'Ah, my dear Persian, your sight is too keen! Ask no troublesome questions, for friendship's sake. Come, let us go back to the maids and the wine.'"

"And you followed him?" asked Darius.

"Yes, lord; but not until I had counted the number of the squadrons and seen that chariot brigades were drilling with them."

"But why should Igas try to conceal this from you? Belshazzar is a great king. We all know Babylon has a powerful garrison ever on duty."

"True; but let my lord take what my bucket drew up from Igas-Ramman's well. He began by vowing he would peril his head if he chirped once about the army of his master; then straightway all this comes out—the garrison of Babylon is being increased, extra chariots are being built, and war horses collected. The troops in Eridhu and Larsam are being sent north to strengthen the frontier posts of Sippar and Kutha. There is a great gang of labourers at work enclosing Borsippa within the outer defences of Babylon. Finally, the militia of the country districts are being armed."

"For what enemy?"

"My lord can guess better than I. When I pressed Igas on this point, he only laughed and brayed tenfold louder than common; but he had become very drunken, and before long fell over upon the bricks."

The prince was frowning darkly.

"Ariathes," said he, "you are a man of nimble wit. Do you think Belshazzar is sincere in seeking peace with Cyrus?"

The other smiled grimly.

"I am only my lord's slave. Who am I to meddle in the affairs of princes?"

"Well, you have a throat that will cut as quickly as any man's; and know this well, if you walk in the steps of Igas-Ramman and chatter loud enough, you will forswear palm-wine forever."

Ariathes grinned and was about to salaam before withdrawing, but the prince spoke again. "Look you; we have been for days in Babylon, yet no courier comes from Susa with despatches. What does it mean?"

"Have I not said I am blind to affairs of state?"

"Then receive sight; for, as you love me and as you love Cyrus, you need two wide-open eyes, as well as a ruly tongue. Cast about and find some means of sending a letter from Babylon without Belshazzar or Avil-Marduk smelling it. My last messenger travelled openly. Do you understand?"

Ariathes replied with a low bow. Darius returned to his seat, took his writing tablet, and deliberately mutilated the letter just completed. In its stead he stamped a very brief message, which he did not place in the chest by the wall, but wrapped in linen and hid in his own bosom; for an uneasy suspicion was beginning to haunt him that the very pictures enamelled on the bricks could see all that befell in this palace of Belshazzar.

"It grows late, my lord," admonished the chamberlain, after a discreet interval; "will you go to the vizier's feast?"

"I will go," replied the master, testily, and he suffered the servants to dress him.

As he went to the palace court to take chariot, the inevitable multitude of palace servants and guardsmen crowded around, bowing and scraping. The press was so dense that the staff-bearers had no little ado before clearing the way. Suddenly, out of the crowd, Darius recognized a familiar face—the old eunuch, Masistes. The two were side by side only for an instant.

"Your lady is well?" demanded Darius, eagerly.

"She is well," was the cautious answer, "but do not seem to speak to me. Read this in secret. It is from her."

Masistes was swallowed in the throng before Darius had time to startle.

"The chariots are ready, my lord," Boges was shouting.

The prince felt something like a tiny roll of papyrus thrust up his sleeve; but he curbed his curiosity and guarded it carefully until he was back at his own chamber that night. Then with all precaution he read this note, written in Atossa's own hand, in their native Persian:—

"Atossa, consort of Belshazzar, to the great prince Darius. Many things hid to the world without are revealed in the king's harem. Do not seek to know how I learn this thing, but wait Ahura's good time. Beware of the royal hunt on the morrow. Of all things beware of the king's tame lions. For *you* they may not be so tame. As you love me, return to Susa when you may, and forget my name, as I pray Ahura I may forget yours. I dare write no more. Masistes' craft will bring you this. Farewell."

Darius sat a long time over this letter, though it was past midnight and he must be up with the dawn. Ariathes had just reported that he had intrusted his master's second despatch to an obscure Jewish caravan merchant, who swore by his God that he would deliver it to the commandant of Cyrus's nearest garrison. If the messenger proved faithful, and eluded the watch, the king of the Aryans and his council would be soon learning wisdom. But what part was left to be played by Darius? Clearly the plot was thickening. For some reason, manifestly, Belshazzar desired him anywhere but in Babylon. Was he suspected of being the eavesdropper upon the king? Should he plead some excuse and refuse to go on the hunting? Should he humour Belshazzar's wishes by hardly disguised flight? The prince was a proud man—proud of his race, his king, his own prowess. The battle spirit was rising in him. Was he not "King of the Bow"? Should he desert Atossa and leave her in the harem of Belshazzar without one friend in all Babylon, saving the eunuch Masistes? The prince, we repeat, loved to dare first, and count the cost thereof afterward. And that night he vowed afresh, "I will brave all danger. With Ahura's help I will not turn back the width of one hair before the guile of these 'lovers of the lie.'"

Long before dawn, Idina-aha, master of the hounds, had emptied his kennels of the fifty black mastiffs who were to accompany the royal hunt; and at gray dawn itself Darius met Belshazzar in the central palace court. A score of trained game beaters were mounted and ready; and what with the escort of dog boys, guardsmen, and eunuchs, the chariots, the lead horses, and the long mule train with the baggage, Belshazzar drove forth with no little army. The monarch had appeared in the best of spirits; had looked Darius fairly in the eye when he told the Persian that they intended to hunt the auroch—the wild bull—whom no dog could face; and that on this account he had with him his pride—his three hunting lions, to whom even the wild bull could have no terrors. When Darius saw the brutes, huge as the beast that he had slain so memorably, he had indeed marvelled, though not after the manner Belshazzar imagined; and the king laughingly vowed to him, that if the Persian should be so fortunate as to slay an auroch, he should have his choice of which of the lions he should take back to Susa, excepting always "Nergal," the royal favourite, whom his master could not spare.

So they set forth, Belshazzar with seemingly one end in the world—to make his fellow-huntsman merry. They passed the great Western Gate, and sped through the pleasant suburbs, past luxuriant gardens, prosperous farm-houses, and innumerable canals fringed with long arbours of trees. Now and then they saw countrymen dragging their hand-carts of kitchen produce to early market, two or three tugging together. As they halted to water beside a little village of dome-roofed huts Darius saw the peasants ploughing in the fields, with the usual team—a mule and a cow—and heard the ploughing song, already thousands of years old:—

"A heifer am I,

To the mule I am yoked.

Where, where is the cart?

Go look in the grass;

It is high, it is high!"

Fields of wheat, barley, and millet waved far and near. Darius grew weary counting the prosperous landed estates and thriving villages. Truly Hanno the Phœnician spoke well, the wealth of the country of Babylon was beyond that of the mine. The corn lands and the thrifty peasants had made possible Imgur-Bel and Belshazzar's kingly glory.

But at last the farms were falling wider apart. The canals were dwindling. The land where untilled was brilliant with spring flowers, and the wind crossing the plain came to the travellers sweet with all the fragrance of the unscorched verdure. The company kept on until, beside the last of the narrowing canals, the king cried, "Halt!" and the weary footmen were glad to drop by the roadside, beside the panting dogs. Then the panniers on the carrier mules were unloaded, wine was passed about, and food. The noon hours were spent in rest and chatter.

Darius had gazed about him curiously.

"So far, and no signs of jungle? Only the open plain."

Belshazzar gave his usual answer—a laugh. "This is not your mountainous Iran. Other gods created Chaldea. Years ago there lay a broad stagnant lake beyond yonder rising, nestled in a deep hollow in the plain. The kings drained and enclosed it, planted trees, and stocked it with game. Here are still found the wild bulls—the aurochs—left nowhere in all Babylonia saving here. To kill one was the glory of the kings of old. The preserve is many furlongs on each side. The beasts run wild, and are fierce as in the virgin forest."

"Ahura grant we meet them!"

The prince had spoken so naturally that Belshazzar darted one glance at him—arrow-swift. But it sped quickly as it came, and Darius added:—

"Yet must you hunt the bull with lions?"

"After you have once faced an auroch you will not marvel that only the king of beasts dare bay him."

When Belshazzar had remounted the chariot, the whole company were away; and once past the hillock, Darius wondered as he saw a sweep of woodland, trees and thickets, stretching north and south far as the eye might reach, the whole enclosed by a brick rampart too high for the bound of the hardiest lion. Merely to enclose so huge an area was a task nigh equal to building the temple-tower of Bel. At a ponderous gate they found a company of soldiers, who opened and saluted. Instantly the forest closed round them. Meadow lands and farms were lost from view. It was like traversing one furlong, yet in that journey entering another world. The paths were leaf-strewn and scarcely trodden. The cypresses and cedars bowed in canopy overhead, and with them rarer trees, native doubtless of India or Ethiopia, but here long grown wild. There were acacias beside the meandering streams, and tamarisk thickets. The woods grew wilder the deeper they penetrated.

"And how old is this strange forest?" demanded the Persian of his Babylonish charioteer, at which the fellow answered:—

"Esarhaddon drained and fenced it more than a hundred and twenty years ago. Since then it grows wild. Except for the guards and gamekeepers no man enters the preserve on peril of his head, unless the roving lions get before the executioner."

The words were broken short by the rush of a frighted creature. "Whir!" quicker than the telling a wild ass had sped across their path: one sight of his shining gray coat—the leaves closed after him. Belshazzar forbade the eager grooms to unleash the dogs.

"No hound can run down an ass, and the game we seek is fiercer."

So they fared onward till, in a clearing, they came to the huts of two old foresters, who, after thanking the gods for suffering his Majesty and his noble guest to deign to visit their forest, reported that they had just discovered an auroch of most marvellous size.

"Marduk grants," ran their tales, "that the beast should be a monster terrible as the 'divine bull Alu' slain by the hero Gilgamesh. To-night he is deep in the jungle; but if the gods favour, his Majesty shall find him in the morning."

Thus the camp was pitched for the night. Busy hands brought bales of linen and tent poles from the pack train. The royal tent—a huge ten-sided structure—was soon ready, its dome-shaped roof stretched above, and within was arranged a complete set of portable furniture, including the ivory throne mounted on wheels, which a mule had tugged all the way from Babylon. Scarce smaller was the pavilion set for Darius, who had brought his own Persian servants with him. Around them the tents for men and horses spread like a little village. At night the king set abundant cheer and fare before his guest, but there was no deep drinking, for sober heads were needed in the morning. Darius bade Boges discover how and where the tame lions were kept, and the good fellow reported that they were safely chained and guarded in a distant tent. The prince contrived that no Babylonian should sleep inside his own pavilion. He kept his bow strung and his naked sword beside him, but nothing disturbed till he woke in the morning.

The foresters had been out very early. They had tracked the auroch and laid a hound on him, but he had distanced them and had hidden in the innermost jungle. Already half of the huntsmen had set forth to make circuit, rout the monster from his lair, and drive him nearer the encampment. After the king had poured libations to Marduk and Istar he mounted horseback and thundered away, the prince and the remaining huntsmen flying behind him.

"And where are the tamed lions?" demanded Darius of a Babylonian riding at his side.

"They were taken away before dawn to aid in baying the auroch. Doubtless they are on him now. Hark! By Nabu, they have found him!"

Through the mazes of the wood reëchoed something deep as thunder, though seemingly very far off.

"Ha!" Belshazzar was crying, "the ox is bellowing. They are driving him from his covert."

"Will they force him this way?" was Darius's question.

"So Bel grant! But you will need no bow, son of Hystaspes," for the Persian was putting on a new string. "The auroch's hide is arrow-proof. Trust to your short sword."

"I do not love the sword. It is the bow of Iran that has made us Persians a great people. It will not fail!"

"I have warned you. You will slay no auroch and win no lion."

The prince answered with silence. Riding side by side with Belshazzar, he had not suffered a word or an act of the king to escape him; but he had not noted how their escort in the rear had gradually dwindled, two falling off here and three there.

"This is the spot. Let us rein and wait the auroch," declared Belshazzar. Darius glanced about, barely in time to see the last of the retinue vanishing behind the trees. He realized, suddenly as a trap locks round its victim, that he was alone with Belshazzar; not one telltale presence to carry report of any strange deed that might befall. He had bidden Boges to keep near him. Gone—diverted by what means, Ahura the Wise alone knew. The prince had many times looked "the Lord of Death" in the face upon the battle-field—what soldier of Cyrus had not? But for all that his breath came quickly, his muscles grew rigid. Here at last was the moment that should prove whether Atossa warned truly, whether the king suspected who it was that had wrestled with him in the garden. Had the letter Ariathes had sent passed through Belshazzar's spies and guards in safety? The Persian needed none to tell him the details of the plot to take his life. Somehow, in the next few moments he was to be murdered. His rashness as a hunter was known in Susa. What could Cyrus say if the Babylonian wrote, "Your envoy was reckless and an auroch killed him"? But Darius's thoughts were not of himself only—the weal of Daniel, of Atossa, of Cyrus and all his realms, hung on his own life, perchance. Oh, the headstrong pride and folly that had rushed him into this hazard!

But these thoughts came and went in less time than the telling. Belshazzar was beside him,—Belshazzar, splendid, arrogant,—and Darius knew the king's heart was harder than hardest marble, while he waited the outcome of his guile. The Persian had his bow in his hand, and his bow was his good friend, part of himself as much as hand or eye. He would not be slain like a snared hare while there were so many keen shafts in his quiver.

The silence seemed growing long. Belshazzar, as if intent on waiting the chase, said nothing. Not even a breeze was rustling the tree-tops. The prince sat and waited.

Presently the auroch lowed again, nearer this time, and they could hear the distant shouts of men and the deep baying of the mastiffs. The scene was no strange one to Darius, but when before had he himself been one of the hunted? A thought flashed across him—to point his arrow at Belshazzar, bid the king swear to send him home scatheless, or take the shaft in his breast. But that were madness. Belshazzar had sworn once and cast his oath to the winds; would he remember it now, if wrung from him by force? The Babylonian must be the first to strike.

A new thunder through the wood shook Darius from his despair. The bolt had not fallen. Ahura grant it should not until he had taught these Babylonian "fiend-worshippers" somewhat. He turned to Belshazzar.

"Why do you wait here? Is not the hunt leaving us?"

"What do you fear?" was the reply, with a smile none too reassuring. "The sport is for us alone. The rest will bring the game to us. Fie on you, Persian, if you fear to be overmatched!"

"Not overmatched by ten aurochs!" cried the Persian, looking fairly in the king's eye. "But will not the chase pass some other way?"

"The game *I seek*," flew the answer, "will pass nowhere else."

Darius's fingers itched to send one arrow through that royal mantle then, and let all Babylon do its worst. Suddenly it dawned on him that if he were tensely strung, the king was likewise. While he ever questioned, "How will the bolt fall?" Belshazzar's one thought was, "How much does the envoy suspect?" They each would have given a hundred talents for one peep into the heart of the other. The thought appeared so comical to the prince that, to Belshazzar's wonderment, he began to laugh; and that laugh refreshed him and strengthened him like a draught of new wine.

"Crash!" A vast lumbering object was dashing through the trees. They heard thickets shivering; birds flew screaming from their nests. The noise neared rapidly. Again the thunderous bellow—close now, and deep. The ground shook with the thunder, and an answering quiver ran through the Persian. Peril or no peril, he had never before faced an auroch, and his hunter's instinct was strong within him.

Belshazzar's horse pricked his ears, snorted, and began to rear and plunge. The king barely controlled him. The Persian's beast started to do likewise, but felt the touch and press of an iron hand and iron knees so powerful that all the spirit was crushed out of him. Not so with Belshazzar.

"Marduk blast me," rang his curse, "if I do not flay Rabit for giving me this beast!" But the horse only plunged more wildly.

One last thunder! Darius saw the saplings bowing, the leaves shook down as a falling cloud; out from betwixt the trees shot a beast the like of which the prince had never beheld before. A bull, but a bull of monster size—his horns the span of a bow, his hide mud-brown; out of his mouth, and with the lolling red tongue, one almost saw the live flames breathing, with more flame in the huge balls of his eyes. To see this took one instant. The auroch crashed on until face to face with the two riders, then halted in his shambling run not twenty paces from them, dropped his horns, and lashed his flanks with his tail. Darius wondered no more that mastiffs did not love to bring him to bay.

The Persian's arrow lay on the bowstring, but he did not shoot. All the trembling had gone out of him. As if by a new sense, he knew that there was something stirring, creeping, in the thicket behind him. Did his ears fail when they heard a human whisper, low, but distinct—a whisper as of a man urging on his hound—"Now!"

Darius did not turn his head. His horse, subdued by his master touch, stood stock still, while the bull glared at them. But Belshazzar was in deadly straits. Try as he might, his beast would not stand steady, and, with the horse plunging underneath him, what chance to strike the bull with the short sword? The king's face turned livid as he struggled.

"Shoot!" he cried, between his teeth; "shoot!"

Darius's hand drew the arrow to its head. The auroch shook his horns, bellowed for the last time, and looked from Darius to Belshazzar, from Belshazzar to Darius. Which should feel his charge? The bull fixed his eyes on the king, gave a snort, a bound.

"Shoot!" cried Belshazzar again. As if in echo came a voice out of the thicket, "Back, Nergal! Woe! The king! Do not leap! Too late! Woe!"

And Darius swung himself in the saddle just in time to see the tawny body of Nergal, the royal lion, launching itself—not on the auroch, but on him. The arrow flew to meet the lion. It was Ahura the Great who shed on Darius the power that sent the startled charger with a wide bound to one side by the mighty press of a knee. The lion leaped. His flying claws tore the leather on the Persian's sleeve. A mighty snarl—the beast dashed upon the turf. The saving of Ruth had been no shot like this. The deed was done too swiftly for thought or fear, while all around the woods were ringing with a fiercer conflict. The auroch had sought his prey the moment Nergal had leaped on his. The king had striven desperately to master his steed, but vainly. The monster caught the horse under his horns and tossed mount and rider in the air. Halting in full charge, he shook his great head and looked about. The horse was disembowelled—dying. The king, cast upon the greensward, was struggling to rise. He had lost his sword. The auroch lowered his head again. Still a foe? He would trample it out instantly!

"Help, in Marduk's name, help!" the king was calling.

Out from the thicket whence sprang the lion sped a man, Idina, master of the hounds, and leaped beside Belshazzar. A brave deed, but foolish. In his hand was only his whip of office.

"All the Persian's skill could not save his horse."

"Help! the king is in peril!" was his shout to the distant beaters. But Belshazzar might have fared to the "World-Mountain" that day had it not been for another. Right at the raging bull rode the Persian, and a second shaft flew, not at the arrow-proof hide, but into one flaming eye. The loudest bellow of all shook the forest when the monster charged Darius. All the Persian's skill could not save his horse. One horn hooked in the belly—the scream of a dying charger, that was all. But Darius was on foot before the bull could turn from his triumph. His short sword was in his hand. He met the charge of the bull on the side where the shaft had blinded. Belshazzar saw him shun the sweep of the terrible horns, and the onrush of the bull drove the steel clean to the hilt in the shoulder. Another snort, a bellow that made the high boughs quiver, and the auroch tore away. They heard him dash down a small tree in his charge, a second, a third; then there was a crashing fall, and silence.

Darius stood staring about and leaning on his bow. Nergal, pierced to the heart, lay twitching, though life was fled. The horses were struggling in their last agony. Belshazzar was trying to stagger to his feet. How long it had seemed since the bull burst upon them!

King and envoy looked upon one another. Darius saw Belshazzar strive twice to speak, but the words thickened in his throat. Then the king's eye lit on Idina, and the royal wrath blew out on him:—

"Verily, as I am lord of Babylon, you shall be impaled! Why not rescue sooner?"

"Lord," replied the other, losing his wits as he trembled, "it was as you ordered. When the prince was confronting the auroch, I was to unleash Nergal—"

The words were like fire upon dry straw; for the king had forgotten all else in the thought of his own danger.

"Nergal? By the Maskim, what is lying there on the ground? A lion?"

"Yes, your Majesty," said Darius, very coldly. "When Idina unleashed him, while they stood behind me in the thicket, he forgot the auroch to spring at me. His claws have torn my dress. I prefer the auroch, my king. *He*, at least, charges fairly and face to face."

The king did not risk himself to reply to Darius, but, turning to Idina, declared icily: "Fellow, for your cursed folly this day, I swear by every god of Babylon, you shall be beaten to death." Then to Darius, in a tone equally icy: "Persian, you have saved my life. Ask what reward you will."

"I ask nothing," replied the other, haughtily, "nothing but this—to meet no more of the king's tamed lions."

Before Belshazzar could answer, the foresters and beaters were all around them. The king and envoy spoke not a word to each other, while the gaping hunters cried out at the hugeness of the slain auroch, and loudly lamented their master's misfortune. There were more wailings over the dead lion.

"The king's trust in these beasts is misplaced," commented Darius, dryly; "Nergal was no less dangerous than the auroch."

The Babylonians who were wise looked at one another slyly. The Persians following Darius soon arrived at a tearing gallop, cursing a forester who had said he was leading them close behind the prince, but only brought them to a halt in a matted jungle.

Belshazzar had to be lifted, and carried back to the tents. His ankle was hurt, not dangerously, but for the while he could enjoy no more hunting. He seemed in no slight pain, and his body-servants were rejoiced when he contented himself with ordering Idina's tongue to be cut out, before the luckless "master of the hounds" was flogged to death, and did not command the execution of any others.

Between Belshazzar and Darius there did not pass one syllable for a very long time. A messenger had come post-haste from Babylon. "Urgent despatches," he announced, "from the chief priest to his Majesty." That afternoon, accordingly, after Idina had passed beyond the reach of the royal wrath, the whole company returned with speed to the capital.

CHAPTER X

Daniel the civil-minister had been arrested on the charge of committing murder by sorcery. All Babylon had rung with the news. Even though the accusers were vouched for by Avil-Marduk himself, the city had received the tale with indignant incredulity. When Sirusur went with a "hundred" of lancers to make the arrest, the burghers would have rescued the prisoner by sheer force, had not Daniel leaned from the chariot in which they were bearing him to the palace, and entreated the citizens to shed no blood. Even those closest to the king shook their heads, and expressed the hope that no ill would brew from the high priest's doings.

But Daniel had spent the night in the palace guard-house, and the rage of the city folk had in a measure subsided. Nevertheless, when the doors were thrown open to the "Hall of Judgment," the wand-bearers had no slight ado to control the multitudes that pressed for entrance. There on the ivory throne sat Belshazzar, in the robes of state, splendid as on the night of the feast in the Hanging Gardens; behind the king stood the parasol bearer and the fan bearers; at his right hand, in his white mantle of office, was the high justiciar of the realm; on his left, in resplendent scarlet livery, was Khatin, statuesque, impassive, save as at rare intervals he stole a sly glance at the ponderous naked sword at his side. On the three broad steps of the throne were arrayed the royal officials, each in due order of precedence, they likewise in glittering array; down the walls the sunlight flashed on the enamelled pictures, the great cedar beams of the ceiling shone with their gilding. The pathway to the foot of the throne was marked by a costly rug. If Daniel was to be tried, it was not to be without due state!

As the old Jew entered, escorted by Bilsandan the vizier, there had occurred something that made Avil-Marduk, as he stood at the accuser's station before the king's right hand, swell with hidden rage. Of all the huge company that thronged the lower hall, scarce a head failed to bow in salutation to Daniel; and not a few were bold enough to shout a "Heaven prosper you!" after him. "Silence! or I clear the hall!" Belshazzar ordered angrily, and the noise ceased; but there was no need to tell on which side was arrayed the people.

Unmoved by all, Daniel, ushered by the vizier, advanced to the foot of the throne, and there, as etiquette demanded, remained kneeling, until, after long silence, a barely perceptible nod from Belshazzar told him to rise. Bilsandan salaamed, and stepped beside the justiciar, at the right of the king, leaving Daniel confronting the monarch.

More silence, and then Belshazzar began abruptly:

"Daniel, otherwise named Belteshazzar, answer: Did you, or did you not, commit murder of late, by spells and witchcraft?"

The Jew, who seemed as composed as the king himself, in the face of that peering company, answered mildly, but without the least hesitation, "that if his Majesty pleased, he would not plead until his accusers had stated their charges."

"And if I do not please?" demanded the king, ominously.

"Then, your Majesty, I shall be constrained to recite to you the law, honoured by all your royal predecessors since its decreeing by Khammurabi, two thousand years ago, 'Let no man be condemned, except he be first accused, and his guilt proven out of the mouths of two unperjured witnesses.'"

"Have a care, Jew! have a care!" warned Belshazzar; "it ill becomes a leopard of your spots to teach the law to the king of Babylon."

"I ask only justice, your Majesty."

"And, by Bel, you shall have it!" swore the king. "Advance, Avil, and produce your witnesses!"

The high priest appeared before the throne, at his back three men and a woman, who bowed themselves most awkwardly in the presence of royalty.

"The wise Gudea," muttered Khatin in his beard, "and Binit his dear wife have scarcely learned courtly graces at the beer-house of Nur-Samas."

But, leaving his myrmidons to gape around the hall, Avil commenced a fiery invective. If his arguments were faulty, his epithets were strong. Daniel, the most impudent blasphemer of Bel in all Babylon, had, he explained, at last carried his impiety so far as to accomplish the death of the most excellent Saruch, simply because the latter forsook his impotent Jewish demon, Jehovah. If the king failed to punish the murderer, the outraged gods would haste to blast Babylon with fire and brimstone.

"Do you still deny the accusation?" questioned Belshazzar, when Avil concluded, and the Jew, all unmoved by the fierce harangue, answered steadily, "Utterly, my lord; my whole life lived in this city denies it."

"Present, then, your witnesses," commanded Belshazzar of Avil, who proceeded to hale Gudea to the front, with a muttered injunction in his ear to "tell a well-welded story, or the 'Earth-Fiends' would have him by night!"

Therefore the exorcist, with smooth countenance and glib tongue, rattled off the tale of the death of Saruch, adding that if the man did not meet his end by foul enchantment, he was willing to bare his back for a thousand stripes.

Khatin had rolled his eyes more than once during this recital, and did so again when Binit was thrust forward after her husband. The good woman's examination was the more brief because the lardy ointment she had smeared on her hair was so pungent that even the king could hardly regard her steadily. She avowed that early on the day of the alleged murder she had sold a quantity of magic wood and magic wax to two men whom she identified as the remaining pair of witnesses. There was an audible titter when she ended.

"Will you cross-examine these witnesses?" asked the justiciar of Daniel.

"My lord," the prisoner smiled quietly, "I can ask these worthy people many things, but since neither have connected me in the least with the death of Saruch, I will only reserve my right to examine them later."

"Come forward, then, Tabni," commanded Avil, confidently; "tell the king the rest of the story, that he may see how the testimony of the most pious Gudea tends to convict the accused."

A more partial judge than Belshazzar, even, might well have looked askance at the personage who now faced Daniel. A squalid dress, an unkempt beard, and a single eye with a most snakelike twinkle, made it difficult for Khatin to swallow his guffaw. Avil examined his witness sharply, and Tabni answered with the readiness of a well-drilled pupil. He was a "charmer," of a profession akin to Gudea's, only he made the spells which the other counteracted. He would supply good crops, profitable investments, or successful love-making as promptly and cheaply as any in the city. On the day of Saruch's death, Daniel had summoned him very early, and told him he needed his services to "wither" a mortal enemy. Tabni had hesitated, and Daniel raised the fee. Therefore, as the witness put it, since it seemed a mere "overcasting," with no impiety involved, he consented, for business had been slack of late, and one must live. He had gone with Daniel's servant Shaphat to buy the needful conjuring material of Binit. Then Daniel took him, in company with Shaphat, into a secret chamber. They made a waxen image; named it Saruch; thrust three red-hot needles through it; and Tabni had pronounced the infallible spell over it,—

"We entwine you with ropes,

We catch you in a cage,

We twist you in a sling,

We drown you in filthy water,

We fling you down from a high wall."

That afternoon Tabni heard that Saruch was dead. He had reflected, and became convinced that he had been privy to a fearful deed. His conscience had troubled him, and he had conferred with Gudea, who advised him to make a public confession.

"And will you examine this man also?" asked the justiciar again, to which Daniel, still composedly, made answer, "May your lordship first deign to hear the other witness."

"It is your right," responded the justiciar; to which Belshazzar added viciously, "I have sworn it, you shall have full justice, Jew; but take notice, your guilt is established out of the mouth of one witness. Let a second swear to his tale, and the case is proved. I give you this opportunity. Confess now, and I will see if I can relax the just penalty of the law."

"I demand the other accuser," answered Daniel, almost haughtily; and Belshazzar nodded to Avil.

"Shaphat, former servant of Daniel, advance!" commanded Avil, peremptorily.

And now there was a rustle and a flutter in the hall indeed. "One of the minister's servants will betray him,—and one who is a Jew, at that!" ran the whisper, while an ill-favoured young man was thrust before the king. But all men noticed that the fellow hung down his head, and would not look the prisoner in the eye. Avil's voice was very stern.

"Now, Shaphat, you have heard all that the pious 'charmer' Tabni has said. Tell the king: Were you not a Jewish servant in the house of Daniel, and did you not quit his service because you grew to love the gods of Babylon, while he worshipped his demon Jehovah and gave himself over to vile sorceries?"

The witness nodded, very faintly.

"You were with Tabni when he bought the magician's material from Binit?"

"Yes,"—the word barely audible.

"You were with him at the making of the waxen image?"

"Yes,"—the word came still fainter.

"Now is it not your oath, taken in the name both of the gods of Babylon and of Judea, that Daniel pronounced the name of Saruch above the waxen image?"

But at this instant the witness raised his head, and Daniel looked him in the face. They saw Shaphat's countenance working in agony; the words were choking in his throat: "I cannot! I cannot!" That was all they could understand.

"Cannot what, knave?" demanded the king, fiercely. But the wretched fellow had cast himself before Daniel, and embraced his knees.

"O master! master!" he groaned, "I cannot lie before your face. I was dismissed justly for my thieving, and only in your mercy did you spare me prison. You are guiltless; Tabni's tale is all perjury: I never saw him; never saw Binit; you never had the 'charmer' in your house. Alas! that I listened to Gudea, and took his money—"

"Silence, hound!" shouted Avil, flinging dignity to every wind, and catching the luckless witness by the scruff; "would you be cut into sandal-leather?"

But a fearful din was rising from the company. Not only the city folk, but the courtiers, were thundering: "Innocent! Innocent! Away with the false witnesses!"

"Silence!" commanded the king, his countenance darkening. "What is this, Avil? What is this witness saying?"

"Your Majesty," answered Avil, barely heard in the tumult, "you see with your own eyes that Daniel is a sorcerer. While Shaphat came forward, he muttered magic spells to force him to utter falsehood!"

The efforts of the wand-bearers had restored stillness. Belshazzar's frown was still very black when he addressed the prisoner.

"That the accused has dealing with demons, who come to his aid, should be manifest to all men. Speak, Daniel; even now I give you chance to show wherefore you should not die the death."

"I stand upon the law, your Majesty." The Jew seemed the soberest mortal in all that excited company. "My past life should be a defence against the slanders of this Tabni; and the king has heard Shaphat and his confession. Even receiving the oath of Tabni, only one witness swears to my guilt."

"And let your Majesty observe," interrupted Avil, angrily, "that the civil-minister, being a Jew, cannot claim the protection of the law of Babylon."

But at this Bilsandan the vizier leaped from his station.

"Are you mad, priest?" he cried. "Deny foreigners our law, and all the great Egyptian and Syrian merchants quit Babylon; our trade is blasted!"

"And will you presume to teach *me* my duty to the king?" retorted Avil, still more wrathfully. But before the tumult could rise higher, the justiciar stepped out before the throne.

"Live forever, O king!" spoke he, salaaming. "Before your Majesty passes judgment, hear this concerning the witness Tabni. Daniel has not yet asked him, but I do ask, whether he was not the 'charmer' who was brought before the 'Tribunal of the Five Judges,' in the past year, when Daniel sat with me among the members? He is silent; he dares deny nothing. No; nor dare he deny that he was convicted first of embezzlement, then of perjury; and that all the judges save Daniel voted 'death,' but the civil-minister persuaded us to mercy. We imposed three hundred stripes. Behold the gratitude!"

The uproar was doubled now, the exertions of the wand-bearers utterly futile. The luckless Tabni cowered behind the chief priest, who still clamoured, "Execute the blasphemer! No mercy to the sorcerer!" While Bilsandan as loudly bade the priest "make an end to his patter!" and to remember the precept in the "Book of Maxims," "Let the king avenge according to the law, or swiftest destruction waiteth upon his city."

Yet, through all the clamour and turbulence, Belshazzar sat upon the ivory throne, impassive, implacable. The very sympathies of the company had made his stony heart still harder. Was he not king? Should any ancient law, from men of ages forgotten, stand betwixt *him* and his own royal will? At the first instant of silence his voice rang clear:—

"Hear my judgment. Daniel is a Jew, and the law does not cover him. His guilt is sufficiently proved. Advance, Khatin; seize the prisoner!"

But it was not merely shoutings now that drowned the king's voice. Right before the monarch sprang Sirusur, "Master of the Host."

"Lord," cried he, hotly, "if your Majesty desires to put crown ministers to death on the word of such as Tabni, let the king find another general!" And he cast his baton of office at the royal feet; so did the justiciar, so the "Master of the Granaries," the "Master of the Treasury," and a dozen great officials more. Khatin, the boldest of the bold, had shrunk from fulfilling the kingly order. But while Belshazzar sat lowering and unbending in the face of every protest, Mermaza had thrust his way through the angry officers, and salaamed before his master.

"Your Majesty," spoke he, and his ever present smile had become dimmed in truth, "I am commanded by the queen-mother, Tavat-Hasina, to say that she has heard with no pleasure of the accusation against that dear servant of her father Nebuchadnezzar, the civil-minister Daniel; that she entreats the king her son to listen to no perjured evidence, and she warns the minister's accusers of her most high displeasure." The colour was leaving Avil's cheek, for Tavat was still a power to be reckoned with. "And I am also commanded," went on Mermaza, more haltingly, "to say in behalf of the worshipful Persian envoy, the Prince Darius, that Daniel the Jew has become most dear to him, and he trusts the king will do nothing hastily, if he desires to retain the ambassador's good will."

They saw Belshazzar's face grow even darker, saw him lift the gold-tipped sceptre, as if to dash it in the eunuch's face. But fewer saw Avil's signal to his lord, as the priest stood close beside the dais, and the muttered whisper, "Yield for the moment." The staff-bearers enforced silence at last. In profound stillness the king announced his decision:—

"In mine own eyes the guilt of Daniel is clear as the moon on a cloudless night; but I perceive that many faithful servants are minded otherwise, and that a question has arisen as to the veracity of the witness Tabni. Let therefore the accused be remanded to prison until his case can be more carefully examined into. And since nothing else is brought to my judgment seat, let the hall be cleared."

The assemblage dispersed. Daniel was led to the palace prison. The king vanished in the harem. Khatin stole away to Nur-Samas's beer-house with very dejected countenance,—he had not taken Daniel's head. Only Avil and Gudea conversed together, but not amiably.

"Scorpion," raged the priest, "what mean you by playing with me thus? To pin half your tale on a creature like Tabni, and then to have the other witness fail!"

"Compassion! my lord," whined Gudea. "Hardly a man would do an ill turn by Daniel, he is so beloved. Even Tabni and Shaphat set their prices high."

"And Shaphat has vanished, after having made sport of me before all Babylon!" fumed Avil. "Better to have Daniel at large, than in prison with so many revilings flung after me as there were to-day! You have failed me utterly, you and your cursed wife. May you never darken my sight again!"

"But your lordship recalls a small matter," sniffed Gudea, as unable as Binit to forget the money-bags,—"a promise, of two talents; merely of two talents. A trifle amongst friends—"

"And I will pay them," swore Avil, "when Allat has requited you in the 'House of Torment.' Therefore, get you gone!"

When Gudea returned to his home that night, he had occasion to meditate long on the ingratitude of the mighty.

CHAPTER XI

If Gudea's heart was sorrowful that night, so were those of greater men than he. Avil had never before found Belshazzar so irascible, as when they conferred in a quiet chamber of the palace, about sundown.

"The Jew is obstinate as an old camel!" cursed the king. "He knows no more fear than a mad auroch. I can do nothing with him!"

"And the king threatened?" insinuated Avil.

"Torture, impaling, flaying alive, hot furnaces,—and all else; yet he will not give me an order on Imbi-Ilu for his daughter."

"Let the king's liver find peace," comforted Avil, sweetly. "Daniel will not torment him long. The feast of Bel is near, when I as chief priest may crave, in the god's name, one boon which you may not refuse. If I ask then the life of Daniel, can the queen-mother complain? You are powerless to deny such a request."

"Ah, well, that will end *him*!" snapped the king. "I seek the daughter."

"Patience, your Majesty."

"No patience, I have waited long. At dawn I will go in person to Borsippa, and demand her surrender. If not—I will find if Nabu can make the hides of his priests too thick for sword-blades!"

Avil shook his head. "Nothing rashly, lord. All the people revere Nabu."

"Let them learn the greatest god in Babylon is its king," Belshazzar threw up his head; "there is too much priestly rule here for my liking." He looked hard at Avil, who bit his lips at the open hint. "You failed miserably in the accusation," continued Belshazzar.

"I did not know Shaphat had so sore a conscience," confessed the pontiff, ruefully; "but once in prison, Daniel shall find it nothing easy to learn the way out of it."

"And the Persian Darius grows more intolerable every day. He has saved my life now. Would that any other had done it!"

"And wherefore should that be an offence to my lord. I never was sanguine the lion would succeed. There are many ways of speeding even so great an archer as Darius out of the world."

"Avil," spoke Belshazzar, eying his minister, "I believe that the gods have set in your breast no heart, but a block of iron; you may persuade me to many things, but not to slay Darius until I stand in sorer need than I stand to-day."

"Ah! well," answered the pontiff, smiling somewhat uneasily, "it is all one whether he lives or dies. My watchers are everywhere; not a letter to or from Susa fails of interception. He is harmless in Babylon. Let us delay the envoy as long as we may peaceably. If he demands to be sent home and seems to know too much, there is but one thing left."

"To clap into prison and prepare for speedy war with Cyrus?"

"The king has said!" bowed Avil.

"Very good," answered Belshazzar, not without bitterness. "I follow your wisdom; but woe to Babylon, and woe to you, if your wisdom prove but folly!"

The king had come to Borsippa with a "fifty" of war chariots, and five hundred mounted lancers. So a frightened underling reported to Imbi-Ilu, just as that pontiff was sprinkling himself with purifying water, before going to the great altar, to proffer the morning "fruit-offering."

"He demands instant entrance," continued the messenger, in no steady voice, "both for himself and the soldiers who follow him."

"Armed men in Nabu's temple precinct!" cried the high priest, dropping the palm branch with which he had been sprinkling his garments. "Never has warrior planted sandal inside our gates since the founding of the *ziggurat*! Surely, your wits are wandering."

"Would to Nabu they were!" groaned the other; "but hearken!"

And Imbi heard the clattering of spear-butts against the portals.

"This is an important hour for the dignity of Nabu," announced he, regaining composure. "We must at once reverence the king and defend the honour of our god. Go, tell his Majesty that we will admit him, as soon as I can array the corps of priests and temple ministers in due order to receive him with proper state."

Then the great gong that hung by the steps to the tower began to clang furiously. The school boys joyously flung away their clay tablets, while their professors hastened to don their whitest robes. The sluggish temple servants ceased dozing on the sunny bricks of the court, and shuffled toward the gateway, where the long lines of priests and other servitors of Nabu were forming.

When the entrance was at last thrown wide, and Belshazzar's chariot entered, the king confronted extended files of "Necromancers," "Libation-Pourers," "Dirge-Singers," and many more sacred colleges, each drawn up in proper order, every man in his snowy garment and peaked tiara, with Imbi-Ilu in his pontiff's goatskin at their head. And at a signal from their chief every knee was bent in salutation, while the temple choir intoned the chant of welcome.

"Grant prosperous life,

Innumerable years,

And children uncounted,

O Nabu, most wise!

To Belshazzar our king!"

The chariot had halted in the courtyard, but the swarms of soldiery without the gate had not begun to enter when Imbi-Ilu stepped before the sovereign, and salaamed almost to the bricks.

"A fortunate day, O Nabu, a fortunate day that brings Belshazzar the heaven-loving sovereign to the 'Eternal House'! Let the king deign to make known his will to his servants; he knows," the pontiff rubbed his hands craftily, "that Nabu is poor, his priests lack corn. Strange and young gods bewitch the pious of Babylon."

Belshazzar leaped from the chariot without waiting for the grooms to set the footstool. He was clearly striving to appear conciliatory.

"I greet you well, you, and all these other venerable priests," nodding to the company. "I have not forgotten that the revenues of Nabu have diminished. I have commanded that the treasurer deliver upon your request a hundred *gurs*[4] of barley and as many of millet, also I deed to you an estate of the crown near Erech of fifty 'great acres' of corn land."

"Blessing to the ever bountiful son of the gods!" chorussed the company, every head bowing again.

"But I have come to make a request," went on Belshazzar.

"The king's wishes are law," smiled Imbi-Ilu. "He desires the supplications of his servants for the continuance of peace; be assured—"

Belshazzar raised his hand. "I crave a smaller boon, that will not take these reverend men from their studies. There is in this temple a damsel—"

Imbi-Ilu bowed yet again. "The king has spoken,—the Jewess Ruth."

"Be so good as to bring her forth immediately. I take her back to Babylon."

Imbi-Ilu repeated his salaam. "The king's word is good. We are all obedience. Where is the letter from Daniel her father?"

"The letter?" there was a dangerous flush on Belshazzar's bronzed cheek; "I do not understand you, priest."

"Let not the king take anger," returned the pontiff, calmly. "Who am I so bold as to remind him that only on command of the father can we give up a maid entrusted to us for asylum?"

"Well," affirmed Belshazzar, tossing his lordly head, "your learning, of a truth, teaches that the king is greater than the father; and it is the king who orders now."

There was a dead hush for a moment, every eye fixed on Imbi. His was the next move.

"Your Majesty," began he, firmly, "*I* am but the meanest of your slaves; but as a priest it is not I that answer you, but Nabu the Wise, making use of my poor tongue." And he met the haughty glance of the king with one as haughty. "Nabu cannot suffer you to take the maiden."

Belshazzar tugged at the sword upon his thigh. "No insolence," he threatened; "I give you one moment to consider. Give up the wench peaceably, or my guardsmen drag her forth by force, and you away to prison, to answer charges of gross rebellion against my will."

Imbi turned to Hasba, the subaltern at his side. "Haste!" was the muttered command, "put the Jewess in the shrine behind the god's own image." Then, still boldly, he confronted Belshazzar. "Live forever, O king! This is my answer. If the king is bent on wickedness, let him proceed in person with one attendant, and search our precinct. If he find the Jewess, let him take her hence with his own hand. Let the soldiers remain without. So shall we be guiltless of resistance to your Majesty, and on your own head shall be all the anger of the god for this insult to his right of sanctuary."

Belshazzar had unsheathed his weapon.

"I will see who is monarch in Borsippa, you, Imbi-Ilu, or I!" sounded his menace. "Forward, soldiers; brush these priests aside! Search the place from pinnacle to cellar; and woe to you," with a scowl at the temple folk, "if you withstand."

But Imbi-Ilu stepped before the gate, where the escort was thronging, and the lances tossing threateningly.

"Hear, ye! Hear, ye! soldiers of Babylon!" rang the pontiff's voice; "ere you obey the command of Belshazzar, hearken to the divine law, revealed to Sargon I. in a dream sent him from Nabu, and confirmed by the kings Sin-iddina and Sennacherib, 'Let him who enters the precinct of the "Eternal House" be devoted to the Maskim forever. Let his sons perish, his daughters remain unmarried, his cattle starve, his enemies prosper, his soul eat mud in the "Abode of Torment."' You have heard the ordinance of the god and of the king; obey you which you list—Nabu or Belshazzar!"

And as he spoke, the lines of priests moved steadily forward, until they formed a solid rank across the entrance way, denying all ingress.

"Advance, men!" thundered the king; "out swords; hew these rebels down, and make a pathway over them, if such is their mad wish!"

But not a soldier advanced. The priests confronted Belshazzar stolidly. Again the king commanded; again mute disobedience. Presently Igas-Ramman the captain took a cautious step forward and saluted.

"Let the king's heart find peace; in other things the soldiers do his least bidding, but they cannot massacre these holy priests in the god's own house."

"Well, then," cried Belshazzar, sending a glance of burning anger through the captain, "be it so. I think the 'king of Sumer and Akkad' has might enough to hale forth a simpering Jewess. As for you, Imbi, in due time I will teach you how foul was the day when you made a foe of me. Who is there who will go with me, and seek out the maiden?"

Not a captain advanced, but into the gate strode a towering giant, Khatin. "Here am I, your Majesty," he announced pompously; "we go together, the headsman and the king!"

"Good, then. Let us find this wench without delay."

The array of priests opened for the twain. Imbi ceremoniously walked beside the monarch, offering no suggestions, but courteously leading wherever the king desired. They searched the college buildings, the quarters of the *kali*, the eunuch priests, of the *zikari*, the "female-recluses," the houses of the married priests, and the great storerooms. Their quest ended in nothing but mortification for Belshazzar. Vainly he threatened and commanded Imbi-Ilu. The pontiff only protested that his lips were sealed—the guilt of outraging the asylum must rest on Belshazzar alone. The king was nigh to returning to the gateway discomfited, when a whisper by Khatin made him turn to Imbi-Ilu.

"One thing more," he ordered. "Lead me to the sanctuary on the crest of the tower. We have not yet searched through *that*."

"The shrine of the god!" cried the pontiff, throwing up his hands in surprised dismay. "What is the king saying? Do my ears deceive?"

"In no way, priest," repeated Belshazzar, sternly; "the sanctuary, and nowhere else."

"Oh, my lord, my lord," Imbi began to groan, falling on his knees, "at least spare our temple this outrage. Forbear—"

"Nip him close, my king," exhorted Khatin, gruffly. "I swear by his own god we shall find the damsel hid under the very image."

"No delaying, Imbi," repeated the king, fiercely. "Your moaning tells too well where the girl is concealed. To the shrine immediately."

"But my lord knows the story," protested the pontiff, leading to the foot of the temple stairs, with all seeming reluctance, "how when King Ourina, twelve hundred years since, sought to drag a suppliant from this very sanctuary, the god smote him with leprosy, and he went out of the temple white as snow."

"A beldame's tale," grunted Khatin; "lead onward."

"Or how King Samas-Nin, for merely saying in his bedchamber that Nabu had no power to defend his servants from the royal will, fell down speechless, and died in three days torn by demons."

"That was many years ago," growled the headsman, "and the estimable god has begun to show old age. Up, priest, up!"

Imbi said no more. He led the two along the lofty flights of stairs toward the upper shrine, deliberately and slowly. As they mounted from terrace to terrace, and the lower world began to drop away below them, an unnatural hush seemed spreading all about, that made even Khatin's river of strange jests and oaths flow sluggishly, and finally cease altogether. Suddenly, when one terrace below the shrine, Imbi halted, and pointed to a black stone, set in the bricks of the parapet.

"Look, your Majesty!" he spoke, in a bated whisper, and pointed.

"Well?" questioned Belshazzar, his own voice husky.

"This stone marks the spot where the impious General Naram-Sin fell down dead when by command of King Esarhaddon he went up to arrest a fugitive in the sanctuary."

The king stared at the stone fixedly, saying nothing; but Khatin gave a loud bray,—too loud, in fact, to be unforced.

"An hundred years ago! As I said, the good Nabu has grown many gray hairs since then. Come, your Majesty, let others quake and gibber. The executioner and the king are of too tough stuff to be thus frighted."

"Silence, impudent villain!" commanded Imbi; "reverence the king, even if you must blaspheme the great Nabu. Shall I lead on?"

"Lead on," ordered Belshazzar, doggedly, but Imbi saw that he was stealing glances out of the corners of his eyes at Khatin, and the headsman seemed anything but at ease. Belshazzar might be "son of Marduk," but it required something better than loud-mouthed boastings to make him advance to a deed like this without a tremor.

They had reached the topmost terrace. Below them lay Borsippa and Babylon, spread like a fair broidered garment. Directly at their feet was the wide courtyard, packed with the gazing priests, and the soldiers before the gate, all staring upward; and Belshazzar knew that not a man of them envied him and his deed.

Imbi halted at the silver-plated door of the sanctuary. His voice was even lower. "At least, let the king put off his sandals before entering the god's dread presence."

Belshazzar and Khatin complied without a word. Even before Imbi thrust in the door, the air they breathed seemed weighted to the would-be violators. Why did the swallows twitter so shrill? Why did their own hearts beat so loudly?

The door creaked on its pivots. Imbi stepped to one side. "Let the king enter," he whispered, "but suffer his slave to remain away from this fearful deed."

The two peered within. The sanctuary was absolutely dark, save for a single bar of yellow light that shot through an unseen opening in the vaulted roof, and did not diffuse the gloom in the slightest. A few jewels on the garments of the idol twinkled faintly. Barely could they see the outline of the great image, looming to monstrous size at the opposite extremity of the chamber. Two steps within, their feet echoed and reëchoed, while the darkness seemed pressing all about them. After the brightness just quitted, no dungeon could have been blacker. Khatin uplifted his voice, throwing into it his last grains of courage. "Boldly, lord. We have her instantly!" And he took a third step, but no farther. His voice was doubled by countless echoes, and scarcely had they died ere a rumbling and muttering as of distant thunder reverberated from end to end of the sanctuary. Khatin felt an icy touch run down his spine in a twinkling: his teeth rattled in his head. There was a quivering at the roots of his hair, as if it were rising.

A second muttering, and to their straining gaze the tall idol seemed rocking on its pedestal. The whole shrine jarred. A pale flicker of light touched the hideous features of the image, illumining the grinning mouth. Then the light vanished, and all the dark seemed alive with writhing demons uncounted, right, left, before, behind,—thronging and threatening. Khatin's feet were frozen under him. He would have given his all for strength to flee away. Suddenly out of the rumbling thunder came a voice, slow, muffled, sepulchral.

"Woe, woe, unto Belshazzar, the impious king; woe, woe unto Khatin, the ungodly servant. For ten thousand years let them eat of fire; for ten thousand years let them drink of wormwood; for ten thousand years—"

But king and headsman had awaited no more. Power of flight returned to each simultaneously. They were outside the doorway in a trice; and Belshazzar had dashed to the portal and bolted it before Imbi might speak a word.

"Away!" gasped the king, all the while shaking as with ague; "away, lest the god pursue us! Back to Babylon with all haste!" He was running down the *ziggurat* with leaps and bounds, Khatin after him.

"Your Majesty leaves his sandals," Imbi shouted, but Belshazzar never so much as heard.

When he reached the courtyard, Belshazzar stumbled. The chariot servants saw that his face was ghastly white, and, fearing leprosy, dreaded at first to help him into the car. With no explanation to any, Belshazzar ordered that they drive at headlong speed to the palace.

It was three days before the king showed himself again in public, and even then all saw that his features were haggard. Khatin had recovered more swiftly. Amongst his cronies, and when well in liquor, he was wont to boast that *he* had been all courage, only the king commanded him to retire just as he was dragging Ruth from behind the image. Be that as it may, on the evening following the attempted sacrilege, Imbi privately commended his faithful Hasba for having done his duty so manfully in the sanctuary during the morning.

CHAPTER XII

Now after the king for the third time had refused the prayer of all the great merchants of Babylon, to accept their security and release Daniel from his prison, Ruth the Jewess declined more and more. Zabini, the motherly wife of Imbi-Ilu, went one day to her husband with no little concern, and told him how the girl was daily becoming pale and languid, her appetite was failing, she took no interest in the songs and dances of the temple women, and how every time a mule-cart rumbled in the streets outside the gates, she would start and shiver, fearing lest it was a new visit from the king to drag her from sanctuary.

Imbi was a kind-hearted man. He directed Bel-Nuri, the oldest and wisest of the temple doctors, to examine the Jewess, and prescribe. The physician did his duty carefully, and announced that the girl suffered from "the wasting sickness," perhaps aggravated by an attack of formidable demons. Ruth accordingly was duly medicined with a paste of "white dogs' brains," supplemented by a most powerful spell, which was chanted over her one whole afternoon by Zabini and six other priests' wives. Privately, however, Bel-Nuri had a long conference with Imbi-Ilu.

"Nought ails the girl," declared the doctor, "except anxiety for her father, now mewed up in 'The House of Walls,' for her betrothed, who you know is now in hiding, and whose arrest has been ordered, and for herself. She trembles every moment lest the king lay hand on her; besides, as a Jewess, our temple rites are most displeasing. She fears the anger of her god if she continues to witness them. We cannot change his Majesty's purpose to imprison Daniel, although, now that Gudea and the other accusers have utterly vanished from sight, it is gross persecution to hold him without cause. But assuredly we may rid her of the last evil influence. Send her away from Babylon and Borsippa; beyond doubt there are some safe and pleasant hiding spots in the country, where she will be happier."

Imbi meditated long on this advice, and consulted Zabini; they both agreed it were best for Ruth that she should be sent quietly away.

Day passed into day, however, with no opportunity presenting, and Ruth drooped yet more. All the bloom had vanished from her cheeks. She spoke little, slept long, yet wakened unrefreshed: therefore it was with a very glad heart that one afternoon Imbi-Ilu went up upon his house roof, where the Jewess was languidly aiding Zabini at her weaving.

"Beloved child," he announced, "I have to tell you that Nabu's house will shelter you no longer. Isaiah your betrothed has communicated with me, and desires to take you out of Borsippa this very night."

"Away from Babylon and Borsippa? Oh, joy!" And it did Zabini's heart good to see the colour return to the Jewess's wan face.

"But how is it to be managed?" questioned the wife.

"I scarce know myself," confessed Imbi; "a strange slave lad left this sealed tablet at the temple gate. You see it is Isaiah's own signet, and cannot be doubted."

Zabini surveyed the tablet critically. "The king may have secured the seal, or it may have been forged by his orders," she objected.

Imbi shook his head. "Between ourselves, I dare not deny that his Majesty is capable of many strange things; but his strokes are those of a lion, not of a fox. I do not believe he would descend to theft or forgery, especially in a matter where Avil-Marduk does not thrust him on. For this pursuit of the girl is against Avil's express advice, as I am surely informed."

Zabini accordingly handed the tablet to Ruth, who read:—

"Isaiah writing secretly to Imbi-Ilu by the hands of a trusty messenger. I have heard how Ruth my betrothed is unhappy in the temple of Nabu, and am resolved to take her to a safe, agreeable hiding spot at a distance from Babylon. Deliver her to-night, at the first 'double-hour' after sunset, to the three persons who shall meet her by the clump of five palm trees before the gate of your temple. They are to be trusted in all things, and will show my signet as voucher. I will be at hand with a closed carriage, to take her away. Farewell."

"Isaiah's seal!" exclaimed Ruth, joyously, recognizing the likeness of the hero Eabani, "and the characters are like those from his hand."

"I have consulted with Hasba," added Imbi, "and we have decided it is best for you to go. Doubtless these persons are faithful servants of your father, though Isaiah would not mention them by name, lest the letter should fall into unfriendly hands."

Accordingly, the rest of the day Ruth passed in delightful impatience. She was to be taken from Babylon. She was to see her betrothed. She was to be put beyond the power of the hated king. Zabini had to urge her that this one time, at least, she should eat heartily; for doubtless she would have to journey the night long, and would need all her strength. When twilight fell, Ruth had gathered her little bundle, said farewell to Zabini and the friendly priests' wives, and restlessly counted the stars as they twinkled forth one by one above the great tower. The time seemed endless before Imbi and Hasba conducted her stealthily through the silently opened gate, and she quitted the refuge that had sheltered so long and well. The five palm trees were just visible in the thickening gloom. Fifty paces brought her to them, and there, as promised, were waiting three figures, the capes of their long mantles drawn so completely across their faces that in the starlight no features were visible. Imbi peered about to see that there were no unfriendly watchers.

"Your business?" he demanded of the three; and one answered, in a husky voice that Ruth did not in the slightest recognize:—

"We are the servants of the good Lord Daniel, and act for his excellent friend Isaiah. Jehovah grant," the wish sounded exceedingly fervent, "that you have brought our adorable young mistress with you."

"You answer well," replied Imbi, "but I must see your token."

The speaker drew back his mantle far enough to uncover a faint rushlight that he concealed, burning in a small earthen jar.

"See this, then," he answered, and held up something in the glimmer.

"It is Isaiah's seal," admitted Imbi; "you are vouched for. Take the girl and guard her well." He was turning to go, when some monitor prompted him to add sharply, "And beware of faithlessness; or, as Nabu liveth, I will make your fate no merry one, though the king himself befriend you!"

"The Lord God of Israel forbid that we should fail even to lay down our lives for our dear mistress!" protested the other.

"Go with these people, Ruth," commanded the pontiff; "and when next we meet, may it be in happier days for your father. And let Nabu and Jehovah, my god and yours, protect and prosper you."

The Jewess murmured a low farewell. The two priests hurriedly returned to the temple gate. She heard it closed and bolted. One of her new companions caught her by the hand.

"Come, little lady; Isaiah is near by with the carriage."

But at that touch, instinct, surer than knowledge, flashed a warning. The Jewess did not follow.

"Who are you?" she demanded, for the first time wavering, "which of my father's servants? Your voices are strange."

"Merciful Jehovah!" protested the other, tightening his grasp at the word, "do you not know the voice of your dear Simeon?"

"You are not Simeon," cried the girl, startled now in truth. "I do not understand. I will not go with you."

But a woman's cracked voice piped at her elbow. "Come, pretty gosling; the carriage is ready. No fears; your friends provide everything!"

It needed no more to make Ruth's lips open in a piercing scream, a second, a third, before three pairs of rude hands plucked her round the throat and almost throttled her.

"Curses on you, Binit," the first speaker was muttering, "for croaking so soon! Off with her; the priests are rousing!"

Force irresistible swept Ruth from her feet. She was carried away by main strength, still struggling feebly, and gasping out little shrieks whenever the grip on her throat relaxed the slightest. There was indeed need of haste, for the gate was opening, while Imbi's voice sounded, "Torches! After the kidnappers!" and a great clamour was rising from the temple compound.

The weakest animal is terrible at bay, and so was the Jewess. Once she almost writhed out of the arms that gripped so fast; but long before the bewildered priests could do more than rush blindly hither and thither in the dark, her captors had hurried her to a closed carriage that awaited under the shadow of the long wall of a granary. The three flung her inside, and two leaped in after, while the first speaker, whom the woman had addressed as Gudea, bounded upon the driver's stand and lashed the horses furiously.

It was some moments before Ruth lay back on the cushions, silent, helpless, too stricken and terrified to shed one tear, but quaking with dry sobs of impotent agony. The carriage flew through the night at a terrific pace, Gudea never sparing the horses. For a time the abductors were content to let their prize lie quiet; then, when the distance from the *ziggurat* seemed great enough to defy all pursuit, and speech became audible, the cracked voice of Binit sounded again.

"Now, my little lady, be reasonable. Harm you? Binit and Gudea and their dear friend Tabni harm a pretty dove like you? We would not ruffle a feather for a talent of gold. Cease crying, then; listen."

Ruth's spasms of sobbing ended; not because she was in the least comforted, but through utter exhaustion.

"You are driving me to the palace, are you not?" was her trembling question. "Are you servants of Mermaza?"

Even in the dark she could see Binit throw up her nose in a crackling laugh.

"Servants of Mermaza? The last person in Babylon we wish to see at present is the 'Master of the Eunuchs.' Eh, Tabni?"

"You are right, by Nergal!" snickered the charmer.

"Where, then, are you taking me?" moaned Ruth, in nowise reassured.

"To a river boat that waits us."

Ruth made a desperate effort to speak calmly. "You imagine I am handsome, and will fetch a great price as a slave. My father is in prison, but he has rich friends. They will pay any ransom you can ask within reason."

"You a slave?" howled Binit; "Istar forefend the thought! Do you think us as heartless as Ninkigal?"

"By any god or demon you fear, if indeed you fear any," implored the Jewess, "tell me, then, for what you have seized me?"

Binit laughed and screamed again. "Verily, you *are* affrighted. Why have we taken you? Because his Majesty loves you, to be sure."

Ruth was smitten dumb by her agony. Binit merely grinned through the gloom, and continued: "You are asking why we make for the river boat. Hearken, then. From the time my pious Gudea parted with Avil-Marduk, after most surly threats on the high priest's part, somewhat has seemed needful to restore us to the king's good graces; for since the examination of your most noble father—" A faint groan from the Jewess induced even Binit to forbear, and she changed her thread of narration.

"Now, if we were to drive you straight to the palace, what would happen? Out would bustle my lord Mermaza, and take you from us, and away you would vanish in the king's harem,—while we would be left with cold thanks and perchance a poor gift of five shekels. But my Gudea is rightly called 'The Wise.' His design is this: Tabni and I put you on a river barge, and embark, professing that you are my slave-maid. We take you upstream to a quiet village near Sippar, where Tabni has a brother-in-law who will be hospitable. When we are well on our way, Gudea, who remains in Babylon, goes straight to the king. 'Lord,' he will say, 'I can get you your Jewess. She is no longer at Borsippa.' His Majesty questions, and Gudea will answer, 'Lord, I cannot tell you where the maid is hidden, but pay me ten talents and I swear I can produce her.' The king rejoices to get you thus cheaply; you will too rejoice, as soon as you learn the sweets of being his favourite; and we rejoice, dividing the riches. Surely, Gudea is a most wise man!"

If a second groan from Ruth meant assent to this assertion, Binit was rewarded. Not iron, but ice, had entered into the young girl's soul. She sat on the cushions, in helpless misery, while Gudea lashed and cursed at the horses.

"But the seal—the letter from Isaiah?" Ruth at last plucked up courage to ask.

"Ah!" chirruped Binit, "for that we must thank the excellent Tabni. Luck sent him a letter from Isaiah his way; and even you must confess that he imitated the hand cleverly, and cut a new seal that would pass in the faint light when we showed it to Imbi-Ilu."

A third groan, and for a long time Ruth gave not another sound. It was a long drive across the breadth of Babylon, from the Borsippa suburb on the extreme southwest, to the river. Ruth hoped against hope that there might be a rescue. Imbi-Ilu was not a man to sit down helpless before a fraud like this. But as the carriage sped onward, this tiny gleam of hope sank to a faint spark indeed.

Once, in fact, as the horses' hoofs beat hollow upon the bridge crossing a canal, they were suddenly halted. It was the guard-house marking the octroi limit to the inner city. Voices sounded and a lantern light flashed through the wicker body of the carriage.

"You are late," a gruff soldier's voice was grumbling. "Few honest people drive at such an hour. I must search your carriage, lest you bring in something liable to 'gate money.'"

Ruth started from her lethargy, opened her lips for a scream, when, before a sound could escape, Binit's fingers squeezed her neck.

"Not a twitter!" murmured the wailer, hoarsely, "though you strangle."

"Friend," spoke Gudea, naught abashed, "I have nothing taxable and am in great haste."

They heard the chink of a bit of silver, an appeased grunt from the official, the lash whistled, and the horses went forward with a bound. Ruth was gasping before Binit relaxed her hold.

"Fool," snapped the latter, "had the guard taken you, what profit to you? Would he not have sent you straight to the king?"

So they hastened onward, Ruth seeing nothing of all the silent streets and market squares they threaded. Presently they rattled over brick pavements, and she knew they were on the quays. Then the carriage halted with a jerk, voices sounded again, and Gudea thrust open the door.

"Out with you," he ordered, "the boat has waited long, and the captain is cursing and impatient!"

"But the girl must be painted," objected Binit.

"Haste, then. Ea knows what will befall if Imbi raises the alarm."

They were in the muddy courtyard of a warehouse, the thatched lofts and storerooms rising in the blackness on every side; two or three swarthy boatmen were standing by in the light of a pair of flickering torches. Binit drew her prisoner's mantle until it covered the face.

"Now, my gosling," squeaked she in an ear, "one little cry, and you feel this tingle!" And she followed up her word by pricking the Jewess's neck with the tip of a very keen knife.

Ruth was silent while Binit hurried her up a dark stairway to an upper loft, full of straw. And there, by an uncertain rushlight, she tore off the girl's white dress, not neglecting to appropriate two valuable rings on Ruth's fingers, smeared the Jewess's body with a red cosmetic that gave her the hue of a sun-tanned peasant; and finally, to complete a transformation, which she accomplished with a dexterity worthy of a loftier cause, threw over her the soiled and sombre garments suitable to a slave-girl.

"A proper serving-maid in truth, by Istar!" asserted Binit, surveying her work, while Gudea summoned from below, "Haste! The boat is departing."

Binit let the cold edge of the knife touch Ruth's throat yet a second time. "Remember," was her warning, "to the boatmen you are my maid. Chatter otherwise—" but she did not complete the promise; the dumb, scared expression on Ruth's face was token that the threat had gone home.

From the warehouse Tabni and Gudea accompanied them to the quay, where, amid a score of dark masts and hulks, they sought a low-lying, clumsy river barge. The exorcist aided the others aboard, while the six boatmen were loosing the tackling.

"We have waited two 'double hours,'" swore the master, "for your wife and her accursed wench. Another half shekel, or I thrust you all ashore!"

"With gladness, good captain," quoth Gudea, complying, and feeling very generous with so much of the king's silver prospectively his own.

"And you will not promise to give the king our treasure," enjoined Binit, in a whisper, "for less than ten talents, not though he rage, and talk of calling for Khatin."

"By Nergal, surely not! I will begin by demanding twenty—"

His words ended with a cry. There was a splash over the low gunwale into the sluggish water that crept around the quay, and a wide ripple spread out under the starlight. In a trice the three friends began to tear their hair and howl piteously.

"Overboard!" groaned Tabni, rending his mantle. "Lost!"

"No, madness," exhorted the captain, coolly, "it was only your maid that missed her balance. She will drift beneath the quay and drown. But another as good is only ten shekels in the market!"

"Ten talents!" shrieked Binit; and she would have leaped in after, but the boatman dragged her back fiercely.

"Do not rave," he commanded; "none of you can swim. She rises yonder a second time. Well, I will save her for five shekels."

"Yours! Yours! Only save!" came from the three in a breath; while Binit threw her mantle over her head, and screamed and moaned.

The boatman flung off his garment, plunged overboard, and presently,—though it taxed all his art,—he was seen plashing alongside, upbearing the Jewess. She was unconscious when they laid her on the deck, and it was no easy matter to revive her. At the first gasps of returning life, Binit hastened her down into the little stern cabin, rejoicing all the while that, thanks to the excellence of the cosmetic, it had not yielded to the water, and the boatman could have discovered nothing.

"She is safe?" demanded Gudea, anxiously, when his wife reappeared, leaving Tabni down below.

"Safe, praised be Istar; but she must hate the king terribly to prefer suicide to his harem. How we must watch her! And remember the price,—ten talents, nothing less."

"Nothing less," assented Gudea; then he gave the master his promised bounty, and leaped ashore.

The hawsers were cast loose; the six sturdy boatmen thrust out their long sweeps, and worked the barge slowly into the current, where the soft night wind, puffing from the distant southern gulf, bellied out the huge square sail, and the barge began crawling northward over the black water. Soon it would be past the river gates, and furlongs away from Babylon. The exorcist stood watching the receding boat for a long time, from the deserted quay.

"Ten talents," he repeated, "are ours as surely as Samas will rise with his sun to-morrow. Verily, O Gudea, the gods have planted in you a most clever heart!"

And then, being a very pious man, he vowed three white heifers to Marduk out of gratitude for this high favour.

CHAPTER XIII

Long after the easy heaving of the boat on the choppy waves told that they were well on their journey, Ruth continued to struggle and moan.

"I swear to you," she would cry again and again to Binit, "I swear by the awful name of my father's God, that if the chance come again, I will fling myself in the river. Death is sweet beside passing into Belshazzar's cruel clutch. Before the throne of the Most High God, whose ear is open to the cry of the innocent, I will stand and curse you!"

"Hush!" vainly exhorted Binit; "think of being his Majesty's favourite,— the jewels, the dresses, the eunuchs to serve you!"

"Away with them!" groaned the Jewess; "if indeed Belshazzar shall love me so well as to grant me one boon, it shall be this, to ask the heads of you two, and of Gudea."

"Be still!" warned the wailer, producing her knife; "the boatmen will hear you."

But, helpless as Ruth seemed, she was not utterly devoid of understanding. "You dare not!" she challenged defiantly, "dare not! Will the king give a shekel for my dead body?"

Tabni produced from his girdle a little flask of blue Phœnician vitrium. "We must quiet her," he remarked grimly to Binit, "or there is trouble yet. She must sleep."

The captive resisted, but her guards forced down the liquor by thrusting a blade betwixt her teeth. The draught burned like fire on Ruth's tongue, but, once swallowed, she felt a fearful languor creeping over her. Vain to resist it: her eyelids became heavy as lead, and even the pain in her heart ceased galling. It was not long before her heavy breathing told that she slumbered.

"What has ailed your maid?" demanded a surly boatman from above. "You made wondrous ado over such a slattern!"

"Alas," whimpered Binit, "the poor thing is tormented by most horrible 'sickness-fiends'; I feel for her as for my own daughter."

Then the good woman, having arranged with Tabni to take turns watching their precious charge through the night, composed herself also for slumber.

But Ruth, as she slept, had all the fair and lovely things that had hitherto made up the gladsome world of her guileless life, return to her. Her father, her mother, who had become only a memory while she was yet a little child, and Isaiah,—all were there. Then she dreamed that some one spoke to her, "Belshazzar the sinful lies with the dead; his power is vanished forever." And she walked in a strange city, not Babylon; and Isaiah was at her side, while all around were fair and lofty mountains. Isaiah's hand was in hers, she knew she was his wife, and he said to her, "Behold Jerusalem! the city which God gives back to us! Here is our home, and let us be glad together!" Before them was a stately temple, but not that of Nabu or Marduk. Whereupon Isaiah said: "Let us enter in and give thanks to the good Lord God." But just as she was passing within the gates, her whole being quivering with rapturous joy, the sweet dream ended; and she was lying on a rude straw pallet, and awakening—where?...

A sudden rasping of tackling plucked her down from paradise to the nethermost abyss. There was a thin streak of twilight stealing through the open hatch. Near her was stretched Tabni, snoring a little louder than a bull. Her misery returned to the Jewess in one awful surge; she pressed her hands to her face. "Lord God, if indeed Thou hast any power at all, have pity," was her murmured prayer, "and let me die!" But a rustle at her side proclaimed the presence of Binit. "The little mistress," purred the woman, "is awaking refreshed and happy?"

Ruth did not answer. "Be comforted," continued the wailer; "we shall reach our destination by noon, and there we shall all delight to serve you. Here, Tabni," rousing the "charmer" with a kick, "go on deck, bring the lady some sweet wine and the cakes of fine barley I provided. She is faint."

Grumbling, and rubbing his eyes, the other was about to comply, when a frightful howl from the deck above made captors and captive startle together. A second howl was followed by a distant shout and yell, then in turn by a furious clatter of the oars upon their thole-pins.

"Marduk defend us!" cried Binit, the most frightened of the three, "what happens? Up, Tabni—" more words were drowned by the simultaneous bellows of the six boatmen, "Save, O Nergal, save!" all the time they were working their sweeps like madmen, while the great sail came down with a crash that made the barge quiver from stem to stern.

Tabni thrust his head from the hatchway, cast his single eye about in the morning half-light, then added his voice to the yell of terror.

"Will you destroy me?" implored Binit. "What has befallen?" But Ruth lay perfectly still; at that moment she was thinking that no human ill could make her condition worse.

Tabni dropped from his station, his face the colour of a whited tile. His jaws twitched so that he could scarce utter a syllable; then came two words, "River thieves!"

"River thieves?" groaned Binit, leaping up as if she had sat on an adder.

"Their boats are hard after us. Two skiffs, ten men in each. The bargemen are straining to make for shore. Then they will only lose the boat. Woe! woe! If we are taken—"

A prolonged screech from Binit, who practised her art in very earnest now, drowned out Tabni's own noise. In the first instant of silence the voice of the barge captain thundered: "Up, all of you, if you would save liberty. Fling these wine-jars overboard, as quickly as if the Maskim were following!"

With feverish haste Binit led or rather carried the Jewess to the deck. A glance told the whole story. Out from the bank of gray morning mist that clung over a stagnant lagoon near the eastern bank were shooting two long reed boats, full of armed men, who came straight on toward the luckless barge. The boatmen had dropped the sail, as useless in the morning calm, and were pulling with despairing energy toward the western shore, in hopes of escaping to land, where they could save their freedom, though the barge was doomed as plunder.

"Every plague-fiend pounce on you, woman," was the captain's greeting to Binit, while he sweated over his oar; "it was waiting for you that delayed us and gave these scorpions their chance." And even while he spoke, a whoop of triumph pealed across the glassy river, and two arrows splashed under the barge's stern.

Yet, despite all the master's cursings and rage, Binit would not aid Tabni in thrusting the cargo overboard, but simply sat on a bale, clutching tight hold of Ruth.

"Ten talents," the wailer was repeating, even while her knees beat together, "ten talents, if only I can hold you fast!"

A third arrow dug into the deck, and the boatmen put forth their last strength. But the two skiffs were flying three cubits to their two. Already they could see the white teeth and wolfish bright eyes of the bandits.

"Yield, yield as you love your lives!" bawled many shrill voices. A new flight of arrows smote down a rower, but at this instant the barge thumped on a mud-bank close to the western shore, and stuck fast.

"Save yourselves!" was the last shout of the captain, and he with his remaining men dashed through the shallow water, and, scrambling up the low bank, were soon on shore, flying inland at full speed, leaving their passengers to the mercy of fate.

"Come, little lady!" Binit commanded; but Ruth hung perfectly limp on her arms, and Tabni and the woman lifted her and tugged her to the shore.

"Run!" exhorted they, setting the Jewess on her feet.

There was no time to be lost. The bandits, leaving the barge to plunder later, paddled straight up to the embankment, and were in pursuit in a twinkling. "Three prizes! After them!" was the general yell.

"Run!" commanded Binit again, when Ruth still dragged helplessly. And at the word she relaxed for a trifle her grasp. In an instant the Jewess had glided out of it, and wheeled, as if in bewildered terror, straight toward the robbers.

"Ten talents lost!" And Binit gave the loudest screech of all her noisy life.

By instinct she and Tabni turned to recover their prisoner, but arrows flew out to greet them, and in a moment Binit was moaning in a heap, as a shaft grazed her shoulder, while ten rough hands were securing the charmer, and as many more were holding Ruth. Then twenty tongues wagged all together, shouting, cursing, laughing, questioning; until, the breath of the robbers having failed, they dragged their three captives back to the barge, which they speedily rifled with a thoroughness born of long experience.

Only when the first flush of victory had spent itself did some order become apparent, and the late kidnappers, with their victims, were ranged before an enormous Amorite, rings in nose and ears, jewels all over his tawdry dress, a tremendous spiked mace flourishing in his fingers.

Binit was so frightened that she had ceased howling; Tabni held down his head as if avoiding scrutiny; while Ruth remained in perfect silence, as if dumbness were her last refuge.

"Well, my brothers," commented the leader, surveying the three, and pulling reflectively at his nose ring, "the gods reward us for the morning's toil. These good folk seem to be worth little for ransoms, but, praised be Moloch! there are Arabian caravan merchants in the next village ahead, who, if they have not started for Egypt, will give silver shekels for three such likely slaves."

The announcement drew forth a new spasm of screams from Binit, who cast herself at the Amorite's feet.

"Oh, kind, handsome, generous lord!" she entreated, "do not sell to Egypt. See, I am wounded; I cannot work; I shall die under the whip!"

"Now, by the Maskim," swore the giant, "this is the first time for long I have been 'kind or handsome' to man or maid!" And he with his fellows brayed together with laughter.

"Pity us," thrust in Tabni, stretching forth his hands beseechingly. "I cannot labour. Alas! I am old; soon I must make my peace with Ea, and prepare to die."

But as he spoke, a bandit leaped forth before the rest. "Do you not know me, Tabni, you half-blind coney?—Eri-Aku the Elamite, whom you drove into this life by your false accusations of murder. Great mercy if I do not commit murder in truth! Give me leave, comrades—"

He brandished his sword over the quivering charmer's head, but his companions plucked him back, while the leader set eyes on Ruth.

"Comely for a swart peasant maiden," he remarked, "but her limbs are frail as lily stems. She cannot work."

"Deliver her to me, noble captain," suggested Eri-Aku; "my hut in the marshes needs a likely wench like her."

The blood came tingling into the Jewess's face, and crimsoned almost under her reddened skin, as the Elamite's words and leer smote her. But the captain shook his head.

"All captives must be sold for the good of the band. She goes to the Arabians like the rest."

Binit commenced to bawl out something to the effect that this was no ordinary serving-maid, and that the king would give for her riches untold. But alas for the wailer's craftiness, Ruth looked anything but the favourite of Belshazzar, thanks to the cosmetic; while to Binit's signs and grimaces to her to declare herself, she answered not one word.

"The woman raves!" declared the Amorite, and he ordered his men to gag Binit and Tabni, and haste away, for there was no telling how soon a king's bireme might be up the river, and their situation become awkward.

Therefore three captives spent the morning very disconsolately, paddling northward by hidden canals and watercourses in the bandits' skiffs. The sun was broiling them at noon when the robbers landed at a squalid mud village, where the Arab caravan train was halting. Fifty odd grumbling, dirty-brown camels were kneeling on the slough of the little square, while their drivers adjusted the last bales of Babylonish carpets and Indian muslins that had just come up from the gulf. The Amorite marched his prisoners before the master of the troop, and the bargain was not long in making.

"These people were come by honestly?" quoth the merchant, with one eye in his head, for he knew his man.

"Honestly, by Moloch!" and the Amorite swore an oath loud enough to make up for all its other shortcomings.

"But these two," objected the Arab, jerking a thumb towards Binit and Tabni, "are too old for hard toil. The risk on the desert is great. I can spare little water. Of the three, one is sure to die."

"Consider how cheaply you get them. The three, and only forty shekels!"

"Not unreasonable, but they look most sluggish for field work."

"'Much scourging, much labour!'" answered the chief, "so runs the old proverb."

"The Egyptian taskmasters remember that, by Baal!" cried the Arab, gleefully, while he counted out the sum; then, with a sudden glance at one of his subordinates, a low-browed young fellow: "Verily, what ails you, Shaphat? Have these creatures the evil eye, that you gape at them so?"

The man addressed only shuffled away, remarking "that he had known something about the prisoners in Babylon, and would tell the leader later."

The Amorite and his following went their ways, rejoicing in the good fortune the god of gain had sent them. The Arabs tied their new passengers upon the backs of camels, and the caravan started; but it did not move rapidly. First a camel went lame, then a girth broke and let a heavy load tumble, then a donkey broke loose and was captured with difficulty. Night caught the caravan at a second little village only a few furlongs above the first.

The master of the Arabs was a discerning man, and he presently called Shaphat aside, and pointed to the youngest prisoner,

"You act strangely, fellow," declared the merchant; "did you know this girl in Babylon? When I engaged you, I understood you were a Jew, once servant of the imprisoned minister, Daniel. To my mind, this maid is of your own race."

"You are right," was the seemingly frank answer. "She is a Jewess, and at some time I have met her in the city; but I forget at whose house she may have been servant. As you see, she is comely. Treat her well, and she will bring twice the price of the two others. And do not bind her. Who dreams that a frail thing such as she can run away?"

"You speak well; she shall not be bound; but cease making eyes at her. Her good looks are not for such as you." Whereupon Shaphat professed himself all obedience.

That night Ruth lay alone upon a dirty truss of straw in a village hut, while without great camels grunted, dogs bayed the moon, and watchmen trolled coarse ditties. First one calamity had thronged upon her, then another, from the moment Isaiah took her from her father's house, only an hour ago it seemed. She had long since passed beyond the solace of tears. She had striven to pray. Her whispered words seemed only to awaken echoes of mockery. Either Jehovah was Himself a fiend, or He was helpless, Bel-Marduk His master. Once a terrible thought crossed her mind. She would curse Jehovah, she would cry to Marduk, to Istar, and to Ramman; the Babylonians called on them and prospered, why might not she?—what good thing had Jehovah granted, that she should love Him? But at the suggestion all the strong forces of the Jewess's nature rose in rebellion within her. Should she, the daughter of Daniel, the betrothed of Isaiah, near and dear to two men who were perilling their lives for the sake of Jehovah, be the one to doubt? No, though the present ills waxed tenfold worse, if such a thing might be! And presently, it seemed as if out of the night a voice was speaking, and she heard it, while an awful stillness was reigning in her heart,—the words of the psalm of her people, the song of David when God delivered him from the murderous hand of Saul.

"The Lord is my rock, and my fortress and my deliverer:

My God, my strength, in whom I will trust,

My buckler and the horn of my salvation, and my high tower.

I will call upon the Lord, who is worthy to be praised,

So shall I be saved from mine enemies.

He bowed down the heavens also, and came down:

And darkness was under his feet.

He delivered me from my strong enemy, and from them that hated me."

The voice was gone. The camp had become very still. A wondrous peace and hope seemed to have stolen over Ruth. She was about to let herself drift away into the arms of sleep, knowing by her pure, unreasoning woman's faith, that One stronger than father or lover was at her side to shield from all real harm, when she heard a guarded footfall on the earthen floor. A figure of a man darkened the little patch of black violet that marked the door; then he spoke:—

"Lady Ruth, dearest mistress, do you not know me?"

It was the voice of Shaphat.

The next morning the master of the caravan and his fellow merchants and camel drivers were scouring all the country round about. They began at last to give some ear to the frenzied protestations of Binit, that the youngest captive was indeed a prize for the king. The Jewish servant, who had hired himself to them at Babylon, had vanished from all sight, taking with him his fellow countrywoman and a round little bag of money. But the merchants could not push their search too far, for the village bailiffs might ask them to explain how it was the maid had passed into their possession; and if they admitted the Amorites' share in the matter, there might be more disagreeable questions to answer. Accordingly, after a bootless search through another day, they set off across the desert, and in due time Binit and Tabni found employers in the Sais slave-market, who taught them the inconveniences of sloth in Egyptian field labour.

But long before these twain had reached the end of their wanderings, their confederate Gudea had been started on a yet longer journey, with even scantier prospects of return. Promptly on the morning after the kidnapping, he had bribed his way through the chamberlains to a private audience with Belshazzar himself. As expected, the king had been stormy at first, but ended by paying the exorcist two talents as earnest money, with promise of eight more when the girl Ruth was delivered. Gudea promptly sent a letter up river, bidding Tabni and Binit return with their booty in all haste. No answer; and a second letter had no better reply. When a third message brought nothing, Gudea began to realize that his associates had miscarried in some unknown manner; while the king waxed impatient, and hinted that the earnest money was best back in the treasury. Then Gudea, being at his wit's end, let all wisdom forsake him. He turned the two talents into gold, and strove to steal out of the city by night, hoping to save at least this fraction of the expected booty. But the crafty gods that had thus far prospered him, at this moment abandoned him. He was arrested at the Gate of the Chaldees, by command of Avil-Marduk, who had not forgotten the affair of the trial, and was not slow in informing Belshazzar that the exorcist had tried to cheat the monarch himself. The case before the high justiciar was brought to a speedy issue, for the defence was the lamest.

"Let Gudea, the exorcist," sounded the sentence, "die the death by the iron sword. Let his head be set above the Gate of Ilu, and let his body be flung to the hyenas and ravens; so shall all men fear to extort money deceitfully from our lord the king."

"Hearken," the despairing exorcist had howled, while Khatin and two assistants pinioned him, before haling him from the tribunal: "Am I not the most pious wizard in Babylon? Shall I sacrifice to all the gods for nought?"

"Off, off!" commanded the justiciar, quitting his seat; "silence this babble!"

Gudea turned to Khatin, struggling vainly to free his hands.

"Ah, dearest Khatin, surely you will not let me die. Remember all the pleasant pots we have drained together at Nur-Samas's; remember our pledges of friendship, and how often I have professed that I love you!"

"And do I not love *you*, my precious jackal?" said the headsman, with a snort. "Have I not many a time said, 'The more love I bear a man, the more joy to see him safely ended.' Bethink you, sweet friend, is it not pleasanter to slip out of the world with the delightful whir of my sword singing in your ears, than to depart as did the lamented Saruch, with Binit and yourself howling above him?"

"Ah," whimpered the exorcist, so limp now that the others had to keep him on his legs, "it is not the dying only, though that is most fearful; but woe! alas! despite all my sacrifices, what will not the gods do to me? How may I justify myself to Ea? Allat will torture me eternally!"

"Fie, my lovely Gudea," belched the headsman, "what expectations for a man of your piety! Yet be consoled; Ea sends every soul to its proper place, and even Allat can be little less handsome than your dearest wife, especially when Binit's palm-wine was heady."

"Cursed be you! cursed with a dying man's last curse!" howled Gudea, all hope vanishing now, as they dragged him away. But Khatin only answered with his mildest chuckle: "I have heard that music whistled by stouter asses than you, comrade. But no grudge; I must drink a double pot to-night at the beer-house,—one for you, one for me,—as token of how I shall miss you."

But Gudea's only answers came in wordless chatterings. And how it prospered him on the rest of his long journey is not written, even in the wisest book.

CHAPTER XIV

On the same night that Ruth lay down to sleep in the mud cottage, Atossa, betrothed of Belshazzar, "queen designate of Sumer and Akkad" not to add titles more, was pacing the leafy avenues of the Hanging Gardens. As the summer advanced she had been removed to the chambers beneath this mountain forest, from the sultrier rooms of the palace. Here, with the cool mould and the ocean of tossing green interposed betwixt her and the parching sun, one could almost forget that out in the dusty world the wretched Jews of the labour gang were panting and groaning, that all the fields about the city were searing brown with the pitiless heat, and the canals were creeping riverward through beds half empty. No sensuous delight was wanting to lull the Persian into forgetfulness of the past. Belshazzar had spared nothing. The maids, the young eunuchs, that served her were the handsomest, the most soft-footed and skilful-handed that could be found in all the slave-markets betwixt Carthage and India; the waters that sprayed from the fountains breathed rare essences and Sabæan nard. There were fresh flowers sprinkled each morn in lieu of carpets, and a cool wreath always ready; the fragrance of the petals wafted on every wind. Each day they brought the mistress some new dance, or some new music. And in the evening, after the sun's copper ball had sunk behind the long shadows of Imgur-Bel, and the broad Euphrates flashed in ever darkening ripples, then it was joy to quit the lower chambers and roam over the wondrous garden domain. There the fireflies would flit out with their beacons from behind fern and thicket, and the nightingale would throb and the thrushes whistle from their safe coverts in the trees, till the night seemed one enchantment, and the Hanging Gardens indeed the Chaldee's "Garden of the Blest."

But on this night Atossa was not watching the stars creep out of the feathery palm trees, nor knew she the silence when the last tired bird ceased trilling, and hid his head behind a wing. She was waiting for Darius.

Masistes had brought her the message, and said he had it from Ariathes. The prince would meet her in the Gardens at this hour, for there was something of weight that he must tell. The dangers, said Ariathes, had all been foreseen and provided for; there could come no peril. As for Atossa, she thought very little of the dangers or of anything else, save this one fact, that speedily she would be face to face with the man she loved.

Atossa was alone in the Gardens. To secure the solitude had been easy. Long since her servants had learned that the Persian desired nothing better than to be left alone of an evening, with only the unseen birds, the whispering trees, and the friendly stars for her company. None wondered when she did the like this evening. The Gardens were safe as the harem, every ingress and exit guarded below by soldiers. What danger to let her roam at will?

She sat upon a moss-bank, and felt for the little cool weeds at her feet, pulling them one by one. There was a sweet northeast wind crooning over the Gardens, and setting all the groves to whispering. "The breeze is from my own Iran," she spoke aloud, while the hidden crickets answered her; "it has blown over Ecbatana and Susa; it has kissed the mouth of my mother, my father; it bears their kisses to me." She shook her coronal of golden hair, and let the soft breeze caress her neck. The Gardens were growing very still. Once or twice arose a distant chant from the river boatmen, singing as they plied their oars. Save for that, she might have dreamed herself a thousand furlongs removed from human kind. As the silent night crept onward there spread an earthy smell about, the smell of green things growing, and the very odour made the breeze a delight. The great trees above her head continued their murmur,—the cadence just varied enough by the puffing wind to make music sweeter than that of harp or flute. She was letting the dreamy mood possess her, when her ear caught the snap of a twig under gentle stepping sandals. Some one had mounted the privy staircase; a form was approaching through the soft darkness.

Atossa sprang to her feet; she gave one little cry. The stranger bounded toward her; and she heard the voice and felt the touch of Darius, son of Hystaspes....

They sat and talked together upon the cool moss, for a long while, in tones so low that the sage old thrush who had stirred on his bough over their two heads gathered nothing, though he listened long. But at last, when their minds passed down from heaven to earth, their voices grew stronger, for their lips were no longer so near.

"Lady mine," spoke Darius, his strong arm still holding fast, "do you know what Isaiah the Jew has told me? Do you know for what end Belshazzar brought you here?"

"Have I not heard from Isaiah's own lips the story of what befell in these same Gardens and of the king's unholy guile?"

"You know all and are yet so calm?"

She looked into his face almost defiantly.

"Because Ahura grants to you the fame of being 'King of the Bow' and of swinging the stoutest sword in wide Iran, has he denied that I also should be strong to bear? Am I not Cyrus's own child, and must I show these 'lie-loving' Chaldees only tears and pain?"

"By Mithra, Lord of Light, I think it is I that must gain the courage out of you, for when I hear of your state, and the treachery with which Belshazzar had ensnared you, I was close to weeping like a maid, and doing deeds of madness!"

A faint sound, as of something moving, startled her.

"What is this?" she cried, leaping from the moss-bank. "There is danger!"

The sound, be it what it might, had vanished. Darius peered into the gloom; black shadows, the dim tracery of leafage, the distant sheen of the star mist—that seemed all.

"No peril," he protested, drawing her back to the soft cool carpet. "Boges is on watch below; the eunuchs proved exceeding corruptible. Naught will be suspected."

"So Ahura grant," she murmured, pressing closer, "yet I hear that spies are all about you. You are in danger, grievous danger. Would that you were back in Susa, were anywhere, save here,—in the chiefest place of peril."

Darius laughed softly. "Are you so glad to have me vanish? I declare to you by all the host of the holy 'Yazatas,' the just spirits who ever wait on God, that where you are, were it in the foulest prison, or parching desert, or in remotest star, there would be my *Garo-nmana*, my 'Abode of Song'!"

"Folly!" she replied, but her laugh was sweet as the dying winds. "What am I?—a voice and a blooming flower; to-day I am joy to you, or to another, because my face is fair to see. To-morrow all is past; faded like every blossom, I lie down and die, and the world knows of me no more. But you," and there was pride in the light of her smile, "there will be other tales to tell of Darius, son of Hystaspes, long after the day when your tongue is cold and still. And that should be your task, doing fair deeds in the sight of men, not wasting griefs or tears on such as me."

But his answer was a hand upon her lips, and he answered her: "I will not give wisdom for your foolishness, the barter is unfair. But this I know, concerning the Great Day when every soul must cross the Chinvat Bridge to enter into the world hereafter (for you have heard our Aryan tale as chanted by the Magi), then to every man there shall come a maiden, in beauty or foulness after his own righteousness or guile. And she shall say to him, 'See, I am thine own conscience, come to meet thee, and to dwell with thee through unending time.' And my prayer to Ahura the Merciful is but this, that when my own dread ordeal comes, and my maiden looks me in the face, her eyes and her smile may be that of Atossa, the daughter of my king."

"Folly!" cried she again, and again her laugh was sweet. But then her mood grew grave. "It is night," she said, "the stars are circling onward; soon they will wonder why I linger here so late, and some will come to see if all is well. Alas! that we have tasted of this bliss; the morsel truly is most sweet, but it is supped and gone. Am I not Belshazzar's betrothed, full soon his bride? And you, what is left save but to speed back to Susa, and tell my father all, and how he robbed me of my joy and all for naught?"

But Darius's voice grew low, he tightened the grasp upon her hand. "You speak but ill. You shall never be Belshazzar's bride. I, son of Hystaspes, have so sworn, though all the Chaldees rise to say me 'nay'!"

"Never?" He felt Atossa thrill. "What is this you say?"

His head was again close to hers when he answered. "Listen, then; for as you say, I must tell all quickly. Belshazzar asked your hand as a pledge of eternal peace betwixt Persian and Chaldee; but to make a pledge there must be no oath broken, and he has broken his. You are his betrothed, but not his bride. No law of man or God binds you to him, nor, as the Most High gives me wit and might, shall it ever bind! My position since returning from the lion hunt, whereof you must have heard the palace rumours, has been intolerable! There is never a moment when I do not tremble for my life. I fear every messenger of mine to Susa is waylaid and halted. Cyrus must not be suffered to remain blind forever. My soul loathes flight from a foe, but what is left me?"

"And have they refused you convoy back to Susa?" pressed Atossa.

"Not once, but many times,"—the prince's voice was very bitter,— "I have been to Bilsandan the vizier, and only met smooth excuses and scarcely veiled lies. Now the Elamite mountain tribes make all travel dangerous; now there is such restlessness in the gulf cities that not a soldier can be spared for escort. And yet, to cast the vizier's words back in his teeth, the garrison of Babylon grows stronger day by day, and the walls mount higher."

"You must go back to Cyrus," spoke she, with beating heart; "you must tell all to my father. But, oh!" and her woman's voice nigh faltered, "his wrath and the war will be most terrible. Aryan blood and Chaldee blood, each poured out in rivers, and my sacrifice will all be in vain. I had one joy left me, that through my own grief I was giving peace to my people, but now at last even this is taken away!"

"Not so," cried the prince, almost sternly, "for out of Belshazzar's cruelty and falsehood shall spring my joy and yours also. For now you are free, and I am free to bear you away in my flight. All is provided, horses fleet as the desert winds, and my Persian followers are with us to the death. Seven days from this night you shall look on your father's face at Susa, Ahura prospering us—my own! Gaze long, gaze hard, upon this city," he pointed over the slumbering vista of *ziggurats*, palaces, and the dark river; "to-morrow at this hour you shall see its accursed beauty no more,—except, indeed, as you ride under its gates at the side of your father when he enters it to conquer."

"Ah!" she cried, his own bright hopes kindling before her eyes, "and how may you persuade him to give me to you?"—she broke short—"Am I wrong? Do I not hear a noise?"

The prince rose once more; again eyes and ears brought him nothing. "There is naught beholding us save God's bright stars; and are not the stars best friends to man and maid in love? How shall I persuade Cyrus? Did you not see how he tossed in his mind, and how his heart was torn almost as yours or mine, when he resolved to send you to Belshazzar? Let him hear the tale we have to tell, the tale that will make every ear in Iran from Media to Bactria to tingle with hot wrath, and I know little of men, if Cyrus prove hard of heart. Let Babylon fall, as fall it will, and in these same Hanging Gardens—not then your prison, but your joy—shall they kindle the torch for our marriage feast."

But Atossa glided out of his clasp.

"Ah!" said she, outstretching her arms in the starlight, "your words are but as words spoken in a vision; I feel such sweetness cannot be. You wake dear phantoms, but they are phantoms still. I know not why; but there is a voice that tells me now, as it has told me long, that I must not look for any sudden joy. I must learn to be yet stronger, and learn to bear not only these, but new ills also. And Susa and my father are very far away."

"And do you doubt my boast?" he flashed, nigh wrathfully, at her failing to warm to his own sanguine joy.

"I doubt you?" she cried, as if scarce understanding his words,—"you? For your least wish, how glad a thing to die! But the power of Angra-Mainyu is strong, and he and his fiends put forth their might against us. Ahura will conquer, but the triumph is delayed. Fly alone; that will be safer—and let the sword of Cyrus be the key to my golden prison."

"Not save *you*?" reëchoed the prince, all the might of his strong nature rising up in refusal at her command.

"Hush! Not so loud!" warned she, and again she started; "surely in the thicket—"

"There may be other eavesdroppers!" spoke a voice from the covert directly behind them, and the words were the words of Avil-Marduk.

A shout from Darius, a cry from Atossa, answered him in the same instant.

The sword shot from the prince's scabbard and flashed in the starlight; one stroke, and Avil would have uttered no more fell counsellings, but the priest stepped deliberately forward and caught the upraised hand before Darius could gather wits enough to smite.

"Nothing rashly, your Highness," was his admonition, he himself perfectly calm. "Your life is in no danger, and I make bold to presume that any hurt that might befall your humble slave would meet with no slow requital."

And even as he spoke there emerged from his hiding-place, or out of the ground of the garden rather, for aught Darius could see in the gloom, the figures of six men, a trembling torch in the hands of one, naked swords borne by the others.

Darius stood facing them, his head thrown back haughtily, his weapon still raised high.

"Do not think to slay me without dear payment!" rang his despairing boast.

But Atossa had fallen on her knees, crying to the Babylonians, "Spare him! Spare!" for her only thought was of Darius.

"And has not Avil already told you your lives are safe?" added a newcomer, who needed no torch-glimmer on his eagle features to proclaim him the king himself. "Put away your sword, son of Hystaspes; it avails you nothing. The Lady Atossa trembles at sight of bare steel, and well she may!"

In the faint light they saw Darius break his sword across his knee and dash the hilt away.

"You are right, O king," he cried, shrill with anger, "for her sake I must bow my neck in peace. Only wreak the vengeance all on me. It was *I* who sought this meeting, who plotted all; she had no part, and is guiltless."

"The noble Persian wrongs himself," spoke Avil, as sweetly as when he commented on his dinner; "neither he nor the Lady Atossa arranged this meeting in these delightful gardens. The author is your most obedient slave." Whereupon he salaamed.

"You?" burst forth the prince. "What snake's part is this of yours? By the aid of what *dæva* came you here with the king? My plans were well laid, my servants trusty."

"Excellently laid, and exceedingly trusty," quoth Avil, still perfectly cool; "alas! that Wisdom is not ever the bedfellow of Faithfulness. It did not need the knowledge of Ea to discover that your Highness would love nothing fairer than an evening's talk with her ladyship. That being the case, and we being greatly desirous to discover your noble plans and the reports you were anxious to transmit to the king's illustrious ally, Cyrus the Persian, I took it upon myself to make this interview in every way most easy. It was I that arranged that the eunuchs and guards should prove conveniently corruptible, that nothing should hinder your easy access to these Gardens, or interrupt your agreeable conversation until you had unbosomed your hearts one to another. I must confess myself deeply pained to have to disarrange the least of your Highness's projects."

"You have overheard?" questioned the prince, controlling himself by an effort. "Be so gracious, then, as to inform a barbarous Persian like myself by what wings you flitted up into these Gardens."

"By the wings of the same privy staircase soon after your Highness ascended. You may deign to recollect you left your Boges on watch below. It was no grievous matter to overpower and gag without a cry escaping. Afterward I conducted his Majesty and these worthy guardsmen to this thicket, whence we could hear all that passed. As Marduk liveth! I believe we could have made more commotion than we did, and to little harm; you two had ears only for each other."

"And you understand Persian, priest?" asked Darius.

"Indifferently well," answered Avil, modestly,—"at least, very little that was said escaped me!"

"Then escape not this!" shouted Darius, and with the word he flung himself bodily toward Avil-Marduk.

The pontiff gave one leap backward, and in the darkness his foe just missed him, but fell with all his might upon an unlucky soldier who interposed. The man went down upon the greensward with a rattle in his throat, as Darius smote him. But the others instantly piled upon him, and after a desperate and aimless struggle the Persian was plucked from his prey. He faced Belshazzar while two guardsmen clung tight to his terrible arms.

"Well, your Majesty," rang his demand, "how long is left to me to live?"

"You are safe," answered Belshazzar, from a distance; "you saved my life from the auroch. I will not take yours at present."

"So I am a prisoner, envoy of Cyrus though I be? You refuse my demand for instant return to Susa?"

"After what has passed here and now," retorted Belshazzar, grimly, "I think you will not marvel if I dare to delay you."

"Better the executioner, and have done!" cried the prince, almost struggling out of his captors' hold.

"We gain little by bartering high words, Persian," thundered the king, in unconcealed triumph; "you are a prisoner. They shall give you the liberty of your rooms, until you prove yourself disobedient to my will."

"Am I then a hostage?"

"You shall see. In dealing with Cyrus—"

But the king said no more, for Atossa deliberately placed herself betwixt the two in their anger.

"Will the king hear me?"

All her courage had returned the instant she knew Darius's life was for the moment safe. She was the great king's daughter still, and she stood before Belshazzar, fair and strong. He told himself he had never seen man or woman more calm, more beautiful.

"I will hearken," was his sole answer, and Atossa continued her speech, that came very slowly.

"Lord of the Chaldees, when my father sent me to Babylon, I loved this man," her eyes were on Darius, "beyond all the Indian's pearls,—yes, beyond very life; but I was content to be the price paid for the peace of my people. I was resolved to be your true and faithful wife. But I come to find the price paid all in vain,—to find treachery blacker than blackest night, to learn that oaths are only to be blown out as a rushlight, at the first convenient season. My love gone, my joy all blasted, for naught, the prospering of the sapient Avil's serpent guile, and that of his cringing master." Avil had winced under the flash of her eye, but now she looked on Belshazzar. "King of Babylon, thus far have falsehoods borne you; count up well the cost. Do not think oath-breaking can prosper man or king forever. Let the walls of Babylon mount yet higher; higher still are God's heavens whence He looks downward, and beholds us all, and all the secrets locked up in the heart. You can still repent. You can send Darius to his own land, and I will yet be to you an obedient wife. You can still regard the oaths taken to Cyrus as sacred, and as such keep them fast. Thus far you have done naught that may not be undone; go no farther. But let the prince, the inviolable envoy, guarded alike by Persian and Chaldee gods, endure one hour of prison, and only heaven shall judge the war. Do not think my father is all blind. The moon cannot fall from the sky, and no man marvel. This is the moment, and the last when you may choose,—the moment which we Persians say to every man is granted,—to make choice of the Right Mind or the Wrong Mind, the great spirits ever at strife. I do not pray this for myself, nor for the son of Hystaspes, but for you, O king of the Chaldees, whom I would honour as husband if I might. To you is this word,—choose the path, of righteousness or guile, of peace or war,—choose!"

The king gazed on her, and she returned his glance fearlessly. Her beauty seemed doubled in that shimmering torchlight, her presence seemed self-illumined, glorious. For an instant, before the eyes of Belshazzar's mind there passed a vision of peace; he saw himself like the great Nebuchadnezzar, fighting as he must, but glorying in peace and not in war. He saw his kingdom prosperous and glad, and Atossa beside him on the throne, his counsellor and guide in all fair enterprise. And on the monuments in the after days, men should grave these words, "In the reign of Belshazzar the land was blessed; no war raged; no mouth lacked corn." Fair vision! And this was truly the moment of choice—to dismiss Darius or to imprison; should he thrust this vision by? But at that instant some demon or god put speech in the mouth of Avil-Marduk.

"Verily by Bel himself," and the pontiff gave a low and mocking laugh, "the Lady Atossa will almost persuade his Majesty to burn his war chariots and set his sword-hands to digging ditches!"

One laugh; did Avil know that the fate of the "Beauty of the Chaldees" hung on that single breath? But Belshazzar spoke now, the spell of Atossa all broken: "Surely as Samas and Sin bear rule in the heavens, so surely have I chosen. I know the path. And who shall teach another way to *me*?"

He made a menacing gesture in Atossa's face. She never quailed.

"You have indeed chosen," said she, in icy tone; "hereafter there is war: betwixt darkness and light, *dæva* and angel, Angra-Mainyu and Ahura-Mazda, implacable, truceless,—till the abasing of the 'Lie'!"

Belshazzar motioned impatiently to the soldiers. "Let the prince be taken to his chambers as commanded, and let the Lady Atossa go below to her eunuchs."

The two Persians sped one glance upon each other—but neither spoke farewell.

CHAPTER XV

Isaiah the Jew, whose arrest had been urgently commanded by the king, continued to defy all the zeal of the royal officers. Truth to tell, that was not great. More than one captain of the "Street Wardens" had been beholden to Daniel or his late colleague, Shadrach, for one service or another, and were loath to bring the young Hebrew within Khatin's gentle mercies. Likewise, not a Jew in Babylon, barring a few recreants, would have betrayed the youth, who passed amongst them as a veritable prophet of Jehovah, hardly less inspired than Daniel himself. When a new levy of forced labour was proclaimed, and scarce a Hebrew but had to choose betwixt toilsome days in a broiling sun and the offering of a little corn to Marduk, Isaiah had gone up and down by night among their little cottages along the Street of Kisch, exhorting, warning, encouraging. "Endure a little longer," was his message, "a few more trials to prove their devotion, and God would recall them to His mercy."

Such was the burden of Isaiah, and to Avil-Marduk's discomfiture scarcely a Hebrew chose apostasy, though the "whip-masters" had been ordered to be trebly harsh. The pontiff gnashed his teeth and swore by all the Anunnaki that he would yet break this Jewish stubbornness.

"Arrest Isaiah, living or dead," fulmined the mandate again from the palace, but the royal thunders spent themselves in noise. Isaiah had found a safe refuge, the house of Dagan-Milki, a Babylonish schoolmaster, and confessedly one of the most devoted servants of the gods in Babylon. Once upon a day Isaiah had saved the goodman's only son from the Euphrates, and now Dagan repaid the debt of gratitude. He conducted a little day school by the Borsippa Canal, where fifty boys and girls buzzed from morning till night, learning their lists of syllables, and the "Book of Fables" and the "Book of Countries and Rivers"; for there were few parents in Babylon that let even a daughter grow up so ignorant that she could not sign a letter, and had to content herself with her "nail-mark." Dagan announced that his scholars had grown so numerous that he needed an assistant, to aid him to correct their tablets. The young man he took into his family seldom showed himself to the pupils; if he had, who would have thought of connecting him with the fugitive Hebrew? Dagan was such a pious man! But a terrible day came to Isaiah when a secret messenger of Imbi-Ilu contrived to search him out, and he heard the story of the abduction of Ruth. Imbi had done what he could, but to have pushed the inquiries about her far would have brought the case to the ears of the king, and that were sheerest madness. Friendly eunuchs reported that no such maid as the Jewess had been introduced into the royal harem. Neither Isaiah nor Imbi knew what to hope or to fear. Isaiah said little of his grief, but he went about with a face seven years older than his wont; and Dagan-Milki, worthy soul, was troubled for him and had wordy comfort.

"Surely, the daughter of Daniel cannot be dead?"

"Would God I knew she had perished, spotless and unsullied; I could then have peace! But into the hands of what human 'Maskim' may she not have fallen!" was the bitter answer.

"But be not reckless in exposing yourself," urged Dagan; "you will not save her by stalking about the streets so boldly. The last time you went to search for her, in the warehouses in the lower city by the temple of Samas, I trembled for your head. The stoutest wine-jar cracks at last, if carried too often. Daniel's plight is miserable, but yours would be worse, if Avil-Marduk once puts the gyves on your wrists. No *Tartan* or vizier will interpose himself betwixt you and Khatin."

"I am in the Lord God's keeping," retorted the young Jew, with a swelling voice; "it is all one whether I live or perish!"

Dagan stifled a cynical sniffle. He did not love Jehovah more than any other Babylonian, but he did not wish to offend his guest.

"My dear Hebrew," he suggested, "at least put by your prejudices enough to accept the aid the gods will send you. Consult a necromancer. I know Kwabta, a 'wise woman' by the temple of Nergal, who keeps a familiar spirit. She can reveal everything that has befallen your unfortunate betrothed."

"Dagan," warned Isaiah, sternly, "speak not of this again, if you would be my friend. Sooner shall the king slay me with tortures than I wilfully break the ordinance of my God."

Dagan said no more. Nevertheless, he went himself privately to the witch, paid her half a shekel, and stated the facts of the case, concealing only the Jewess's name. Kwabta left him in an outer room, bidding him cover his head and mutter certain powerful spells, while in an inner chamber she conferred with her demon. She came back, reporting that the question was a difficult one, but that in ten days Dagan should have a dream, which she could interpret for a second half-shekel, and this dream would reveal all he desired to know. The schoolmaster accordingly had few hopes to bring back to Isaiah, whose mood grew blacker than ever. Another day passed, and Dagan saw that the young Hebrew was unwontedly preoccupied.

"I have been to Borsippa," he explained at length, "and talked with Imbi-Ilu. Daniel's life is in grievous danger. Avil-Marduk is preparing to demand his execution on the day of the feast of Bel, and the king will only rejoice to comply. Nevertheless, Daniel shall be saved."

"From the power of the king himself?" quoth Dagan, pricking up his ears.

"From Belshazzar's own power," assented the Jew, "but the manner is hid. I have another task, however, to-night. I must see Daniel himself. He has asked to see me."

"Daniel himself? Daniel in prison? Are you mad?" almost shrieked the schoolmaster.

"I was never in sounder mind. Zerubbabel, my friend who brought the message, keeps the prison watch to-night. The eyes of the other warders can be closed with a little silver."

Dagan argued and besought in vain. Away went Isaiah soon after nightfall, and Jehovah, or some other power who loves the bold, protected him. He had his hour alone with Daniel.

The dungeon of the palace prison was fetid, the straw damp, the only light that of a single shivering candle. At sight of his friend and all but father in chains and amid these squalid surroundings, the younger Jew burst into tears.

"Alas! my father," was his cry, while he knelt for Daniel's blessing, "what is this I see? What does the Lord God suffer? He who has served Him beyond all others, whose life has been naught but holiness, in the state of the vilest felon!"

"Peace!" commanded the old man, never more calm and majestic than now; "what is there to fear? Did God simply go with me when I was 'civil-minister' of Babylon, and cannot His goodness follow within this prison?"

"Ah! father," protested Isaiah, "I do not doubt God's power, yet how can I trust His mercy? First you, then Ruth, the guileless of the guileless, have been brought to bitter grief,—and lo! the wicked wax fat and prosper!"

"I know it well," answered Daniel, his voice unfaltering; "but all is not yet ended. I have heard of the abduction of Ruth, of the malice of Belshazzar and Avil-Marduk against me; yet neither for myself nor for her have I any fear."

"Would God you could teach me your own trust!"

The old Jew smiled gently. "You are yet young, and I an ancient river, close upon the sea. The wisdom that you ask is not written in all the books of Imbi-Ilu at Borsippa, nor can a treasure-house of silver buy. But as you fare onward with obedient will and open mind, you shall yet see the vision, and shall hear the message from on high, and know that all is well. The Chaldee's power passes not beyond the grave, and there are no griefs in Abraham's bosom."

Isaiah lifted his head, and shook the unmanly tears from his eyes.

"I have put by my faintness," spake he, as if in anger with himself; "who am I to stand as prophet to our people, when my own faith in God grows pale? You have sent for me, my father, on some weighty errand, for I know you never summon me to needless peril. Declare; I am all obedience."

Daniel spoke with bated breath. "Dearest son, Jehovah is speaking again to me in visions, as in the former time. Again His command has come upon me, and with a message which your mouth must give."

"I am unworthy to be the mouthpiece of God Most High."

Daniel smiled again. "Who of living men is worthy? But be confident and strong; fear nothing, and He will lead you out of all perils. Is the Persian Darius still in prison?"

"Closely guarded, and they watch all persons that pass out of Babylon, lest they be secret bearers of news to Cyrus. But there is a report—"

"Of what?" asked Daniel, as eagerly as ever was his wont.

"That Ariathes, the favourite servant of Darius, was not arrested with the other Persians of the prince's suite, and there is a chance that he has fled to Susa, bearing tidings of the outrage done the envoy."

"Jehovah's name be blessed, your task is made easy!"

"*My* task," cried Isaiah.

"Yours," again Daniel's voice sank low. "This is what is commanded you of God: On the day of the feast of Bel cast all fear from you. Trust in the guardianship of Jehovah. During the festival the customary watch will be relaxed. You know the great tunnel beneath the Euphrates, from the palace to the Eastern City?"

"I have been through it twice. It is treading amongst the dead to traverse it, but I do not fear."

"By means of it you can pass unnoticed to the very temple of Marduk. Take your stand upon the terrace of the *ziggurat*, before all the thousands when they approach with the ark of the idol. Cry aloud against Belshazzar, against Avil-Marduk, against the sinful city and its evil gods. For Jehovah commands that they shall not be cut off unwarned. Bid them repent, and to cease the persecution of the Lord God's people. Nevertheless they will not hear, for they are to be cut short in their sins. But though they rage against you, they shall not harm you. You shall escape. You shall go to Susa, and stand before Cyrus the righteous king, and give him the mandate of Jehovah, for God has summoned him to bring low this Babylon. The words which you shall speak to him, God will put in your mouth in due season; for He has chosen you out of all the sons of Judah for this high honour—the freeing of His people."

"My father! my father!" again Isaiah fell upon his knees, "who of all am I to do this deed? Again I cry, 'unworthy.'"

"And again I say to you, not righteousness, but obedience, is demanded. Go forward with all boldness."

"Hist!" warned Isaiah, "Zerubbabel approaches to warn us that we must part. When shall I see you again?"

"In His own good time," answered the old man, sweetly; then he laid his fettered hand on Isaiah's head, "the God of our fathers keep you, my son, in His service, and teach you that nothing truly evil may befall."

The door opened. "The guard changes," announced Zerubbabel; "away, quickly, or all is danger."

Isaiah embraced the prisoner once, and followed the friendly guardsman out of the palace precinct. Then he wended his way alone back to the house of Dagan-Milki, through the silent streets of the capital.

At the schoolmaster's door the good man himself confronted Isaiah with a beaming face and a voice that trembled with agitation.

"Glory, glory to every god! Praised be Nabu and Nergal! Compose yourself, my dear Isaiah, be collected; do not grow excited; bless your god with calmness—" but here the exhortations ended in a new shout of "Praised be the name of Bel-Marduk!" and Isaiah stared at Dagan, wondering if his kind host had been blighted in his wits.

"I would fain rejoice!" remonstrated he, coldly, for in his heart he was telling himself that he must have no other joy now save the labour for his people.

Dagan almost dragged him across the threshold, and led through the courtyard of the little house.

"Rejoice!" he was commanding, almost angrily, "rejoice! Do you not wish to be glad?" tugging Isaiah behind him, as he strode feverishly forward.

"Now, as Jehovah liveth!" protested the Jew, beginning to wax furious in turn, "shall I make merry against my will? Wherefore this cry, 'rejoice,' save for one dear thing the good God will not grant?"

"And will He not grant it?" fumed the schoolmaster, forcing on his unwilling companion. But while he spoke he felt Isaiah totter on his feet. By the light of the copper lamp he carried, Dagan saw the Jew's face turn very pale.

"Friend," Isaiah spoke hoarsely, "do not mock me if you wish to live."

"By Ramman!" swore the Babylonian, not a little fearful, "I think you are in earnest." He pushed in the door of a little sleeping chamber, and waved the lamp, sending a wan flicker around, that now hid, now revealed, all the room.

"Behold!"

Dagan pointed downward, where a mattress was spread upon the floor and on it the form of one sleeping. And as they looked, there was a rustle upon the pallet, two little hands unclasped across the breast, while Dagan saw that again the Hebrew was trembling.

"Dagan," commanded Isaiah, still hoarsely, "set the light upon the floor and get you hence." Which injunction, the schoolmaster, being a wise as well as a kindly man, hastened to obey.

"Shaphat," said Isaiah, later that same night, in another chamber of the house, "tell me the story of your flight with the Lady Ruth, for I would not suffer her to speak long, but bade her go back to rest."

Whereupon a young man, who had been dozing in a dark corner, shuffled to his feet; but he would not look Isaiah in the eye.

"Ah, lord," stammered the fellow, "who I am to tell my master,—I on whose head rests untold guilt? Who will believe, though I swear by every god? Even these Babylonians, if they know me, will cry 'bricks for the perjurer,' and will pelt me in their streets."

"And well you say," muttered Dagan, who stood by,—"the servant who robbed so kind a lord as Daniel, then conspired with that viper Gudea to work his death. By Marduk!" and he turned to Isaiah, "I will not trust him;

no, not till cockcrow! If he has saved the Lady Ruth, it is but to serve some dark and hidden end. He knows your secret. Let him never quit this house alive!"

The renegado cowered at Isaiah's feet. "Woe!" he groaned, "I am undone utterly; accursed on earth, and accursed in heaven! If such is the wrath of man, what is not God and His just and holy anger?"

But Isaiah deliberately stooped and raised the wretched man by the hand. "Peace, Dagan," he commanded, and then he looked sadly but calmly upon the apostate. "Shaphat," his voice was very gentle, "I have but just stood beside Daniel, the most righteous man in all Babylon. He is in chains in a noisome dungeon. If God suffers him to undergo this, what punishment is left for such as you to endure, were we all rewarded after our ill-doings? But were He to remember all the foul deeds in even the most righteous, who of us shall stand? Rise up, and speak with boldness. You are rewarded, not of man, but of God. *I* will hear and believe your story."

"Master," cried the penitent, the big drops on his cheeks, "your words are precious beyond seven talents of gold. Yet have I not sinned beyond the Lord God's mercy?"

"You have not if by your future deeds you atone as in you lies. And now I am hearkening."

Whereupon, with many groans and protests of sorrow, Shaphat told how, after the trial, and his almost forced exposure of Gudea's infamy, he had rushed away and hid himself in the vilest quarters of the city, amongst the bargemen and sailors. Often he meditated slaying himself, but the fear of the angry Jehovah passed his fear even of his stinging conscience. Daniel lay in his prison, and Shaphat knew that up to the last moment he had been consenting to the "civil-minister's" misfortune. His own scanty means were soon ended. Avil-Marduk was his enemy, and desired his arrest. As a last recourse, Shaphat hired himself to a band of nondescript Arab caravan merchants, who were about to set forth for Egypt. Perchance, he vainly argued, he would find that the goad of memory might not follow to the strange Nile country, and he could commence life there afresh. But on the day after setting forth, while the caravan halted in a village, lo! after the manner already told, the Amorite bandit came with his three captives, nor was Shaphat long in recognizing.

And then began his new agony. Well he knew that Ruth was all Binit protested,—worth her weight in silver to any who might deliver her to the king. And first he resolved to tell his employers that Binit's ragings were indeed truth, and they had great prize. But the serpent of guile brought him yet darker thoughts. Why should he not flee away with the Jewess herself, deliver her to Belshazzar, claim the royal reward, and drown his remorse in the delights of riches? It was with this thought uppermost that he suffered himself to drift into new falsehoods when the leader of the caravan questioned him as to their youngest captive. All that day he adhered to his black purpose, and the delays which prevented the advance of the caravan were largely of his contriving. In the evening, as soon as the camp grew still, he filched a bag of money from an Arab and prepared to make off. The flight was not difficult. Ruth obeyed him implicitly when he promised he would conduct her back to safety. They wandered onward toward the city until the Jewess's feet were so weary she could trudge no more, and she slumbered out the remainder of the night in a farmer's stack, while Shaphat remained on guard to beat off the wild dogs and jackals. In the morning he contrived to purchase some millet bread in a village, and they plodded southward.

"But now," continued Shaphat, while his voice once more was near to breaking, "I found all the demons of the Chaldees rising up within me; for it seemed impossible that I should refuse life riches, and yet a voice spoke ever goading, warning, torturing, 'Better a life of beggary and rags, than do this deed which will cry out to God.' But then I answered myself, saying: 'God is already angered past all atoning. He can never forgive. Let me make joy to-day, for to-morrow is only endless gloom.' And so I continued debating long and bitterly, while we measured the long road. But when we drew near to Babylon, the Lady Ruth spoke to me, after her gentle way, 'Good Shaphat, what are you fearing, and why does your face become so sad?' Whereupon I answered her: 'You know I have promised to deliver you to some friend who will keep you safely. Do you put trust in me, seeing that I have done great wrong to my lord, your father?' And she looked up at me, and said, in her innocency, little knowing all the evil that was passing in my breast, 'You have truly done great ill, and on this account I will put trust in you yet more, for I know you will not wish to anger the good Lord God for yet a second time.'—'Alas!' cried I, 'have I not so angered Him that I can never be forgiven, though I had all the riches of the Egibi bankers, and spent them in alms-deeds on the poor?' But she said, and her voice was like a cool hand laid upon my brow, 'And wherefore should the good God not forgive? for I know that I, since I see you truly sorry, have forgiven, and so, surely, has my father; and have we more of pity than Jehovah the All-Merciful?' Then," but here the apostate must needs stop and weep hot tears indeed, "as I looked down upon her, and saw how fair she was, how her face was pure as a summer's cloud, and her heart guileless as a bursting flower, and when I told myself how selling her to Belshazzar would be selling her to worse than death, I said within my soul, 'I cannot do this evil deed in sight of God; no, though I die this hour, and descend to

Sheol forever, I shall yet have this to comfort me, that I am free from this great sin.' For I felt as if ten thousand talents from the king would turn to fire in my hands. All the rest of the way to Babylon the fiends pressed close to tempt me, but they had lost their power. I fought them all away. I scarce knew where to take the Lady Ruth, but I remembered that Dagan-Milki was your friend, and unsuspected among the Babylonians. I little thought to place her in your keeping. When I gave her to Dagan, for a moment my soul had peace. Nevertheless, when I saw how even he, a Chaldee, turned the back on me, and I thought on my great sins, my sorrows all returned, and I have been fearfully tormented. But as Jehovah is my judge, I have told all truly."

He was weeping once more, but Isaiah stepped beside him, and took him by the hand.

"The Lady Ruth is right," he said simply; "God is more merciful than man. You are forgiven in His pure sight. I believe all your story."

"Blessings upon you for the word!" cried the penitent; "you make me your slave forever. How may I serve you, even unto death?"

But Isaiah only smiled. "Fear not that through me God will not find you ample chance for service. But the present duty is rest. Sleep to-night, and wait His commands for the morrow."

CHAPTER XVI

Upon Ai-Bur-Shabou Street, not far from the Northern Gate, called the Gate of Ilu, stood the barber's shop of Mulis-Assur. A shop, we say, though in truth it was only an open booth, thrust in betwixt two houses, and its sole furnishings were two low stools, a reed carpet, a little chest for the razors and silvered mirrors, and a brass brazier, over which at this moment curling irons were heating above the smouldering charcoal. Mulis-Assur was neither the first nor the last of his kind whose principal staple of sale was gossip. At this moment, as the worthy man stood patting the lump of melted butter upon the black locks of Gabarruru, the corn merchant, who occupied one stool, his head was turned to reply to Itti-Marduk, the banker, who was lolling on the other stool. It was a great festival day—the day of the procession of the patron god of Babylon, of the "going forth of Bel-Marduk," and for once the broker had forgotten his jars of account books.

"Well," Mulis was declaring, while he lifted the irons from the brazier, "I am the last to chatter treason, but may the gods ward off from his Majesty the consequences of listening to that frog Gudea's croakings, and casting the civil-minister into prison! Not one man can say a fair word for the deed."

"The more particularly," thrust in the merchant, "because Gudea himself has died the death not long since. I saw the crows around his skull the last time I passed under the gate. Jew or Chaldee, no man ought to suffer bonds on such evidence. The minister is no more guilty of slaying by sorcery than you or I. A trick of Avil-Marduk, I say; there is too much priestcraft loose in Babylon. My head already sits overlightly on its shoulders."

"Peace!" conjured Itti, "never will I, a loyal and pious citizen, suffer such treason to be prated against my betters!"

"No alarm," answered Gabarruru, feeling that perhaps he had gone too far, "we are all loyal and obedient men. Daniel, at least, has been saved for the present by the queen-mother."

"The queen-mother saved the Jew for the moment," replied the barber, "but I think his neck will last through to-day, and no longer. You know the custom. When the ship of Bel reaches the foot of the *ziggurat*, the chief priest can demand of the king one boon, and the king cannot refuse it. You may imagine what that boon will be."

"The life of Daniel?"

"Nothing else, by Marduk! But I imagine there is likely to be another part to the tale. Imbi-Ilu, the chief priest of Nabu, is Daniel's good friend. Mark my words, the priests of Nabu and of Samas and Nergal of Kisch hate Avil, and his designs to make all their temples subordinate to his own, more than they do the harmless Jehovah worship of the minister. I look for a spark on the firewood in Babylon, and strange sights this very day."

"Ramman protect us!" muttered the banker, uneasily. "I have put down fresh loans only last night. I shall lose all."

"Yes," continued Mulis, who was happiest when peddling bad news that did not touch himself, "we must prepare for grievous times. Now that the king has clapped the Persian envoy in durance, and keeps him prisoner in his chambers at the palace, I think we may see a war the like of which was not since the brave days of Nebuchadnezzar. Ea, the God of Wisdom, alone knows what it was that befell during the royal hunt. Forth goes his Majesty and Darius, boon companions as Gilgamesh and Eabani; they come back eying each other like two cocks in the farmer's yard. The next thing we hear, the Persian is a state prisoner. Woe, what wretched times!"

A groan cut the barber short, for a hot curling iron had tingled on Gabarruru's neck.

"Nergal blast you, chattering sparrow!" was his curse. "Must I be roasted like a stalled ox every time I seek your shop?"

"Mercy, gentle sir," soothed Mulis; "I was but saying to the noble Itti, that the evil omens which have plagued the city of late, seem too nigh fulfilment. Piety declines, the gods are neglected—"

"Small loss!" growled the corn merchant, who was a very impious man; "the gods are of little use. They may be all-wise, and know each secret we would give everything to learn, but they are most inconveniently silent when they might serve us. My brother spent half his estate on priests and exorcists; much favour heaven gave him—he died childless and poor! While I, who have not given one of Avil's cattle two shekels in ten years, wax prosperous and fat!"

"Hush," exhorted Itti, horrified, "do not blaspheme before me! Doubtless heaven will, with one clap, smite you down for your wickedness—"

A second touch of the iron and renewed curses interrupted the broker. And before the conversation resumed, into the shop came Hasba, the tall, gaunt priest of Nabu, his costume very threadbare, and his eyes glittering as if with ill-concealed excitement.

"Well, Hasba," cried Mulis, pausing in his curling for the twentieth time, "you are in a strange robe for a festival day. Is Nabu so poor a god he can give his priests nothing better?"

"Nabu is very poor and hungry—to-day," responded Hasba, with a significant cough, which made Itti look at him very hard.

"But not yesterday or to-morrow?" pressed Mulis, pricking his ears.

"Quietly." Hasba's voice sank very low. "You are all good friends, and will leak nothing. See!" He showed a short sword girded under his mantle.

"Istar help us!" cried the broker. "What will happen?"

"Patience, worthy Itti. Avil-Marduk is likely to learn strange things before nightfall. We have sworn loyalty to Belshazzar, but not to Avil. His Majesty loves the priest of Bel-Marduk too well. Why is Daniel in the palace prison? Not because he 'kills by sorcery,' as that scorpion Gudea charged, nor because he is a Jew. He stands betwixt Avil and his design to make Belshazzar his tool, to make all the priesthoods of Babylon slaves of Bel-Marduk. Imbi-Ilu is not a man to see the deed done in silence. To-day we of Nabu appear in tattered mantles that the people may see how the king is starving us. And as for Avil, if he seeks Daniel's life, let both him and the king beware!"

"Ramman protect us!" muttered Itti again. "When was ever such strife in Babylon?"

"A strange case that of Daniel's," commented Mulis. "I hear that the king was very desirous of laying his hands on his would-be son-in-law Isaiah, who was so loud in denouncing the gods, and more than desirous of getting the minister's daughter (the maid was called Ruth) for his own harem. Yet both have escaped him, though their arrest was ordered."

"Vanished utterly," replied the priest, gathering his robe tightly, to guard against an unfriendly eye upon the sword; but his tone and wink made the others stare at him, then exchange knowing glances.

"As for the young Jew," continued Hasba, with the air of a person who knows far more than he is likely to tell, "he is a man of great resources, and knows the city as a bird the way to its nest. All the Jews reverence him as a prophet of their Jehovah, and protect him when they can. My own master, Imbi-Ilu, esteems him highly, notwithstanding his absurd devotion to his native god. But the Jewess," Hasba's lips curled in a very bitter smile, "she is safe also, and Nabu grant shall remain so long, for the man who prompted his Majesty to try to take her by force from our temple is devoted to the 'Maskim' if the gods keep any power to punish sacrilege. Better worship a thousand Jehovahs, than do one deed like that."

"You of Borsippa do not hate this Jewish god so very fiercely?" remarked Mulis, shrewdly.

"He is a harmless demon. We of the temple of Nabu only know this,— that we have no hate to squander on any, saving Avil-Marduk and his underlings."

"Be that as it may," was Mulis's answer, "Isaiah and the maid have been in marvellously safe hiding. The king threatens Mermaza's head if she is not found."

"Then may the chief eunuch's pate topple off quickly!" swore Hasba. "Next to Avil we love him the least."

Gabarruru's tortures were at an end at last, but just as he was about to quit the barber's shop, the sudden rush of people to the street from all the adjoining alleys, and the din of distant horns and kettle-drums, told that the long-waited procession was at hand. Hasba excused himself and was off, leaving the others to meditate on his warnings and await the issue in what peace they might. The clangour of cymbals grew louder continually. The street was becoming one sea of heads. By standing on the little raised platform of the barber's shop, it was possible to gain a fair view up the avenue, where one could see standards tossing, and the shimmer of steel.

"Way! way!" rang the familiar cry at length, and a squad of scarlet-robed wand-bearers began forcing the people backward toward the house walls. After this advance corps streamed the priestesses of Istar, tall, comely women, their heads and necks wreathed with flowers, their dresses of tinted Egyptian gauze floating around them in bright clouds, the transparent web falling in folds none the most prudish. The older priestesses walked in well-drilled files, bearing gay banners, and keeping up an incessant clatter upon their tambourines; but their younger sisters would break ranks, time and again, and whirl in voluptuous dances, joining hands, shaking out their streaming black locks, tearing off their coronals to cast amid the admiring crowd, or even when they saw a handsome youth, would pluck him from the multitude by sheer force, and whirl him with them; then, at a change in the music, all released their captives, and marched demurely until the spirits moved them to new madness.

So the "Maids of the Grove," to the number of many hundreds, passed. But when the soldiers of the palace guard followed, each in his gayest mantle and brightest helmet, Mulis whispered in the banker's ear:—

"A costly blunder, unless there is no fire under much smoke. Look at the guard!"

"What is amiss?" demanded Itti, rubbing his eyes.

"The troops have neither shields nor spears with them, only their parade arms, sword, and helmet. His Majesty may have cause to rue this blunder."

"Ramman protect us!" implored Itti yet another time. But now fifty squeaking pipers headed the files of the priests of Samas from the southern city, a notable array of handsome men, white robes, and nodding banners. After them marched their brethren of Sin, the moon-god; then those of Nergal from the Kisch suburb; then the priestesses of Nana, consort of Nabu.

Suddenly a great shout began running down the street in advance of the next contingent.

"Hail, Nabu! Hail, son of Marduk! Hail, Imbi-Ilu, holy priest of the god!"

"Nabu, they say, is the son of Marduk," commented Gabarruru, dryly. "He bears dutiful love for his parent, if what Hasba says is true."

"Do not blaspheme him," implored the broker; "he is a great god, the peer of Marduk almost. The son has the place of honour in the father's procession. Pity the two must quarrel."

"Bow down! The knee! The knee!" rang the shout, and the multitude (all that had room) knelt on the stone pavement, while from a distance sounded a mighty rumbling as of clumsy wheels. Soon there lumbered into view an enormous wain, dragged by long cables like those for a stone bull, but no sullen labour gang was tugging now. Many leaped from their knees and contended with the priests who were toiling at the ropes, for the honour of drawing the god. Upon the wain rode Nabu's "Ship of the Deep," a goodly-sized galley, fitted with a towering mast and tackle. Upon her decks swarmed a score of priests in lieu of crew, and perched upon the upcurved stern was the idol of the god, a block of black stone, human size, but with features of such ugliness that the very fiends beholding might well have trembled. Yet at sight of that image even Gabarruru bowed his head, for it had been the guardian genius of Babylon and Borsippa for more generations than the wisest could tell.

Yet a great wail of wrath and disappointment seemed rising from the people. "Nabu's priests are threadbare! Where are their robes of honour? Where are the jewels once on the gunwales of the ship? Where are the golden dresses of the image?" The three in the barber's shop rubbed their eyes. In the crowd they saw Hasba and others, doubtless fellow-priests, bustling about, whispering in the ear of this burgher and of that.

Imbi-Ilu, second pontiff of the realm, the friend of Daniel and the arch-foe of Avil, stood handsome and erect beside the image of his god; but there was no tiara on his head, his robe was torn and sombre.

"Marduk is robbing Nabu!" some bold spirit in the crowd was shouting. "The priests of Bel-Marduk grow fat; those of Nabu starve! Down with Avil!"

But the servants of the Borsippa god marched on in silence, each man smiling grimly when he saw how their pitiful display was working on the crowd, and pressing his mantle around his hidden sword. And there were other cries at times:—

"Release Daniel! Release the good minister! Release! Down with Avil!"

"Evil times!" muttered Itti. "While Nabonidus was king the processions were suspended; now they become mere occasion for tumult."

"Well," protested the cheerful barber, "here comes his Majesty and the car of Bel-Marduk. We shall soon see now."

A new corps of musicians, new guards. A second boat creaked past on its many wheels. High above the noise of the crowd sounded the hymn chanted by the choir of chosen priests and priestesses in praise of Bel-Marduk, smiter of the great dragon.

"Look favourably upon thy dwelling-place,

Look favourably upon thy city, O Lord of quietness!

May Babylon salute thee, and thy temple,

May the city find safety under thee!"

After this choir moved the car, and, unlike Nabu's, it was a single blaze of colour. The four snow-white "sacred horses" who aided to drag the ship tossed their bridles of silver chains, and champed on bits of pure gold. The sail and pennons were covered with the rarest embroideries, the gunwale glittered with precious stones—agate, onyx, lapis-lazuli. The idol on the stern wore a robe that was one sheen of golden lace. But Belshazzar the king, who sat under his purple umbrella upon the prow, scowled at Avil, his prime counsellor, who stood beside him.

"The people give thrice as many cheers for Nabu as for Bel. The gods reward me if I do not make Imbi-Ilu pay the price for his mummery! To appear with his priests in tatters, and his car all stripped of decoration, at the moment when the procession was about to start! He knew well I would never have suffered his company to march, had it not meant a riot to leave behind the car of Nabu!"

Avil deliberately cast his eyes down over the swelling crowd, and readjusted the horn-set tiara that crowned his head.

"The more reason for striking down Daniel, my king. His fate will be a mighty warning to Imbi-Ilu."

"Once you advised me to move gently with him, yet you are bold now."

"True; but I have set my feet on the path, and see no danger to-day."

"Release Daniel! Release! Release! Down with Avil!" broke in the bolder spirits in the crowd, as if to give the lie to the hardy pontiff.

Avil spat at them in contempt. "Stingless drones!" commented he. "They will forget the Jew by another Sabbath."[5]

"I am led in all things by you," replied Belshazzar, in a tone that showed he nigh felt himself overpersuaded. Avil only salaamed, and turned to pay his respects to the Princess Atossa, whose chair was upon the prow, close beside that of her royal lord.

"My princess sees a sight that must be rare in her native Persia," began he, blandly. "If my information does not fail, the worship of the Persian Ahura and his archangels does not demand such elaborate processions as these."

Atossa turned upon him haughtily, and from under her veil shot through him a glance such as can dart only from the eyes of a great king's daughter.

"Assuredly, worthy priest," and Avil winced before her disdainful patronage, "it is true our prophet Zarathushtra[6] enjoins no processions where the populace heap personal revilings on the chief of our Magian pontiffs."

"Down with Avil! Release Daniel! Nabu is outraged!" buzzed from the crowd.

"Ah, my princess," said Avil, smiling, "the king is overkindly disposed. Could I persuade him, these seditious fellows would soon shout otherwise."

"His Majesty is too kindly disposed?" replied she, removing her veil that Avil might see the unconcealed sneer on her lips.

"His heart is a mountain of compassion," asserted the priest, who felt that he was being made sorry sport of, yet would not retire from the encounter.

"But not so merciful as my Lord Avil," interposed Mermaza, the oily chief eunuch, glad to prod his comrade, "for his heart is one sponge soaked with magnanimity."

"Marduk blast you, Mermaza!" muttered Avil under breath.

"I trust not," replied the smirking eunuch, "the excellent god, my dear Avil, will need all his powers for weightier things to-day. Hear the people—"

"Avil conspires against Nabu! Rescue for the good minister! Release Daniel!"

To reënforce the shouts, a brick flung by some mad rascal in the crowd dashed against the car.

"Be persuaded, Avil," urged Mermaza; "make no demand for Daniel's life."

"Spare the Jew? Never will I yield a 'finger breadth.' Having gone thus far, it is self-destruction to turn back."

"Nevertheless, I wish we had brought more soldiers from the palace."

Belshazzar was beckoning to the priest, and he turned away, whereupon Atossa addressed Mermaza wearily:—

"Is it far now to the temple of Marduk?"

"Not far; yet why is my mistress so tired? The under eunuchs tell me she did not sleep. The king's Egyptian doctor must prepare a night draught."

"Alas! that can profit little when I consider that Prince Darius's life is in danger while he is a prisoner."

"Danger?" Mermaza's smile was radiant as the moon. "Has not his Majesty pledged that he is perfectly safe? His life is more precious than the gems in the royal treasure chamber."

Atossa fixed her clear eyes straight upon the eunuch, and even he glanced away from her uneasily.

"Mermaza," said she, very coldly, "I think it will be better for both of us if we hide fewer black thoughts under smooth protestations. You know as well as I that Darius is held as a hostage, to tie the hands of my father in requiting Belshazzar for his dark intrigue."

"I am only your ladyship's slave," the eunuch bowed obsequiously. "Who am I to say my mistress 'nay'?"

"And for once you speak well in very truth," answered she, the hot colour of anger rising at last; "for to a man I would bow as to one mightier than I, and to a woman I would answer wrath with wrath. But to you, who are neither man nor maid, but only creature, I will vouchsafe not one curse; one does not bend the bow to slaughter gnats!"

Mermaza's smile had become sickly indeed; but she deliberately turned her back upon him, and kept company with her own gloomy meditations.

She had not seen Darius since that evening hour when they were surprised in the Hanging Gardens. Report in the harem had it that the prince was under close ward in his own chambers, and that all the Persians of his suite had been arrested. All save one: Ariathes, the crafty and the nimble, had passed from sight as completely as if he had never been born. Was he escaped to Susa, and had the truth come to the mighty Cyrus's ears? It was a faint hope, but all that was left in the princess's despairing breast. The seizure of Darius, just at the instant when the future seemed bursting fair before her, and escape so close at hand, had almost blotted out the sun for Atossa. It had taken all her womanly strength and royal pride to bear up in the presence of her oppressors. Yet at that moment she had become possessed with one deep desire,—to see that Babylonian mob rise and take vengeance on Avil-Marduk and his grim master; and the howls of the multitude sounded sweeter in her ears than all the harping.

The great *ziggurat* at last! They had passed up the "Procession Street," the broad avenue that led past the temple of "Istar the Foe-smiter." There had been howls, ever increasing, from the multitude. Once the soldiers had charged with drawn blades to clear the way for Bel-Marduk's car, but there had been no bloodshed. Avil, Mermaza, and their royal lord breathed easier. Before them was rising "*E-Sagila*," "The Lofty House," queen of the temple-towers of Babylon. The seven terraces of the great cone were all decked with flowers and streaming banners, the parapets of the different stages were swarming with the people, flowers were festooned over every pinnacle and battlement.

There it uprose against the azure, a vast mountain of brick, its lowest terrace painted white, the second black, the third purple, the fourth blue, the fifth vermilion, the sixth plated with silver, the seventh—the day-beacon first hailed by the Persians—was glittering with its sheen of gold. The bull-guarded gates had opened wide for the ship of Marduk. Inside the vast courtyard at the foot of the tower had arrayed themselves all the priests and soldiery that had preceded the car of the god. All but those from Borsippa stood on the left of the gateway; but the servants of Nabu, with their ship, were arrayed silent and sombre on the right. Imbi-Ilu's company thus kept an ominous peace, but there was no lack of cheering for Bel-Marduk now. Even the disaffected multitude that had tried to attack the procession grew hushed and quiet when it passed within the sacred gates.

Loudly rose the well-drilled acclamations from the thousands of gentlefolk and temple servants perched upon the heights of the terraces above.

"Hail, Marduk! Hail, Dragon-smiter! Hail, Belshazzar, beloved of the gods! Hail, Avil, servant of the Guardian of Babylon!" There were more cheers for Atossa, for the vizier, for the "commander of the host." Then, just as the ship of Bel-Marduk reached the foot of the great stairway leading to the first stage of the tower, the corps of priests marching before the god suddenly raised a shout that had not been heard before that day:—

"Death to the Jew! Death to Daniel the murderer! Death! Death!"

Instantly the crowds of Avil's underlings upon the tower caught up the cry. But though the noise swelled to a deafening clamour, and all the files of the soldiers joined, Atossa heard no priest of Samas or Sin or Nergal open his lips. They were every man silent, like their fellows from Borsippa. And the great multitude that had trailed into the gate at the tail of the procession was silent also. Yet from Avil-Marduk's supporters, and from the throng of courtiers about the king, the outcry continually increased. Belshazzar, she divined, must be able to say he sacrificed Daniel to quell the general clamour.

Louder, ever louder, "Death to Daniel! Death to the murderer! Extirpate the Jews!"

Atossa saw men with speaking trumpets stationed at advantageous points to roar across the sea of heads, and make one voice pass for twenty.

"Death to Daniel! Death to the civil-minister!"

The heads of the sacred colleges of the temple, the chief "libation-pourer," the chief "demon-restrainer," and their peers, had come to lift the idol from its station in the car, and bear it to the summit of the *ziggurat*; the king had descended from the ship to follow them. Their feet were on the first stair, when across their path stood Avil-Marduk, in his hand the long white staff of his office, and obedient to his gesture the clamorous underlings and soldiers were silent instantly.

"Hearken, O Belshazzar, lord of Babylon and Akkad. On the day of the great feast of Bel, when the image of Bel is borne to the crest of the Lofty House, is it not the right of the god—a right, and not a boon—to demand of the king of Babylon one thing whatsoever the god, even Bel-Marduk, may desire?"

It was so still that the thousands could hear Belshazzar's answer:—

"It is so, O Avil, mouthpiece of the 'Lord of the Lofty House.'"

"Therefore I, O Belshazzar, do demand, as a thing not to be denied, the life of that enemy of the god, that guilty murderer, that impious blasphemer—"

But the high priest said no more. Every eye had turned, his own also. Directly above him, at the head of the steps to the first terrace, had stepped forth a young man, who beckoned to the people. And a hundred whispered to their neighbours:—

"Isaiah! Isaiah the Jew, who prophesies for his God, Jehovah!"

CHAPTER XVII

Isaiah was robed in spotless white. His station at the head of the broad stairway to the lower terrace of the temple-tower raised him full thirty cubits above the multitude. With the myriads packing the area below, the glittering array of the procession at his feet, the shining crest of the *ziggurat* towering above, no marvel he was the one figure on which a thousand eyes were fastened. And as they gazed on him, the crowds grew still. Who was this that stayed the hands of Bel-Marduk's own priest, in the god's own dwelling? Men felt their hearts beating loudly, their breath was bated; and each passed to each the whisper, "Either the Jew is mad, or the spirit of some mighty god possesses him. Let us listen."

The king was silent, Avil-Marduk was silent, and the chiefs of the sacred colleges, the captains of the army. Only the spell of power passing human—every heart was confessing—could make the high priest's words die on his lips, his eyes hang captive on the compelling power sped from the eyes of the youthful Jew.

In the profound silence Isaiah spoke. Clear and strong his words sounded across the packed enclosure.

"Woe, woe, woe unto Babylon! Unto the great city, the cry of whose sins is gone up to heaven! Whose evil deeds are uncounted! Woe unto Babylon, and woe to her base priests and baser king!"

Was it not a god that dared to revile the lord of the Chaldees before his face? The silence was not broken. Isaiah spoke again.

"Woe unto Belshazzar and Avil-Marduk, who seek the blood of the innocent for their own dark ends! Whose power is born of treachery and lies! Who spare neither the hoary head, nor the guileless maid! Woe unto king and priest and to all who walk after them!"

Men saw Avil-Marduk turn away his gaze as from a sight of ill-omen. Those near by heard him mutter to Sirusur, commander of the host:—

"This is a madman! Pluck him down, and end his ravings!"

But Sirusur only stood and stared dumbly, and Avil was impotent.

"Hear ye, hear ye, men of Babylon!" thundered the prophet. "Hitherto the spirit of Jehovah, the Lord God, has sent me to my own people. This day His message is to you and to your sinful king.

"Come down and sit in the dust, O virgin daughter of Babylon! There is no throne left to you, O daughter of the Chaldees. No more shall you be called tender and delicate; therefore take the millstones and grind the meal in hard labour. Your vileness and shame shall be revealed; for I, Jehovah, will take vengeance. I will bring the strong races that serve me, and the king that worships me, against you. I will abase your pride. Therefore sit you in silence, and get you into darkness, O daughter of the Chaldees, for never again shall they declare you 'Lady of Kingdoms'!"

By this time the most hardened scoffer felt his knees beating together in dread. The rumour of evil omens that had shaken the city of late, the suppressed excitement of the morning, which all now expected to end in a tumult, the sudden apparition of this Jew, whose arrest had been diligently sought—what more was needed to spread a trembling among the thousands? And when Isaiah paused, there came in answer many gasps and cries: "No more! Woe, woe! Heaven is wroth with us, and with our children!" But the Hebrew had not finished.

"You have trusted in your strong walls, men of Chaldea; in Imgur-Bel, in Nimitti-Bel; in the breadth of your rivers. You have filled your granaries, you have numbered your chariots, you have gathered your captains. But I say unto you, except you put away the oppression from your midst, except your king spares the innocent, and turns back his lust from the helpless, and makes end to the captivity of the people of Jehovah—I, even the God of gods, will mock your rage; will bring low your pride; will make a way for your enemies through the deep waters; will go before them; will prevail with them, and give the empire unto another who shall be my servant, who shall execute righteousness toward my people, and judgment toward their oppressor. Thus, thus is the word of Jehovah, before whom Marduk is less than dust, and Istar than hoarfrost beneath the sun at the noonday."

Isaiah had ended. He swept his robe about him, and stood silent, steadfast, neither advancing nor trying to flee away. Whence he had come, Ea the Wise alone might tell. There was stillness one instant, till the first magic of his spell had passed. Then, following the impulse already strong in their hearts, and trebly strengthened by the Jew's inspired warning, most of the multitude broke into the howling cry:—

"The gods are angry on account of Daniel! Spare Daniel! Spare! Spare!"

The yell was the signal for the loosing of pandemonium. Instantly, with a din redoubled by the strange interruption, the priests of Avil resumed their opposing clamour.

"Death to both Jews! Death! Death! Marduk is enraged! Away with Daniel!"

The two shouts rose in one deafening babel. But in the midst of the din the chief pontiff had made himself heard by the king, and a "ten" of guardsmen sped up the stairs, seized Isaiah, who had waited them in perfect passiveness, and hurried him down to their royal lord. Belshazzar was standing beneath his purple parasol at the foot of the steps, close by the car of Bel. Ramman, spreading the hurricane clouds, was never blacker than the king's face when they dragged the Hebrew before him.

"Kill! kill!" that was all they could hear him shout, striving to be heard above the increasing din.

"In what manner?" demanded Sirusur, barely heard, salaaming respectfully. "I wait my lord's command."

"Hew off his head; let the dogs fight over his body!" came from the king in one breath.

"Ah, Jew!" sneered Avil, during a lull; "it would have been better to have been led by me, to have forgotten Jehovah for Bel-Marduk. Will your god save you *now*?"

"If it be His will He can indeed save me!" flashed back Isaiah, unflinching. "When my father Shadrach would not bow to Nebuchadnezzar's great statue of Bel in the plain of Dura, did he come from the king's furnace living or dead?"

"Fairly smitten on the very thigh," grunted Bilsandan, who took small pains to conceal his enmity toward the pontiff. But Avil's flushed face only turned the darker, as he threatened the prisoner.

"By every god of Babylon you shall nevertheless die a jackal's own death!" he shouted, while Belshazzar still thundered, "Kill! Kill!" But Sirusur stood hesitant; for if his lord had cast off the Jew's spell, the general was still under it.

In his fury Belshazzar tugged at the short sword at his side that he might become himself executioner, when a new shout of the people finally drowned his commands.

"Spare Daniel! Spare the good minister! Do not anger Heaven!"

Avil's underlings were fairly howled down at last.

"Except the king promise to spare Daniel, I look for a riot instantly," remonstrated Bilsandan, the vizier, in the first instant of silence.

"Better let Babylon flow with blood, be he ten times innocent," blazed the wrathful king, "than I give way to these hissing geese. Khatin ends him to-night."

Avil-Marduk sped to the terrace where Isaiah had taken station, and beckoned in vain for silence.

"Away with him!" roared the crowd, led on by Hasba, the bold priest of Nabu. "Away with the king's evil councillor!"

Belshazzar had mounted to his friend's side.

"Well," cried he, in Avil's ear, "Allat has loosed all her fiends! Let sword and spear quiet them!"

"So be it, my king," answered Avil, putting on a bold face, though quaking within.

Belshazzar turned to Sirusur, the "Master of the Host," "Hark you, general," stormed the king, "this is more than half your own doing; it was you and Bilsandan who favoured that accursed Daniel, gained his reprieve, and left these geese chance to hiss so loudly. Chase them outside the temple grounds, and that quickly, or I call you my enemy as well as Avil's."

"I am your Majesty's slave," retorted the general, colouring angrily, "not this man's," with a menacing scowl toward Avil. "I have been Imbi-Ilu's friend, but while he raises hand against the king I become his enemy."

"Prove it, then," enjoined Belshazzar, fiercely; "form your men! Charge!"

"And Isaiah?" the general asked.

"Spare now. We must torture him to learn where that wench Ruth is hidden, for she is no more at Borsippa. Now silence this hubbub."

A hubbub, indeed. The people were flinging dust in the air and calling ominously for "bricks." Just as Sirusur had formed his men in a solid body by the stairway, a priest of Nabu drew forth a short sword, and the rest, with their brethren of Sin and Samas, imitated him instantly.

"Down with Avil! Away with Avil, the king's evil councillor!" swelled the shout.

"Charge! Drown out this yell in blood!" commanded Belshazzar. And with this command winging them, the guardsmen hurled themselves on the mob. But Mulis, the barber, had warned truly, that the king would repent that the soldiers had marched with only their parade swords. Charging in a solid body upon the disorderly array opposed to them, they had small difficulty in beating down the first rioters they encountered; slew some, arrested others, and drove the whole multitude—rebellious priests and lawless city folk—backward toward the temple gates. Flushed with their triumph, Sirusur's men even surrounded the ship of Nabu, and dragged from his high car Imbi-Ilu, author of the outbreak.

"Ha, good pontiff!" the general laughed, covering his real sympathy with Imbi-Ilu's cause under a mighty show of zeal, "you are not likely to find this day's sport cheaply bought!" And he called to two under officers to hale the arch-malcontent before the king.

But even as Belshazzar was foaming and threatening over his captive, the tide of conflict turned; for, led by Hasba, the priests of Nabu rallied to a man for the rescue of their chief. The ranks of the soldiers had been broken as they followed up their victory. And once their solid array shattered, their advantage was gone. The priests and rioters were all around them, almost crushing them with incessant volleys of bricks, and guardsmen as well as the mob were now falling fast. The rioters tore down the copings of the enclosure walls, securing an exhaustless supply of missiles. The troops were brave. They charged this way and that, but every time their companies were shivered into smaller fragments, around which the multitude rolled like the billows of an angry sea. Sirusur was in the act of re-forming his men to attempt a second charge, when a brick smote his helmet, and with a great yell of triumph the priests of Nabu leaped on him, plucked him out of the midst of his men, and dragged him away safe prisoner. The soldiers made one last effort to rally, but with their leader taken, and outnumbered ten to one, they were swept back to the stairs of the *ziggurat*; and in a moment the exulting priests of Nabu were charging after them, forcing them upward step by step, and making straight for the lower terrace of the tower, where the royal party was stationed. Only when they saw Sirusur taken had their own peril dawned fully on Belshazzar and his suite. The riot was taking alarming proportions. A new king might be proclaimed ere sunset—who could say?

"Glory, glory to Nabu! to Samas! to Nergal!" a thousand throats were yelling. "Rescue for Imbi-Ilu! Death to Avil!"

The troops, desperate now, turned at bay halfway up the wide staircase, and for an instant their close array of swinging swords made the rioters recoil; but what with the bricks' constant pelting, no men without armour could hold such a position long.

Avil had turned to the king. The haughty pontiff fell on his knees, his face ashen with terror.

"They did not know the lion spirit within the king, that made him as steeled against fear as against mercy."

"Protection, lord! Save me! Save! They will pluck me in pieces!" And he caught at the hem of his master's robe. But if any had reckoned on Belshazzar's quailing at that dread moment, they did not know the lion spirit within the king, that made him as steeled against fear as against mercy. Atossa had never seen him more kingly, more truly the incarnation of his arrogant, indomitable race, than now, when he leaped upon the parapet of the terrace, and faced that screeching, raging mob.

Three bricks brushed past him in a twinkling, a fourth smote the purple and white tiara from his head, but he would have heeded snowflakes more. And at sight of him, the king, "lord of Sumer and Akkad, who had taken the hands of Bel," even this foaming multitude gave back, and grew quiet. The king spoke to them as to crouching hounds.

"Back, imps! Do you so love Allat that you seek quick voyaging to her? Get you gone, or by the Anunnaki, the dread spirits, I swear the kites shall eat you all by morning!"

A moment of hesitation and silence. "And you, spawn of Nabu," thundered the king, "advance one step farther, and the head of Imbi-Ilu, your chief demon, is flung down to you!"

Untimely boast, for Hasba instantly howled back: "Be it so, and we of Nabu swear that Sirusur, the general, dies when Imbi-Ilu dies. Life for life, and death for death!" And to this all the priests answered; "It is so! We hold Sirusur hostage for Imbi-Ilu!"

The king gave a fearful curse. "So be it!" cried he, in his passion, "but if the general loses an hair, he shall be terribly avenged. Execute Imbi-Ilu this instant!" He had leaped down from the parapet. The bricks were flying again. He repeated his command to Igas-Ramman, the captain now heading the troops, but Igas had salaamed before his lord, saying:—

"Live forever, my king! Your slaves, the guards, will die for you; but they will throw their swords away rather than see Sirusur, their leader, sacrificed. We dare not touch the high priest of Borsippa."

"Have you, too, the hearts of conies?" warned Belshazzar. And they saw his hand go to his sword, as if to smite Imbi with his own arm. But the instant he had sprung from the parapet the attack had been renewed. The troops, cowed and ill-led, broke under the pressure, and the volleys gave way; and in a twinkling the rioters were on the first terrace. It was a moment of uttermost danger for king and courtiers. The mob swept up upon the platform in a single human wave. "Back, my lord! back!" exhorted Igas-Ramman, thrusting himself with a handful of men betwixt the rioters and Belshazzar; but the king brushed him aside.

"Where is Isaiah?" shouted the monarch, casting about one glance. "Though I perish, let not *him* escape!"

But while the words quitted his lips, a young man in the foremost of the assailants, had bounded past the demoralized soldiers, and in an instant loosed the Hebrew's bands.

"Shaphat! Shaphat the accuser of Daniel!" howled many voices together; but rescuer and rescued were already swallowed in the sea of writhing, fighting forms. A moment later, the victorious priests of Nabu had plucked their leader out of the hands of the panic-struck guardsmen, and Imbi-Ilu once more headed his cheering followers.

"Away with Avil-Marduk!" rang the shout, never louder. "Fling him over the *ziggurat*!"

The pontiff barely saved himself by most headlong flight up the next stairway to the second stage of the tower. After him fled Mermaza, and many a dignitary followed them. But there was one who did not fly, and that was the king. Marduk, guardian of his house, cast his shield indeed before him, and saved him, for he was foremost in the press of death; and more than one stout priest of Nabu and riotous burgher howled no more after the royal sword smote them.

Atossa had watched the first moments of the battle with keen delight. The hated Avil and the scarce less hated king were the assailed; their enemies were her friends. But now that the strife was all about her, she was whirled from her place by a sudden rush of the rioters; an instant more and she was in rough hands, the veil rudely torn from her face, with ten brutal voices crying in her ear:—

"Praise Istar! A prize! A prize! Off with her!"

They should have guessed from her dress who she might be; and she declared herself haughtily, but her voice was drowned in the babel. Atossa was feeling herself hurried down the stairway to the temple enclosure, the whole rude scene enacted so swiftly that she scarce knew what had befallen, when suddenly a strong arm was thrusting aside her excited captors.

"Fools!" a loud voice was crying, "are you bat-blind? Release! she is no spoil for you. Wrong her, and you bring Cyrus down on Babylon!"

The hands upon Atossa relaxed, as her captors stared into the face of the young man who had awed them so shortly before—Isaiah the Jew.

"She is ours," commented the leader of the band, little liking to let so fair a bit of spoil slip through his fingers. "Who are you, Master Hebrew, to give the law unto us?"

He flourished a cudgel in air, when a second cudgel, wielded by the same young man who had released Isaiah, smote the weapon out of his hand, and left him disarmed and cowed. The brutish weavers who had taken Atossa blinked at one another in confusion.

"This way, lady," commanded the Hebrew, taking Atossa by the hand, "and those who lay finger on you shall pay right dear."

The weavers stared at him, but Shaphat's cudgel was waving very close to their heads. One fellow, bolder than the rest, stretched forth a hand to seize the Persian again, but he only earned from Isaiah a buffet behind the ear that laid him prone on the pavement.

"Be warned," exhorted the Hebrew. "I am your friend, and the king's enemy; but as Jehovah my God liveth, you shall not do violence to this woman!"

"We meant no harm," protested the leader of the band, cowed and sullen.

"Good, then; she is safe in my hands. Go again to the struggle, for by the Lord of Hosts, Belshazzar is far from mastered."

They were gone, rushed back to the conflict now raging at the foot of the stairs to the second temple stage, whither the king had retreated with the soldiers. Isaiah caught a dusty robe from the bricks, where it had lain since being rent from its owner's back, and threw it over Atossa.

"Cover your gay dress and your face, my lady," commanded he, "so none will recognize, and I will conduct you back to the palace. This is truly proving a day of deeds fierce and terrible."

Many rioters stared at them, but as soon as they recognized the prophet, they made way rapidly, and Isaiah led on unhindered, Shaphat following silently after, and guarding their rear.

Thanks to this half-reverence, half-dread, the two were soon clear of the tumult within the temple enclosure and were threading the city streets. Here everything was nigh quiet as the grave. Sober burghers and shopkeepers had long since barricaded their houses and closed their booths, lest the malcontents turn speedily from sedition to pillage. Once Isaiah led into an alley while a chariot corps from the Northern Citadel thundered past at headlong speed, bearing belated succour to the hard-pressed king.

Isaiah guided the princess westward, past the temple of Nana, and down the great street until they reached the river, the bridge of boats; and that once crossed, Atossa saw before them the stately gates of the palace, within which was her safety.

"Declare yourself fearlessly to the sentries, my lady," said the young prophet, "and your danger is at an end."

"And you?" said she, while he turned to leave her; "where is your safety? What may I do in reward for this peril run for me?"

The Hebrew smiled gently. "I shall be scantily welcome in the king's house, I fear. And in serving you I have but repaid in part the debt I owe Prince Darius."

"Yet you must not go without one token. What may I give?"

"Some talisman, then, that shall be known to all Persians to vouch for my truth, if I say I bring word from Babylon of you and of Darius."

Atossa tore a gold locket from her neck. "Take this, then," and she held it out; "it was given me by my father on my last birthday. It is marked with the winged likeness of Ahura the Great. Cyrus and all his lords will recognize."

Isaiah and Shaphat were salaaming again to make farewell, but Atossa had one more appeal.

"Ah! brave Jew," spoke she, "if the one God leads you—and He must—to let you do the deed you have done this day, do not forget my wretchedness, or the peril of Darius. Do you verily purpose to stand before Cyrus my father?"

"As speedily as the Lord God shows me the way," assented Isaiah.

"Oh!" she cried impulsively, "am I not for the instant free? Can I not trust you in all things? Why may I not flee with you to the city of my father, and see this wicked Babylon no more?"

The young Jew smiled. "Spoken like a king's own child, in very truth! But such things cannot be. You cannot go where I may go, or endure what is as naught to me; that were not trusting, but rather tempting, God."

"But you will tell all to Cyrus,—of myself, of Darius, of Belshazzar and his guile. You swear that you will conceal nothing, that my father may dash from power this evil king of the Chaldees."

There was a strange light on Isaiah's face when he answered: "Fear not, lady, Cyrus shall hear. And think not that the one God will forget the wickedness of these servants of stone and brass; for I say to you, He shall turn all their guile against themselves, and shall humble them utterly."

"Alas! brave Jew," Atossa cried, at parting, "would to Ahura your faith were mine. My own faith in Him grows weak, but my faith in you, who can dare so much, is very strong."

"Put no trust in me," Isaiah replied, kissing her mantle; "but trust much in the Spirit that moves in me, and in every soul whose love is light and truth."

How Belshazzar made good the tower of Bel-Marduk that day against half of Babylon, how soldiers came at last from the garrison cantonments to the aid of the hard-pressed royal guard, how the king slew his tens and surpassed all his captains in valour—of this there is no place to tell. Save for Belshazzar himself, the priests of Nabu and the rioters would have stormed the *ziggurat* to its topmost stage, and flung monarch and chief pontiff upon the pavement below. But Nergal, or some other divinity of the bold, watched over the king, and saved him from mortal wound. The malcontents gained the second stage of the tower after a bitter struggle, so that the steps of the *ziggurat* flowed with blood. But here their progress was stopped. Companies of soldiers, arriving outside the temple enclosure, threatened to cut off the retreat of those rioters who had entered, and the troops within turned at bay, and held their own at last. Then, finally, the tide seemed to have turned. The valour commenced to ooze out of the undisciplined priests and burghers. Only one thing prevented Belshazzar from making good all his threats, and causing the brethren of Nabu to curse the day they had lifted their heads against his power and the supremacy of Bel-Marduk. Sirusur, the general, was still captive in the malcontents' hands. Let them be pressed too hard, and his life was not worth a shekel. The king raged at his captains, but they were obdurate.

"Rather than sacrifice Sirusur," declared Bilsandan, the vizier, bluntly, when his lord gave orders for a final charge, "the soldiers will declare for Imbi-Ilu. The rebels are desperate. We can ill afford a victory that will plunge half Babylon in mourning. It will sow ill feeling to blossom into twenty new revolts. We dare not do it, your Majesty."

And so the king had been persuaded. The criers had made proclamation, and the decree had been promptly published, that his Majesty, out of the goodness and benevolence of his heart toward his subjects, would proclaim amnesty to all who had taken part in the day's riot, from Imbi-Ilu downward. As for Daniel, the king gave his royal word that he should be kept in honourable custody, and no attempt made against his life. This concession ended the tumult. The rioters dispersed. The priests of Nabu returned—as many as were yet alive—to Borsippa. They were not completely satisfied, for Avil-Marduk was still living and in power; but a great blow had been struck at his prestige. The lower temple of Bel had been thoroughly sacked. Avil would have to mortgage all the lands of his god to make good the damage, unless the king was generous out of the treasury. Daniel had been saved from death. Belshazzar had been taught a lesson, likely to be remembered, that Bel was not the only god worth conciliating. So on the next day peace reigned in Babylon.

There had been one exception to the amnesty, however. Whatever the secret thoughts of many, none dared openly to express sympathy for the mad Jewish prophet. Belshazzar had desired to make a notable example.

The next night, as the boatmen warped their barges into the current to drop down the river to Erech, they heard the criers upon the quays shouting across the water:—

"Two manehs of silver! Two manehs from the king for the body of Isaiah the Jew, alive or dead! Two manehs for Isaiah the Jew!"

Yet, though the silver was coveted by a host, the gods strangely suffered their blasphemer to remain at large, and the money to lie safe in the royal coffers.

CHAPTER XVIII

The seventh day of the month, sacred to the dread goddess Sapanitum, and by every calendar pronounced an unfortunate day. The king had been forbidden by divine law to eat cooked food, change his dress, mount his chariot, or approach an altar for sacrifice. As for his subjects, they dared not, however sick, call in a physician or conjurer lest the wrathful goddess turn the remedies into poison. Nor had they ventured to breathe a curse against the bitterest enemy, lest the malediction be visited upon their own heads. It was a day of gloom and anxiety in all Babylon.

Graver things than the calendar were troubling Belshazzar and his ministers. Yet Khatin, the headsman, who waited beside Neriglissor, at the door of the king's council-chamber, while their betters deliberated within, seemed in an unwontedly merry mood for so black a day.

"I profess, dear priest," chuckled he, "his Majesty's humour has most happily changed since the riot. He orders beheadings by the score, not of whining bandits, but of stout guardsmen and fat temple folk like yourself. By Samas! I shall need an assistant to aid me."

The old "anointer" looked at him out of the corners of his eyes, and sidled away, fearful of too close company.

"Yes," he assented, "since the riot the king cries 'kill!' every time a fly hums past his ears. The eunuchs who serve him every morning vow a goat to Sin if they are kept safely through the day."

Khatin was just beginning some impious remark to the effect that "the worthy god was being over-fed with goats' flesh," when Igas-Ramman the captain burst in upon them on the run, and flew up to the sentry guarding the council-chamber door, almost before the two others knew his presence.

"Hold, friend!" shouted Khatin, a ponderous hand clapping on Igas's shoulders; "your business? The headsman is better than the king. Give him the news first!"

"Allat wither you!" growled Igas, writhing out of his clutch. "Do not stop me! Such tidings for his Majesty!"

"Speak, rascal!" Khatin was thundering, when the door suddenly opened, and Bilsandan, the vizier, admitted the messenger instantly, then slammed it in the others' faces. Those without stared at one another for many minutes, until the door reopened suddenly as before, and Bilsandan called for Khatin by name.

"Your slave waits my lord's orders," began the executioner, gleefully expecting the vizier was going to ask for a head.

"Go with Igas to the chambers of Darius the Persian. There is no time to summon a regular guard; but on your life do not let the prince escape you. He is active and daring. Watch him well."

"Be he strong as Tiamat the dragon," laughed Khatin, gruffly, "he shall find me almighty as Bel." Then he strode away after Igas, wondering vainly what this strange summons of the Persian might mean.

Since his arrest Darius had been confined in easy captivity in the tower of the northeast angle of the palace. The king's eunuchs had supplied every physical want; but he had been separated from his suite, and allowed no communication with the outside world. At sight of the royal signet borne by Igas, the subaltern commanding the squad of troops guarding the tower promptly led forth his prisoner. Darius appeared little the worse for his imprisonment. He bore himself haughtily, and was silent when Khatin croaked in his ear, "that, in his opinion, the king was about to have the envoy's throat sundered." In fact, the Persian carried himself so arrogantly, and showed his guards such supreme contempt, that they in turn had come to feel some little awe of a man who dared treat them thus; and they were glad when they had marched their captive into the council-chamber, where Khatin, to his great delight, was bidden to remain and witness the scene to follow.

Neither the room nor its company was large. Belshazzar occupied an ivory chair on a low dais. At his right hand two white-robed scribes were ready with clay tablet and stylus to take down all that passed. On other stools facing the dais were seated the coterie of magnates who made up the privy council—Avil-Marduk, Bilsandan, Mermaza, Sirusur the general, and a few colleagues. Behind the king stood the inevitable pair of eunuchs with their fly-flappers. As for Darius, he had been placed directly facing the king; and to the surprise of all he remained standing with folded arms, without any obeisance, during a silence that soon became awkward.

Belshazzar had heavy rings beneath his eyes, as if he had drunk overdeeply the night before; and when he turned to motion to Bilsandan, his hand was seen to tremble. Seemingly, he was deeply moved. Then, while the vizier was feeling around for words, Darius broke forth rudely:—

"Well, your Majesty, this bullock here"—with a nod toward Khatin—"says you desire my head. By Mithra! I wonder that, after imprisoning Cyrus's envoy, you hesitate to kill him also."

Belshazzar, by an effort, ignored the taunt, and with uncommon smoothness answered: "Noble prince, few have deplored more than I your nominal imprisonment. I have summoned you here to declare that you are shortly to be set free."

Darius looked gravely into the king's eyes.

"I rejoice to hear it, my lord," said he, sternly; "yet more would I rejoice to know how your Majesty will account to Cyrus for this outrage upon the person of his ambassador. A strange story, surely, to send to Susa!"

"If the noble prince," commenced Avil in turn, speaking gently, as if treading on slippery ground, "will deign to listen to his slave—"

"Ugh!" grunted the Persian, turning his back on the pontiff, "what foul *dæva* told *you* how I was to serve the king of the Aryans?"

"Do you speak for us all," Belshazzar nervously commanded Bilsandan.

"May it please the preëminently noble son of Hystaspes," began the vizier, also timidly, "there has just come to Babylon a courier saying a second embassy from Cyrus is close to Babylon, and has sent so unfriendly a letter on before it, that we are fain to ask my lord to explain it to us."

"Ha!" They saw the prince's lips curl in half-suppressed triumph; but he demanded, "And what proof, wretched oath-breakers, have you to lay before me, a prisoner, that you are telling me one morsel of the truth?"

Bilsandan flushed, but tried to keep his temper.

"Believe me, my prince, we have nothing to gain by concealing anything. We had expected no new embassy from Persia so quickly. Now, all unwarned, comes Igas with tidings that Gobryas, the general of Cyrus, is within a hundred furlongs of the city. And doubtless if he is not persuaded to alter his mood, as shown in his letter, we fear Cyrus, your master—"

"Will take swiftest vengeance on Belshazzar, lord of Babylon, and all his guileful race!" shouted the Persian, triumphing at last. Then, with a step straight toward the king, for he had not been fettered, he shook a knotted fist in the royal face. "Give me the letter, the letter," he commanded, "or, as Ahura reigns on high—"

So fierce was his passion that for the moment king and council quaked before him. It was Belshazzar himself who commanded, "Bilsandan, give him the tablet." So Darius was suffered to take it, and read:—

"Gobryas, servant of Cyrus, king of Persia and of the Aryans, to Belshazzar sends greeting:—

"Know, O king, my master has sent me to inquire into the strange tales that have come to his ears touching his former envoys, and their treatment. Why have their couriers been halted when bound for Susa? Why does Belshazzar negotiate with Pharaoh Amasis, Cyrus's foe, and gather soldiers in time of peace? Why does he speak 'peace' with his lips and in his heart weave war? I have come to demand an answer of you, O Belshazzar; do not think to hinder my return. For if in twelve days I come not back to Susa denying the tales of treachery, the hosts of the Aryans are in arms. Farewell."

Darius turned again to Belshazzar. His smile became yet haughtier. "Your Majesty," declared he, "the meaning of this letter is plain as the moon on a cloudless night. Cyrus has caught scent of your plottings, ere their completion. Instead of Persia being in danger, the peril confronts Babylon. Yet doubtless the worthy Avil is ready with his serpent's craft. Look to him, Belshazzar, for escape from a net of his own making!"

But the king in turn had put on his arrogancy, and spoke back in wrath:—

"Have a care, bold Persian. You are utterly in my power. I did not send for you to have you revile me to my face."

The prince only stood more proudly than before.

"Well said, my king; I am summoned here to aid these wise Chaldeans in devising an escape through the blasting of their own plots. I am to yield myself a tool to Avil-Marduk and his fellow-crows. I am to excuse my own letters of warning, and the tidings borne by Ariathes, who it is plain escaped your spies and guards, and reached Susa safely. I am to profess to Gobryas and Cyrus, 'I was mistaken. The stories are false. Trust Belshazzar in all things!'"

It was as if he had taken the words out of the king's own mouth. All the council stared at him. "And if not?" he demanded, suddenly stopping.

"If you will not," threatened Belshazzar, blackly, "prepare to die. We know a Persian's word can be trusted. Once give your pledge, you will explain away everything—"

Darius almost shouted his reply:—

"And I know that it would be better to groan in 'The Land of the North'[7] for years uncounted, than to put trust in *your* word. From your own mouth I know how your oaths are sworn only to be broken, how you have prated 'friendship' in my ear, and all the while plotted death. Therefore take my life. I do not fear to cross the Chinvat Bridge, and stand before the throne of Ahura. But rest assured, Cyrus will wreak full vengeance!"

When Darius ended there was silence in the council, for every man knew they had laid hands on a monster, equally dangerous to release or to retain.

"And what, then, would my lord have us do to preserve the peace?" faltered at length Sirusur the commander.

"Let your king send an embassy in sackcloth to Susa to confess his fault and declare his penitence. Let him send to Cyrus the head of Avil-Marduk, chief begetter of these falsehoods. Let him send me back safely with the Princess Atossa, and present my king with a great treasure. Finally, let him throw down two furlongs of the city walls of Babylon, to show he meditates no war. Do thus, and you preserve the peace; and thus only."

Belshazzar had risen on his throne.

"Let us have an end to this," cried he, darkly. "I see the prince's wits have been blasted, or else he has fallen in love with death. I have spared his life, because he saved me from the auroch; but my forbearance is near its end. Yet he shall have chance to reflect on his madness. Hale him away, clap him in the lower dungeon, beside that of Daniel, double-fetter, and let him prepare to die!" Darius neither salaamed nor gave other sign when his guards stepped beside him to lead him away. Having delivered himself to the council, he became silent as a stone idol.

When the prisoner and his escort were gone, there was yet again stillness in the council. When presently the storm broke out, it was upon Avil.

"Cursed are we, priest," growled Bilsandan in his beard, "for listening to your counsels. It is you who poured the oil on this fire. It is you that advised the sham treaty, then browbeat the king into arresting the envoy. Whither are we come, indeed? The Pharaoh still holds back. Cyrus knows all, and it will take more than smooth words to stop the charge of his lancers!"

"We have the prince as hostage," retorted Avil, trying to retain his composure.

"Pliable hostage, indeed!" snarled the vizier; "catch the lion cub, as hostage for the friendliness of the lioness. We may cut off the prince's head, but such a deed is little suited to make Cyrus more friendly. You temple folk, Avil, will be the first to whimper when your crafty deeds return one and all to nest on your own heads. I love wisdom, but not the wisdom that is like to ruin all 'Sumer and Akkad.'"

Avil kept his temper by a manifest effort. It had not escaped him that Belshazzar was staring at him very fixedly, a most ominous sign of royal displeasure.

"Noble Sirusur," spoke the priest, turning to the general, "surely you and all the king's sword-hands have not waxed so unvalorous that you dread the war. Has his Majesty only harem girls for an army?"

"The sword-hands of the Chaldees," retorted Sirusur, testily, "are able to fight for their king, and, if needs be, die; but I say only truth when I tell you, the host is in no condition to meet the Persians in pitched battle. Madness to risk it."

"I congratulate our lord," flashed back Avil, "on the heroic spirit of his gallant *Tartan*."

"Aye!" shouted the "Master of the Host," "the taunt comes right well from such as you,—you who have lit the blaze, and fain would see others quench it now. I know your prowess. While I was risking my life in that mob, all say the valiant high priest was cowering like a cornered hare."

But it was the king who terrified the pontiff most; for, though Belshazzar spoke not, Avil-Marduk saw his eye fixed on him, full of that cold menace which, he knew well, had often preceded a curt command to Khatin.

"You may speak, Avil," remarked Belshazzar at length, his tones icy as a blast of the north.

But the courage of Avil-Marduk, if not that which might carry unblenching through the ragings of a hostile multitude, was yet courage after its kind. He had turned pale in the face of the furious rioters, but he was steadfast before the hostile council and angered king.

He rose and addressed Belshazzar almost as haughtily as had the Persian.

"Do you well, my Lords Bilsandan and Sirusur, to revile me?" retorted he, hotly. "Am I not a man of peace? Is it my business to see that the royal guard does not fly like sparrows at the yells of an unarmed rabble? As for this coming of the second embassy, who save Anu and Ea could know that a letter of Darius could pass through our watchers—so many were they—even had some foul demon whispered the truth in the Persian's ear? I am not a god, your Majesty; but what human wit has done, I have done also."

"But human wit," quoth Belshazzar, grimly, "has not sufficed to avert an issue with Cyrus. What are we to do now, my dear pontiff?"

When the king became affectionate, men said he was not far from ordering an execution. Avil knew his danger, but he only let his voice rise higher.

"O King Belshazzar," cried he, "Bel-Marduk, the sovereign and guardian god of Babylon, even he and none other it is that has set you upon your throne of Sumer and Akkad. Did he not clothe you with power that he might bring all nations in subjection unto you? That the gods of the Persians and of the Medes should be brought low before the power of his servants? Is Cyrus the first king who has raised his head against Babylon? Where is Sin-shar-ishkun the Assyrian? or Zedekiah the Jew? or Necho the Egyptian? Gone, all of them. Their gods have brought them no help, but Bel has fought for his servants. And will you now, King of Babylon, distrust the god that has protected you so long? Will you cringe to this Ahura of the Persians, that we may be taunted before every nation, 'Bel of Babylon is subject to the god of Cyrus the barbarian'? The gods one and all forbid that Belshazzar should do this thing! Let him be strong. The guardians of Babylon shall yet show how much mightier they are than the weakling spirits of the Persians, before whom also the spiritless Jews shall whine in vain."

The priest paused a moment. The swift rush of his speech had borne away all the hesitancy that had risen in the heart of his lord. Avil knew he had saved himself and had triumphed. He went on boldly:—

"Trust the strong walls of Babylon, my king. They can mock all Cyrus's thousands. There is yet time to assemble a great host. The warriors of Chaldea have not all waxed cowards. Meet the Persian fairly in the field, and if fortune there fail, Imgur-Bel and Nimitti-Bel will not fail. There is provision inside the walls for a siege years long. Before many months the Aryan hosts will be dissolved for lack of forage. Revolt will kindle in Cyrus's provinces. The Pharaoh will take arms. Be bold and the gods will bless you. I speak not of myself, for is the king of Babylon a dog that he should submit to the commands of Cyrus or his envoys? Take my life, if so your Majesty will, but bow the knee to the Persian?—never!"

The king's eyes were flashing. He had risen again on his throne.

"And the high priest counsels well!" cried Belshazzar, doubting no more. "We will put the might of Bel-Marduk to the test! Bel-Marduk against the puny god of the Persians and the Jews! Bel-Marduk, who rules forever, against the god who might not save Jerusalem to his servants, who shall not now save them Susa. In Darius we have a hostage that will make Cyrus hesitate long before taking the field against us. Away with all fears, my lords. I, the king, have spoken, and my word is 'war'!"

That same day there went a letter to Gobryas, the new Persian envoy, who had just arrived outside the city, bidding him return to his land with all speed. "Belshazzar," wrote the Babylonian ministers haughtily, "would not receive any embassy sent on so unfriendly an errand as this. The king would make due explanation to Cyrus for the detention of Darius; but if Cyrus would not accept it, let him be warned that the first hostile move on his part would be followed by the execution of the son of Hystaspes. And in the war that might ensue Belshazzar shunned no issue."

That night also an order went forth for the arrest of Imbi-Ilu, chief priest of Nabu, on the ground that he had violated the terms of the amnesty, and was conspiring against the king; but the next morning found all Babylon astir with the news that the threatened pontiff had already escaped to the Persian envoy outside the walls. Gobryas had taken no risks of detention. The instant the letter of Belshazzar reached him he had started straight homeward, outstripping any chance of pursuit.

A second fugitive likewise fled with Gobryas. In the second Persian embassy Isaiah had beheld the opportunity divinely promised through Daniel; he should stand face to face with Cyrus the Aryan, and deliver the message of Jehovah. There was no longer any refuge at Borsippa for Ruth, but he counted her safe at the humble house of Dagan-Milki. Shaphat would be her guardian, and if needs be die, to save her from the hand of Belshazzar. Very beautiful and strong had been the smile on the Jewess's face when she kissed Isaiah farewell.

"Go, beloved, go," were the last words the young prophet carried on his journey; "who am I to give you care, when God has called you to His service?"

"Ah!" thought Isaiah, many times while on the way, "if the prayers of the pure and good avail anything with the great Lord God, I have already persuaded the king of the Aryans."

CHAPTER XIX

Another king, another council, another palace. The twilight was creeping over Susa, the city of Cyrus, over the blue Choaspes winding southward, over the rambling town, with its shops and bazaars, which stretched away to eastward, and over the great mound betwixt river and city. High above dwelling and street loomed the ramparts of the palace fortress of the king. Complacent Babylonian envoys might sneer under breath at the barbarism of the decorations, but under the failing light the palace wore a glory all its own, the like of which was nowhere else save at its prototype in Ecbatana, city of the Medes. The citadel was natural, but strengthened by human art. Twenty furlongs and more was its circuit; its sheer height rose for fifty cubits. On its summit spread the Aryan palace. Original in nothing save truth-speaking, the Persian had been a borrower from many lands. A stranger would have declared the house of Cyrus like that of Belshazzar, yet in manner unlike it. Endless colonnades; huge courts, unroofed save for the Tyrian purple tapestries on great feast days; giant-winged bulls; walls brilliant with innumerable processions of huntsmen and spearmen, wrought in blue and green enamel,—all these from Babylon. But Greek chisels had given delicacy and grace to the sculptures; the conceit of India had set the four heads of griffins on the corners of each stately capital; Median ostentation had plated the ceilings of many of the chambers, as well as the cornice and parapet without, with the pale lustre of silver, or even with garish gold.

He who entered would have lost himself in court after court, hall after hall, each a-swarm with its hordes of guardsmen, eunuchs, and courtiers. His feet would have trodden priceless Bactrian carpets; over his head would have twinkled a thousand silver lamps and red resinous torches. Yet had he kept onward, he would have at last come to a door guarded by a score of watchful "eyes of the king," and then, if some talisman suffered him to pass them, have stood face to face with the lord of the Aryans.

The king was taking counsel with his peers. The Tartar on the chillest steppe, the Brahmin by the hoary Indus, might quake at the name of Cyrus, son of Cambyses; but the six princes of the tribes of Persia and of Media were suffered at all times to speak their word to the monarch, and he must hear them.

There was no throne in this chamber. The king sat in a ponderous arm-chair, at the head of a long table, his fellow-councillors ranged on lower seats at either side. They had long since cast off ceremony. Cyrus's cone-shaped tiara was taller than that of the others, the embroideries on his flowing Median robe richer; these alone distinguished him. There was no scribe present, nor other attendant. After a long silence the king was again speaking.

"My friends," Cyrus smote a fist on the table with a buffet weighty enough to fell an ox, "you seem to have suffered Apaosha the 'Drought-fiend' to dry up all your thoughts. I called you for counsel; I meet silence and black frowns. Have you nothing to say?" The king looked from face to face; his own was troubled. There was care spread upon his high, bronzed forehead, care was in the lines of his mouth under the flowing gray beard, care was dimming the genial lustre of his keen blue eyes.

A man at the king's right hand made answer, and all heard respectfully, for he was bowed with age and its wisdom.

"Live forever, King of the Aryans! Do not blame us if Ahura denies us the presence of Vohu-Manö, angel of good counsel. What is left to say? Yet let the king know this—determine the fate of Darius, my son, without thought for my own private loss or grief. The honour of Persia and of Persia's king is more than the safety of forty sons of mine."

But Cyrus shook his head, replying sombrely: "You are a true friend, Hystaspes; but understand that the honour of Persia and of Cyrus demands to-day that Darius should come harmless from that snare to which I, in folly, sent him. The blame is mine. Belshazzar has deceived me. Would to Ahura that I alone might bear the calamity, and not the noblest of our youth!"

But the dark-eyed Median prince, Harpagus, who sat at the king's left hand, broke forth hotly: "Now as Mithra rains light from the heavens, I protest the Babylonian will never dare to make a hair of our prince to fall. Belshazzar and his pack of snivelling priests and paltering corn-merchants put to death a prince of our blood royal? The Chaldeans will love well to see our Aryan cavalrymen eating up all their dear farmlands like locusts! Belshazzar's was a coward's threat. He will make it good—never!"

"Peace," commanded the king. "You do even that *dæva* wrong. We have Gobryas's letter and cannot doubt. Belshazzar has a city nigh impregnable. His army, if not so large as our Aryan hordes, is well drilled, valorous. His capital is provisioned for a siege of years. Only a man who had resolved to follow his path to the end would dare to utter this threat."

"True," Hystaspes looked down, grievously tormented; "yet for the honour of our people and our god, there is but one answer to make to this defiance."

Cyrus was standing erect and confronting his council.

"Do you, princes of Persia and Media, bid me to sacrifice Darius, son of Hystaspes, proclaim instant war, and send our forces over the Tigris to strike Belshazzar! An answer,"—the king's voice grew hard,—"peace or war?"

Stillness for a moment, and then Harpagus was thundering:—

"War, in the name of every archangel! Tell Belshazzar that if Darius dies we will beat down Babylon till she be a city for wolves and jackals."

"And you, Hystaspes?" demanded the king.

"I have spoken," replied the old prince, wearily. "Not to save my own child can we cringe to Belshazzar, that 'Son of the Lie.' There is no other way."

Cyrus was looking wistfully from one to another.

"And is there no word for peace?" he was asking, almost eagerly. "The power of Babylon is great. If we fail, the empire will depart from us. On such a war we stake our all."

"And our all truly is lost," Harpagus replied, nigh fiercely, "if the king of Persia crouches trembling under a threat like this!"

"Your voices then are all for war?" was Cyrus's last appeal.

"For war," was the sullen answer of many, none looking upward. But Cyrus smote again upon the table, making the firm oak quiver.

"But I, Cyrus, son of Cambyses, king of Persia and all Iran, am very ill content with your counsel. We all will be partners in Darius's blood, if he is left to die. I, the king, have chief blame in sending him to Babylon, but you all were consenting. Would to Ahura I had followed my own heart, and given him Atossa! Of her fate in the clutch of Belshazzar I say nothing." It was the first time he had mentioned his own child that day. The princes saw a tear on the iron cheek of the conqueror of Mede and Lydian. None answered him. The king ran on: "Our debate ends as it began—in darkness. I will not act on your advice to-night. Orasmasdes, the chief Magian, shall pour libation to the great star Tishtrya[8] and all the other heavenly powers, that they may incline the Lord God to favour with his wisdom. I am no 'Father of the People,' if, to spare my own dignity, I suffer the bravest and choicest of our Aryan youths to die miserably."

The king had thrust back his chair, and motioned to the others to rise also. They were obeying, in moody silence, when the door was flung open, and Phraortes, the high chamberlain, was kneeling before Cyrus.

"Live forever, O Bulwark of the Nations! May your slave speak?"

The monarch good-humouredly motioned to him to say on. Phraortes arose, and punctiliously hid his hands in his flowing sleeves—token that he meditated no attack on the royal person.

"Your Majesty, the General Gobryas sends in advance a young man who demands instant speech with my lord."

"Does he come from Babylon? Who is he?"

"He brings a letter from the general, that he is in all things to be believed. He also bears a token from the ever-to-be-reverenced Lady Atossa."

"From Atossa?" They saw the king's grip on the arm of his chair grow hard as a vise. "Bring him in instantly."

Cyrus had reseated himself; the rest imitated perforce.

A moment later Phraortes ushered before them a young man in Babylonish dress, handsome-visaged, but now dusty, unkempt, travel-stained. The stranger did not cover his hands, Persian fashion, but fell on his face and kissed the rugs at Cyrus's feet, nor did he arise until Cyrus bade him to fear nothing.

"Your Majesty understands Chaldee?" began the stranger, his eyes still on the carpet.

"I understand and speak it," was the answer. "Do not tremble. We Persians forgive all else so long as men speak the truth. Who are you? Not a Babylonian?"

While the king spoke he had sped a glance keen as a spear through the newcomer, as if searching every recess of his soul. But the other, unconfounded, lifted his own gaze and met Cyrus boldly eye to eye, a glance in turn so penetrating, yet so winsome, that half the suspicions of monarch and princes were disarmed.

"I am no Babylonian, O king!" The young man tossed his head proudly. "My people are the Hebrews, whom it pleases the Omnipotent God should suffer oppression at the hands of these servants of speechless brass and graven marble, but who would not exchange the Lord God of their fathers for a thousand Belshazzars and his kingdoms. Know, your Majesty, that my name is Isaiah, son of Shadrach, the Jew, though born and bred in Babylon, city of darkness. And in proof of what I may tell you, receive this."

He was extending something which Cyrus caught eagerly.

"Beware," admonished Hystaspes, in the king's ear, "this may be but a spy of Belshazzar." But the young man overheard and answered boldly:—

"I a spy of Belshazzar? May Jehovah the All-Seeing smite me as I stand, if I speak one jot or one tittle more or less than truth!"

Cyrus had raised his head, and looked on the Hebrew again.

"And I believe you," swore the king; "for as Ahura reigns, I do not deem he could set deceit behind so frank a face and eye. This, my lords"—he held up the trinket—"is the locket I hung on my daughter's neck before you all. And now, Jew, say on."

And long the council sat and listened while Isaiah unwound to them the tangled web of Belshazzar's and Avil's intrigues and ill-doings—the sham marriage treaty, the attempt on Darius's life, the plottings with Egypt, the preparations for war.

They had gathered much from the tale of the fugitive Ariathes, and the hasty despatch from Gobryas; they saw all clearly now. But when Isaiah had finished, Cyrus asked simply:—

"One question: By what means did you gain this locket from the Lady Atossa? Can you enter Belshazzar's own harem?"

Whereupon Isaiah told very modestly the manner in which he had saved the princess during the riot; and despite his slackness in self-praise, as he ended, the king demanded of his lords:—

"Men of Persia, do you now believe this man?"

"Every word," came from Harpagus, and he spoke for all.

"How, then, shall the great king reward him?"

"Let the Jew take three talents of gold," answered the councillor, and Cyrus nodded approval.

"So be it. Son of Shadrach, you shall have as Prince Harpagus has said."

"The king jests with his servant," and again the Hebrew looked downward.

"Not so, on the inviolable pledge of a king of the Aryans!"

"Your Majesty," Isaiah spoke very rapidly, as if to escape repentance for his boldness, "if I rescue Prince Darius from his dungeon—what reward then?"

The eyes of the Jew were very bright. They could see he was hanging on the king's every word. Cyrus had lifted his hand in an oath.

"The man who saves Darius shall enter my treasure-house in Ecbatana, where are stored the jewels taken from the Assyrian by Cynaxares the Mede, and bear thence his own weight in precious stones, though he take rubies and diamonds only!"

They who watched Isaiah saw him sweep his hand, as if in high disdain.

"Keep the jewels, O Cyrus!" cried he, nigh passionately. "I have not come to sell my service like a huckster, to bargain for gems or gold. Yet would you truly see Darius free?"

His voice had risen almost to a menace, but the king was not angry.

"Good, Hebrew!" Cyrus was smiling. "I did not think riches would tempt such as you. You seek something nobler—and by Ahura's great name, I declare that if you may save Darius, you may ask anything in reason, and it is yours."

Isaiah's eyes glittered even brighter than before, but his voice grew calm.

"King of the Aryans, the one God, whom you worship under the name of Ahura-Mazda, and we as Jehovah, has given my people now for fifty years into the power of the idol-worshipping Chaldeans. Fifty years long have we bowed beneath this yoke, and besought our God that he would forget our sins, would restore us to His mercy. Now at last the hour comes when it shall be proved before all nations which is the greater, Him whom we serve, or Nabu and Marduk and Samas, the demons of the Chaldees. For the rage of Avil-Marduk, the chief pontiff, and of Belshazzar is gone out against my people, and the oppression they suffer is more than most may bear. Either my people must bow the neck, must forsake their God, must teach their children to serve the idols of Babylon, or you, O Cyrus, must hear the summons of the Lord Most High, and make the oppressed go free!"

"I? What are you saying, Jew?" The king had leaped from his seat. They faced one another, monarch and prophet for the instant equals.

"Sovereign of Persia,"—Isaiah bore himself as proudly as if he were the "King of kings,"—"the God of nations has clothed you with power, the like of which he never shed on mortal man before, not on Assur-bani-pal, the great Assyrian. The tribesmen on countless plains are yours; your horsemen He alone may number. Belshazzar, the Babylonian, casts defiance in your teeth. You hesitate, for you fear for Darius. Were he free, the perjurer would already see from his walls the sky lit with the villages blazing under the Persian torch. And *it is I* that may set Darius free. Jehovah has set in me a spirit of craft and wisdom that with His help shall not fail. Though they seek my life in Babylon, I know how to avoid them.

Be this the reward for the rescue of Darius: you shall call forth your myriads and dash Belshazzar from his ill-gained throne, and then"—brighter than ever were the Jew's eyes now—"you shall restore my people to their own land, that they may rebuild their desolate Jerusalem. *This* is my reward!"

Stillness, while many heard their heart-beats. The rest saw Cyrus approach three steps toward the Jew; the two were yet looking eye to eye.

"Hebrew," Cyrus was striving to speak quietly, "a great thing you propose, a great thing you ask. How long a time will you require to return to Babylon and do this deed?"

"In forty days I pledge my head to show you Darius safe and free, here or in your camp. In Babylon I have two fellow-countrymen who will peril all to aid me." And Isaiah thought of Zerubbabel and of Shaphat.

"By Mithra! you speak of return to Babylon as of returning to a feast!"

"Fairer than a feast, my lord. I return to the fulfilment of my heart's desire—the winning of freedom for my people."

"Yet though you prosper, what if we fail? We may drive Belshazzar from the field, but the ramparts of Babylon—"

Isaiah took the words from the king's mouth.

"Shall lie smooth as the plain to the feet of Cyrus, the called of Jehovah!"

Cyrus looked again, and very earnestly. "One thing more, Hebrew—my daughter, in Belshazzar's harem?" His voice sank exceeding low. "What will be her treatment? Answer me truly this."

"Your Majesty," was the unfaltering reply, "even the Babylonian is not in all things a fiend. Belshazzar does not carry his villany so far, that if Darius escape, he would wreak vengeance on his own betrothed wife. I grieve for the Lady Atossa, but the swords of the Aryans are the only talismans that will make her lot less wretched."

Cyrus moved another step nearer. He had raised his hand toward heaven.

"Then in the name of Ahura, One God of All, and the Ameshaspentas, His archangels, I swear that if you save Darius, I will lay low Babylon and set your people free. And you, princes of the Persians, are my witnesses."

When he looked downward, he saw Isaiah kneeling before him, kissing the hem of his mantle.

"Do not fear, my king," he was declaring; "Jehovah, who has plucked me from so many perils, will not fail me now, when I speed upon His service."

But Cyrus had turned to his council.

"Men of Iran," said he, simply, "Ahura has not forsaken us. He has sent us Vohu-Manö, the spirit of wise council. We need linger no more here."

CHAPTER XX

Avil-Marduk had visited a strange place for the chief priest,—the nethermost dungeon in the palace guard-house, by the royal quay. Here one could hear the river brawling against the slimy walls. The black murk of the sunken galleries leading to the cells had been charged with a damp and sickening odour. The light from the slits against the ceiling was just enough to suffer one, with eyes accustomed to darkness, to grope his way. When the chief warden put his key in the ponderous wooden lock of a door, the pivots creaked and a whiff of air drifted from within, but so stifling that for an instant the priest recoiled.

"Who is here," demanded he of the warden, "the Persian or Daniel? My errand is to both."

"The Persian, my lord. Your eyes may not see him, but he is crouched in the farther corner. He is dangerous. Seven men had to hold when we put on his fetters. Shall I stay by while you speak with him?"

"Wait within call, though I must talk alone." Then, raising his voice, he jeered boldly: "Ha! noble prince, do you find the raw millet and canal water of this guard-house daintier than the fare on Cyrus's tables? Be comforted; twenty-seven years did Zedekiah, the Jewish king, languish in this very cell. You are not likely to enjoy its hospitality so long."

Out of the dark came an ominous growl.

"Take care, *dæva*; come within reach, and chained though I be, I can kill you!"

"I will keep a safe distance from your Highness," was Avil's undisturbed reply.

"And now, son of Hystaspes," he continued, dropping the catlike purring from his voice, "let us understand one another. You are utterly in our power. By this time, at least, you will begin to confess it."

He heard the chains begin to rattle from the corner.

"By this time, O Prince of Treachery, you begin to hear the roar of the Persian lion. Do you confess it? Has the news that comes of late to Babylon been sweet as Assyrian honey?"

Avil let a moment pass before he answered:—

"It is true that Cyrus is massing soldiers," he admitted.

"It is true that Kutha has surrendered, and Sirusur the Tartan suffered a defeat. Make your toads, these jailers, keep tighter mouths, if you would have them leak no news to me."

"If those turnkeys chatter, the stakes are ready to impale them," cursed Avil, under breath. Then, returning to the charge boldly: "Yes, it is true, war has blazed forth. No profit to deny. But nothing decisive has befallen. The king leads his host into the field in a few days. If Cyrus be the first to attack—"

"I shall be put to death?"

"Unless you will serve our ends. Are you bent on destruction?"

"I am in Ahura's hands. It is His, not yours, to give life or death."

Avil incautiously advanced a few steps into the darkness.

"The 'suicide-demon' possesses you, Persian," he was asserting, when with a clatter of chains the prince bounded from his corner and dashed the priest to the bricked floor.

"At last, adder!" snorted he, uplifting his manacled hands, and smiting once and again.

"Rescue! Help! Murder!" bawled Avil, helpless on his back.

Well that the jailers ran swiftly, or Bel would have lacked a pontiff. They plucked the prince from his victim by sheer force, and dragged Avil away, covered with bruises. He stood, invoking upper and nether powers to blast the Persian race forever. They put a shorter chain on the prisoner, but he still challenged out of his gloom.

"Closer, friend! Closer! I dearly love a fair wrestle!"

But the priest turned away, quaking, and bade the others open the door of the adjacent cell, for he desired speech with that second prisoner of state, the Hebrew Daniel.

Darius was left in his dungeon; the bolts clanked into place, the footsteps died away. At first he heard only the swash of the current against the oozing bricks, and the shouts of bargemen forcing their craft up-river. But the prince did not rage in his fetters, as a month earlier, when first they cast him into this "death-in-life." Laying his ear against the partition, he could hear voices uplifted—Avil-Marduk in angry colloquy with Daniel, who, contrary to Belshazzar's pledge in the proclamation, had not been kept in light captivity, but in heaviest durance. Darius caught no word, but he guessed that the priest was ill satisfied with his errand when Daniel's door clashed to suddenly, and Avil's voice sounded in the gallery:—

"Now, as Bel is lord of Babylon, we will find straiter quarters yet for this stiff-backed pair!" Then there were more steps, and again silence; but presently a soft rattle at Darius's own door, and the prince crept toward it, as far as his chains suffered. Some one spoke at the ample keyhole.

"Listen well, my prince, the other wardens are all around us."

Existence in such a prison had taught Darius to catch every whisper.

"I hear you. You are Zerubbabel, the Jew. Where is Isaiah?"

"He is more suspected than I; and even my fidelity as turnkey is half in doubt. Isaiah is looking to the locks on the tunnel. The escape must be to-night or not at all. Shaphat is arranging to have horses waiting beyond the gates." Feet sounded once more in the gallery. The speaker moved noiselessly away. Again silence and again the voice:—

"The chief priest swears that longer parley with you is useless. He urges the king to cast your head into Cyrus's camp. That would bar the last door to peace, and spur on Babylon to resist to the uttermost."

"And Daniel?"

"Avil would love to slay him with you, but dare not. News of his execution, were it to leak out, would still raise the city in riot. But we hope to save him with you."

"Till when shall I wait to-night?" The words came eagerly.

"We cannot stir before the third 'double-hour'[9] of the night. All is ready."

Shouts sounded down the gallery; Zerubbabel was gone, and Darius sat in his gloom. How many times since he had been thrust within that cell had he watched the bar of pale golden light, which drifted through that chink against the ceiling, creep, silent as the tread of a dream, across the floor! It was his only sun-dial. Pictured in its brightness he had seen many a sight he had told himself he would never see more with mortal eye,—his father, the hills of his native Iran, and Atossa, always Atossa, fair as on the night of their meeting in the Hanging Gardens, when for the last time he had looked into her dear eyes.

Interminable waiting! All the hard-learned lessons in patience, in which Darius had schooled himself since existing in that dungeon, forgotten in an hour! But, nevertheless, the day *did* wane. The little bar of light crawled snail-like across the wet bricks of the floor, and began to climb the reeking wall. It mounted higher, higher, then began to fade, and for once the

Persian's heart commanded "go quickly," though the ray had ofttimes been his dear friend. The chief warden entered with eight men, examined his captive's chains. Intact. He and his band with their blinding torches were gone. Once more stillness, and only the monotonous music of the great river fleeting seaward.

The last daylight had long vanished before Darius heard again—how gladly!—something stirring in the gallery without. There were a shout and a challenge when the guards were changing, the trample of heavy sandals, silence again, then Zerubbabel's voice close to the door.

"Quiet, my prince, my watch ends at midnight. We must be all haste."

The bolt was withdrawing noiselessly; the door crept open; inside glided a man with a flickering lamp that shed a red, uncertain light, leaving half the cell veiled in its shadows. Darius started, but a warning "Hist!" fixed him.

"Where is Isaiah?"

"In the next dungeon, releasing Daniel. The sentries have been drugged. Now off with these chains."

Babylonian fetters needed no key; the bronze circles, never locked, were simply hammered together around wrist or ankle. Happy mortal was he who, having felt them close upon him, could feel them also release. The turnkey set down his lamp, drew forth a stout iron bar. One twist of the lever freed the Persian's good right arm, and like an unchained lion Darius tore his other limbs free, almost with his empty hand. The Persian's heart gave a great bound as he sniffed a clear, sweet puff of night air, while ranging the gallery. A second lamp and two more figures came out of the gloom, but it was no place for stately greetings.

"The noble Prince Darius!" exclaimed Isaiah, softly, advancing from the darkness. "Jehovah be praised!"

"And with you is my Lord Daniel?"

"Safe and free, Jehovah willing," answered the older Jew, stepping forward.

"Good, then," replied the Persian. "Lead the way, for I am helpless here. Next to Ahura, I owe all to you, Isaiah, and to your friends!"

"Fear nothing." And Isaiah trod forward into the dark. "Few know the secrets of this city and palace as do I. We must haste to the tunnel."

They advanced in silence. The prison seemed empty of all life. Their feet awoke loud echoes down shadow-veiled galleries, but nothing hostile started forth to greet them. Presently they began ascending stairways, and the foul stench of the dungeons grew yet fainter.

Then a door swung open before them, and a cold breath smote their faces. A strange form thrust itself across their path.

"Who comes? Shaphat?" demanded Isaiah, never off his guard.

The newcomer stared about him in the dark.

"I am he; the guards are quieted. There is no danger. But where is my Lord Daniel? Let me fall at his feet."

And recognizing the older Jew, he cast himself then and there upon his knees.

"O lord, gracious master, who was as a father to me and whom I have requited after the manner of demons, speak to me one word. Declare that you forgive, for the blackness of my sin is ever before me!"

Daniel beckoned him to rise.

"You are forgiven long ago; I have heard of the atonement made by saving Ruth, and by rescuing Isaiah in the riot. You have sinned and have repented. The Lord God requires nothing more."

"Speed," interrupted Isaiah, "we must be all haste."

Then without another word he led the way over the threshold, past the ponderous prison gate, and Darius rejoiced yet again when he found himself beneath the glittering canopy of the stars. No moon. Under the starlight he could see the vague white tracery of the great palace to his left; to his right the outlines of the *ziggurats* beyond the river, trebly tall in the darkness, and before the temples the opalescent twinkle of some wavelet of the mighty Euphrates, where a constellation was mirrored. Isaiah hastened northward. They saw, far off, a form pacing the embankment above the stream. The starlight touched something that glittered—a soldier's helmet. Darius heard the chanted call pealing over the sleeping fortress:—

"The Ninib-star[10] rises. Midnight approaches. Marduk prosper Belshazzar our lord!"

"They change sentries soon. Speed!" urged Isaiah. And he led faster along the deserted quay. Soon before them rose a low, square building, and they halted.

"The entrance to the tunnel beneath the river," whispered Zerubbabel. "Now, if at all, let Jehovah show His mercy. All other exits from the palace fortress are too well watched."

"The starlight touched something that glittered—a soldier's helmet."

Isaiah, who had kept his lamp pricked down to a bare flicker under his mantle, boldly thrust in the door. They were in a small, bricked guardroom. Directly before them was a second door, small, ponderous, and heavily barred. Across the threshold lay a man in armour, but snoring in the slumbers of the just.

"This is the passage to the great tunnel of which I have heard so much?" asked Darius, softly. "Is not the exit guarded?"

Isaiah shook his head. "That, too, is provided for. The guard across the river is more lax than here. But now we must push away this dolt and force the door."

Darius motioned with his hands, signifying that one twist of his fingers around the sentinel's neck would speed him past mortal outcry; but when they rolled the rascal over, his guardian god favoured him. He grunted once, folded his hands, and fell again to snoring. The drug had done its work.

Isaiah, Shaphat, and Zerubbabel applied themselves to the massive door. Its bolts and bars yielded one by one. They were about to put their strength against it and thrust inward, when the turnkey stepped to one side into a darkened corner. One step, but the mending or ending of five human lives was hanging on the planting of that foot. He trod on something soft, something living. In a twinkling there followed a howl, a yelp, a prodigious barking.

"Fiends of Sheol blast the cur!" swore Zerubbabel, his iron bar clattering from palsied fingers. "All is lost!"

Darius leaped upon the dog, caught him, strove to throttle; but the mongrel brute writhed from his grip, bounded to the outer door, and lifted up his muzzle, howling. Instantly a second dog answered, a third, a fourth, and more, till they seemed encircled by dogs uncounted. Human voices were beginning to swell the din.

"Alarm! To arms! Turn out the guard!" The distant sentries were passing it one to the other.

The five stood and stared in one another's faces. The hopes of the night had been utterly dashed. What was left save death? But Darius, ever the soldier and leader, tossed up his head, and demanded fiercely: "Why gape and gibber here? Down the tunnel! We can cross before they reach the exit by bridge or boat."

"My lord," answered Isaiah, sadly, "below this door, on the staircase, is machinery to the sluice, whereby the tunnel can be flooded. We cannot bar this entrance from within. To descend means drowning beneath the river."

The drunken sentinel stirred in his slumber, but did not waken; yet the others heard the nearing shouting. The sleepy soldiers were tumbling from their barracks. The five heard the clangour of the great brass gong at the palace gate. The Lord God knew how soon a "ten" of infantry would be on the fugitives. Darius had possessed himself of the helpless watchman's sword.

"By Ahura Most High!" was his desperate oath, "it is better to mount aloft with seven foes sped on before me, than to drown beneath the river. They shall not take me unresisting!"

Feet approached rapidly. A new cry was rising, "The state captives, the Persian and Daniel! Escaped! Pursue!"

Isaiah dashed to the door of the tunnel-house and bolted it. It would take a few moments to force. Darius had turned to the others.

"I am a man of war, and know the look of death. If two men were to remain in the narrow entrance to this stairway, they could defend it long. Five must not perish where two suffice." He was stripping the drunkard of helm and shield. "I and one other will defend against pursuit, the rest flee!"

But Isaiah threw up his hands in dismay. "Folly, my prince. Your life is worth a thousand such as mine. I am no weakling. Shaphat shall guide you to safety. Leave the defence to Zerubbabel and to me!"

A thunderous beating on the door, and Igas-Ramman, the captain, was clamouring, "Open! Open! In the king's name!"

Isaiah reached to pluck the sword from Darius's hands. "Haste!" he exhorted, but another hand caught his.

"Folly again." It was Daniel who cried it. "You are all young. Life is sweet. God will give you many days and power to do great deeds. *I* will defend the entrance."

"You?" The others were staring now in truth.

"Open! Open, or you die the death!" howled the soldiers without; and Igas commanded fiercely: "Beat in the door! Hew it asunder!"

The stout portal shook on its pivots, battered by spear-butts. It could not last long.

"This shall never be!" shouted Darius, while the deadly clamour increased. "Who will abide with you? You are the least fit of us all."

But at this instant Shaphat spoke forth boldly: "If my Lord Daniel remain, he shall not remain alone, nor shall my betters be brought to death. Of us all, I am of least worth. I have but one life to proffer, as sacrifice for my sins, let it be offered now!"

"Dare you trust this man?" cried the prince, nigh angrily, while the door leaped inward with every stroke—"a confessed perjurer?"

But Daniel answered, with his wonted calm majesty: "Yes, as the Lord God liveth, I can trust him. He and I shall cover your retreat as long as Jehovah grants us strength."

But still the friendly rivalry went on, until Shaphat plucked away Zerubbabel's own sword, and set himself boldly across the doorway. Daniel turned to the others imploring.

"Away! away!" he prayed; "do you not see delay only ruins each and all?" And with a marvellous strength that white-haired man had wrung the weapon from Darius's grasp, and was putting on the helmet. As he stood in the wan lamplight, his form loomed erect, powerful. He seemed to have cast off the weight of twenty years. Woe to the first to meet him man to man!

"Bring a beam!" raged Igas to the soldiers. "Shatter the door!"

"Off!" urged the minister, tears now in his eyes. "Will you cast yourself away, Isaiah, and leave Ruth desolate when I am taken? Will you leave the Lord God's purposes for you undone, my prince, by dying here in vain? I am old. I have done His work. I live or die by His will. I do not fear."

Crash! Before the battering beam the door was splintering.

"We will never leave you!" came from the young men; but Daniel answered with a gesture of command. It was he who was prince, not Darius.

"Go! I command it!" cried he, almost arrogantly; "or your own blood and God's wrath are on you."

The tone, the majesty of his presence, these made his words as law. Darius's heart cried out in revolt, but he bowed his head and obeyed. They thrust open the inner entrance, and a dank stairway wound down into the darkness. They kept Zerubbabel's lamp. Isaiah left his for Daniel. No instant for long partings. Isaiah strode over beside Shaphat—"You are a true son of Judah," said he simply. But Shaphat only bowed his head.

"The One God spare you, my father!" came from Darius's trembling lips, though the fear was not for self.

"And you, my son"—like words between Daniel and Isaiah, and that was all. They saw the civil-minister standing, sword in hand, across the narrow entrance, hoary, but then, if never before, terrible. And at his side, steadfast and unflinching, was Shaphat, the one-time recreant.

A last crash—the beam, swung by twenty arms, beat the outer door inward. It toppled on the bricks. Half a score of torches tossed together and flickered on bared blades and lance-heads. A great yell of triumph, followed by a howl of surprise. A last vision was branded on Darius's memory. He heard the clash of steel above him, the crash of conflict. Then the stairway turned, cutting off sight and sound, and all about was blackness.

CHAPTER XXI

The last glimmer of light from above had vanished. The darkness, deeper than that of deepest night, crowded about the three. The little lamp in Isaiah's hand shed only a tiny gleam that made the shadows behind and before tenfold the blacker. As they descended the air grew foul, so that the lamp sank to a poor spark, and all were gasping. It was like passing alive into Sheol, and threading the avenues of the dead. No word, save when Isaiah halted an instant and pointed to a ponderous bronze lever set in the brickwork.

"This controls the sluice," quoth he, in a whisper; "we pass beneath the river soon."

Darius had caught the lever in a giant clutch, and twisted it in its socket; it would play less easily now, and delay the flooding. Then the air around them grew yet more foul, so that they were fain to bow their heads and haste onward, catching the purer breaths that hung along the slimy bricks at their feet. And above him, and all around, the Persian heard what sounded as a rushing wind—yet not a wind, for it sang and sang, without gust or crooning, one ceaseless, monotonous murmur, and he knew that it was the great Euphrates speeding above his head. No longer any stairs—their path led right onward.

So narrow the way that they could have reached to each wall at once with outstretched hands. But they seldom did so, for all the bricks were slimy with an ooze that made the flesh creep to the touch. And Darius trod through a plashing mire, cold, fetid, unsunned for many a long year. What monsters lurked in the all-encircling dark? Did not the dread "Scorpion-Men" of the Chaldees' tales here find dwelling? Were they not near the gates of Ninkigal, "Lady of Torment," of the Anunnaki, the "Earth-Fiends"?

Once Zerubbabel, just ahead of Darius, had stumbled; they heard a splash and clatter of some object escaping into the dark—some vile, light-hating creature that loved this pathway of the dead. Yet there was no time for halting or even for trembling. Above them the rush of the river became a maddening torture. Every heart-beat seemed long, every breath of the death-laden air bought with a pang. And behind them at the mouth of the tunnel was the old man Daniel with Shaphat,—renegade once and hero now,—sacrificing themselves for the fugitives. But how long might such as they hold back Igas-Ramman and his scores? How long before hostile hands would be wresting on that sluice lever and this thoroughfare of the dead become a tomb indeed?

Darius knew that Isaiah was counting the brick piers bedded in the casement; but, though he stared into the blackness ahead until his eyes nigh throbbed with the pain, he met only darkness and ever more darkness.

Once he cried aloud to Isaiah, "How many piers are yet to pass?"

His words seemed to have awakened all the ghosts and ghouls of this foul country. Echo pealed upon echo, his words were multiplied a score of times. Hidden voices flung back his question out of murky deeps. And he thought (for what were not his thoughts at such a moment?) that these same tongues were answering for Isaiah: "Forever! Forever! You must run this course forever!"

Onward and ever onward, till senses reeled and ears were filled with a buzzing that dimmed the fearful music of the river. Almost was Darius ready to pray for death, if life were longer to be this. But still Isaiah's lamp went on before him, and still the Persian followed, his feet obeying his instinct, not his numbing will. The Jews wasted no breath on speech. The journey was seeming interminable, when Isaiah uttered a great cry of relief: "Praised be Jehovah. The last pier is passed; we soon mount upward!" But the words had just crossed his tongue when the three groaned together, "Hark!" And blended with the steady rushing of the Euphrates swelled another rushing, as of water, splashing and swirling rapidly in the tunnel, but far behind.

"They have opened the sluice at last," came from Isaiah, with awful calmness; "we must haste, and may the Lord still speed us!"

And haste they did, human feet pacing against the tread of the waters. They stood erect despite the deadly air, and ran—ran, while the swirling behind them grew to a roaring; and of a sudden the slimy pools at their feet, through which they stumbled, began to swell from their soles to their ankles; and all the water, once chill, grew warm, rushing fresh from the sun-loved current. Then all around the air began to whistle past them in stifling blasts, heralds of the conquering river, blowing as swift as the waters chased them, and hurrying the fugitives onward. The roaring behind rose to reëchoing thunder, cavern answering to cavern, till it seemed that all the demons of the deep were howling after as for their prey.

The stream had risen from ankle to knee—now higher. Isaiah stumbled; his lamp was quenched, and all was noise and utter darkness. Darius's voice sounded above the swirl, his firm spirit bent at last: "Let us make our peace with Ahura! That only is left!" But the Jews caught him by the hand; he saw nothing, but under foot he felt a stairway. They were rising, rising; the waters raved after them, loath to quit their spoil. But the air—praised be the Merciful!—was growing sweet. The crash of the element was dimming below. The Jews were halting on a platform, and groping about for a keyhole. A rattle of bolts, a creaking of the pivot—Isaiah was withdrawing the huge wooden key and relocking. The three trod the embankment on the eastern side of the river. The moon was creeping up above the tracery of the tower of Bel-Marduk, and spreading her mellow light over the sleeping city. For a moment it seemed still—still as the peace of the Most High. They saw no one, they feared no one; but each fell on his knees, and after his own manner prayed.

Yet they had scarce risen before Isaiah was plucking the Persian's mantle, while Zerubbabel stretched a finger toward the river. Gliding from the royal quay, now hid in shadow, now clear in the glistening moonlight, was something black, crawling,—a huge beetle as it were upon the glancing river—a boat and their pursuers. But Isaiah was calm as the heavens above him.

"Fear nothing. We have by far the start. The gates are open. My friends are ready with the horses. Jehovah, who has saved us out of the clutch of the great Euphrates, shall He not much more save from the feebler wrath of man?"

"I fear nothing," answered Darius; for after that journey what were swords and spears for him to dread?

"Come, then; we go the Gate of Kisch."

The boat had crept out into the current when the three sent a last glance across the river. A red beacon fire was flaming on a tower of the western palace. Soon the guard in the "Old Palace" on the eastern bank would be stirring. But they did not tarry for the alarm. The three followed the length of Nana Street, silent and desolate, and for a time heard only the soughing of the kind night wind from the balmy west. The vision of the tower of Bel faded into the star-mist. They crossed the bridge of the East Canal, where no drowsy watchman challenged them. As they passed the gates of the temple of Beltis, a dozing soldier cried, "Your business!" from his guard-room; but he was too fond of his warm mat to sally into the dark and pursue possible robbers.

The Arachtu Canal was behind them, behind them the shops of the great merchants, the still bazaars. Once two men sprang out of the dark before them,—street thieves, perchance, lurking for the unwary; but one sight in the moonlight of the stalwart shoulders of the three, and the others vanished without a cry. A faint light gleamed from the steps of a low beer-house; they heard brutish laughter and more brutish jesting as they sped onward. The tall houses were beginning to lessen, the moonlit alleys to widen. Another canal and another bridge, and the houses were breaking away into vague masses of shadowy villas and gardens. Still forward; and now behind, and far off, came a roar and a clattering,—the sound of horsemen at their speed,—and the sound lent wings to their going. But Isaiah, who paced even the prince as they ran, cried across his shoulder:—

"No peril! Jehovah is with us! See, the walls!"

And lo! as Darius gazed upward, above him was rising the naked height of Imgur-Bel, the black battlements clearly outlined against the roof of heaven.

Far above their heads, as the voice of a sky-dweller, came once more the call of a sentry, "The morning star rises! Sleep holds the city! Marduk shed favour on Belshazzar the king!"

The loud noise of hoofs behind was ominous, but Isaiah led unfaltering toward the gate. There stood the portal, at either side a soldier in his armour, but here also prone on the ground in sleep; and the great bronze-plated doors were unbarred, and opened wide enough to give passage to a man. They glided through them without a word. Twelve paces more and the drawbridge was cleared. Suddenly forms rose up out of the gloom before them—five horses, and at their heads as many men.

"Who comes?" cried a voice, and Isaiah halted.

"This, my Lord Prince," he announced to Darius, "is that Abiathar in whose behalf I had attacked Igas-Ramman when you saved me. He is not ungrateful." Then to the others: "We are here, Abiathar, though late. You and your friends have not failed us; Jehovah reward you and give His mercy!"

"And my Lord Daniel and Shaphat?" answered the other, grieving to find three, not five.

"In the Lord God's keeping," was the solemn answer; no time for more. "Save yourselves, for all Babylon will ring with this, and rigorous search be made."

"Farewell!" The strange forms vanished in the darkness. A cry was rising from the gate: "Treason! Escaped! The guards are drugged! Pursue!" Darius had leaped, and felt betwixt his knees a blooded Assyrian horse. The Jews had mounted. The three together felt the good steeds spring under them. Down the brick-paved way they flew, whirlwind-swift, the reins lying slack on the manes. The portal of Nimitti-Bel, closed and guarded only in actual siege, stood wide before them. They saw it come and saw it vanish. Shouts behind, and a raging gallop also; but Darius knew a horse by a touch, and he knew the best in Belshazzar's stables might run long before breasting the Assyrian that was speeding beneath him. Before the three spread the Chaldean plain-country, lulled by the moon into that last hush before the bursting dawn. They heard the pursuers follow a little way, then deeper silence. The Babylonians had found their chase was vain. The three rode for a long time without speech. Once Darius glanced across his shoulder—walls, palaces, temple-towers, had sunk to a shapeless haze. He had left "The Lady of Kingdoms," "The Beauty of the Chaldees." Stars and moon above, a soft west wind, and the sleeping country—that was all. But a strange exhilaration possessed the prince. He was saved; he was free; he had still the might of his good right arm, the keenness of his unerring eye.

"Hebrews!" he cried, tossing his head proudly, "behold the man you have plucked back from death unto life. Hereafter you shall learn how the son of Hystaspes can reward his preservers and their people. But now—" he flung his voice to the arching heavens—"to Cyrus! to Cyrus, the avenger of all the wronged! And then war—for the abasing of 'The Lie,' and the love and the joy of Atossa!"

There had come a Tartar cavalryman into Babylon, a small wiry man on a bay horse fleet as Bel's lightning bolt. When he cantered up Ai-Bur-Schabu Street and turned the head of his Scythian toward the king's house, a great crowd had gaped at him. "This," ran the whisper, "was the bearer of the last message from Cyrus before the bursting of war!" He had ridden straight up to the palace gate, and flung his lance against the bronze-faced doors, turned the head of his steed, and galloped headlong from the city, no man molesting. Thrust on the head of the lance was a leaf of papyrus, and they had brought the letter to Belshazzar, after which he and his ministers wagged their heads in long debate.

"Thus says Cyrus, King of Nations, to Belshazzar his perjured and unfaithful slave. Your guile and your plot is known unto me. Would you live and not die? Disband then your armies; throw down your walls; send me your treasure, and your choicest harem women; likewise restore unharmed my daughter and the Prince Darius, my servant. But if you do otherwise, behold! I will make Babylon as Nineveh, a dwelling for starving wolves; and as for you, I will cut off your ears and nose, and chain you forty days at my palace door, that other perjurers may see and tremble, and after that you shall be crucified. Farewell."

When this was read Avil cried out to burn the last bridge and cast Darius's head into the Persian camp. So would Babylon be goaded on to resistance to the end. But the king had shaken his head. "The prince was a hostage,"—he repeated the word often,—"Cyrus would never dare to pass beyond threats." Therefore the ministers departed and Belshazzar sought to drown his fears in wine. He had called for Atossa to come and drink with him. He told her brutally, as if she had not heard it before, how the game stood betwixt him and her father. When the colour mounted her white cheek he brayed with laughter; when it fled he had new jeers. To save the life of Darius, he asked her, would she not write in her own hand to Cyrus, and warn him to postpone the war? But Belshazzar, who had known only the simpering women of his seraglio, was cowed at the burst of womanly passion he had raised. Under his blows the sparks flew from the anvil, and that anvil was Atossa.

"I am Persian, O 'Fiend-lover,'" and Atossa stood before him raised to queenly height; "kings were my ancestors, men beloved and prospered of Ahura. When the Assyrian oppressed my people, he sank back smitten. Where now is Crœsus the Lydian, or Astyages the Mede, who defied Cyrus my father? Sooner let your lions growl above my bones, than a daughter of Cyrus make herself wax to such as you!"

"But you have loved Darius," the king protested, sorely abashed; "I saw you in his arms in the Gardens."

"Yes,"—Atossa's anger was becoming terrible,—"I *have* loved him. But I do not love his poor body more than his Aryan honour. To us death and life may be a very little thing; but outrage, insult, oath-breaking—Ahura may forgive such things, not we!"

"Out of my sight, woman!" thundered Belshazzar; and he had spurned her. The eunuchs took her away. The king drank alone, draining goblet after goblet of the most heady "Elamite"; but though he wished it, he could not grow drunken. His body eunuchs put him to bed. He tossed long on the India-web pillows and the Sidonian purple. They had bathed his feet in perfumed water at last, and very late he fell asleep. The little group of servants had gathered outside the door of the chamber, squatting in silence on the tiles, each inwardly blessing some god that he had been spared the royal wrath that day....

Midnight. The king turned once on his pillows, and the eunuchs' hearts commenced quaking. Anew he slept soundly, and they were again rejoiced.... But what was this hasting of feet on the stairway, this thundering summons to the guard below not to hinder? "The king! The king!" Sirusur the *Tartan* was before the eunuchs, sword drawn, fully armed.

"Rouse his Majesty," commanded the general, halting his run. "Rouse instantly! Darius the Persian is fled!"

A eunuch stood by the bedside, awoke the king, and told him. The fellow had vowed a sheep to Samas, but the god did not favour. The king caught the short sword, ever ready, and smote the messenger of ill tidings to the floor. Then he raged from the chamber, and even Sirusur fell on his knees, cowering, for the king's wrath passed that of bayed lions.

"Not I—O awarder of life! I was not guards-captain; no blame is mine!" The general's teeth chattered as he spoke.

"Who commanded the watch?" came from Belshazzar, in a voice betokening the bolt impending.

"Zikha, 'captain of a thousand.'"

"Go you," Belshazzar addressed Mermaza; "have a stake made ready. Let Zikha be impaled at dawn. And now, Sirusur, where is the fugitive? By Istar, you deserve death likewise! Whither fled? Is pursuit made? Speak, as you love life!"

"He fled by the tunnel, lord. The guards were drugged. Traitors aided. Daniel fled with them also, but he has been retaken."

"Daniel? Namtar, the plague-fiend, destroy him! Is the tunnel flooded?"

"Not so wrathful, lord." Sirusur was still trembling. "Your slaves did all in their power. The old man Daniel remained in the entrance to the tunnel with Shaphat, his one-time accuser; they made desperate resistance."

"Shaphat defend Daniel? You are mad, Sirusur."

"Alas! no. Shaphat slew with his own hand two men, and as Bel reigns his master fought valiantly as Gilgamesh the hero. You will not believe there was such might in so old an arm. We killed Shaphat at last, and disarmed Daniel, after nearly every man in the squad had his wound. Then finally we were able to flood the tunnel, but I fear too late. The Persian had a long start. The exit is poorly guarded. The bridge is raised, so we sent soldiers across the river by boat. Nergal grant they nip Darius ere he pass the city gate!"

"Bring Daniel the Jew before me!" and Belshazzar's teeth shone white, hateful. The men obeyed silently. The king stood in the palace gallery, the light of one red torch touching the blood of the slaughtered eunuch on his sword-blade. The anger on his face was fearful. The old Jew's dress had been torn to shreds, his white hair fouled by blood and mire, his left arm hung limp at his side. Two petty officers upbore him. They thought to hear Belshazzar cry "Slay" at first sight; but the king reined his passion enough to taunt bitterly:—

"Ha! is it custom to quit the king's house with so scant leave-taking?"

The old man shook back his bloody locks and looked straight into Belshazzar's rage-shot eyes. "As you have kept faith to me and mine, so have I to you, O king!"

"Revile me now!" Belshazzar's sword whistled as he brandished. Before a mere reed Daniel might have winced not less.

"I do not revile. True servant have I been to you and your fathers. My reward is this!" He held up his right arm, with the red ring marked by the fetter.

"And this"—Belshazzar swung the sword higher—"one last mercy—death."

But Daniel had shaken off the soldiers. He stood erect. Some power from his eyes stayed that upraised hand as by a spell. "No, lord of the Chaldees! You cannot kill me, nor all your sword-hands, for I am mightier than they."

They heard the king laugh, but—wonder of wonders—the weapon sank at his side.

"Sorcerer! By what magic can you make your old neck proof?"

Belshazzar had moved two steps backward, turning his head to escape the Hebrew's compelling gaze, but could not; and he watched with a fascinated, uneasy smile.

"O king, as in former days the word of Jehovah, One and All-powerful God, spoke through my lips to Nebuchadnezzar the Great, so now again His spirit comes upon me, and puts these words into my mouth. And this is the word,"—Belshazzar was uttering a formula against the evil eye, but he could not look away,—"There shall come a time when I, whom all your wrath cannot destroy, shall stand again before you, shall declare to you the mandate of Jehovah, and when you and with you all the world shall know that whom He wills He saves, whom He wills He lays low, and whoso blasphemes Him He rewards utterly; that all may fear the Lord God of

Israel, before whom Bel-Marduk is less than the small grains of the threshing-floor!"

Then they saw a strange thing. They saw Belshazzar, that man of wrath, shrink back step by step before the blood-grimed, aged Jew, until from a long way off the king laughed again a shrill and direful laugh: "Away with him! Back with him to his dungeon! Keep him fast, till he longs for death, till he knows that his puny god is helpless before Bel-Marduk!"

But all the strength seemed passed out of Daniel. The soldiers caught him as he fell. The king was staring wildly from one servant to another; he was as a man awakened from a frightful dream.

"Wine!" he demanded. "I cannot sleep. Do you, Sirusur, pursue the Persian. Hound him down. But wine, more wine! My head throbs!" His gaze wandered; he in turn was tottering.

"The king is ill," declared Mermaza, just returned; "bear him back to his bed."

"Allat consume you, eunuch!" Belshazzar buffeted him in the face. Then the royal gaze lit again on Daniel.

"Off! Off! What hinders that I kill you? All your babbling is folly. You shall cry to your Jehovah many times, and cry in vain!"

The aged prisoner shook off the soldiers; once more he stood fast. "Remember the prophecy, King of Babylon! Remember! You shall with your own lips summon me; with your own tongue pray to me; with your own hands stretch forth imploring me to speak the mandate of the God you now blaspheme!"

"Silence, dotard!" Belshazzar smote the captive on the mouth. Then again the king reeled, and did not resist when Mermaza caught him. The eunuchs carried him to bed. A frightened page roused the Egyptian court physician. "Raging fever," quoth that wise man gravely, and ordered "poultices of lotus leaves, well soaked in lizards' blood and in the fat of sucking pigs' ears." Before long the king was in violent delirium; his servants had to hold him on his bed, while he made the chamber ring as he cursed them. But one word was uppermost in the royal mind as he raved—"Jehovah, Jehovah!" When he repeated the word he would foam in hate. "Let me master Cyrus; let me conquer in the war, and I swear by every god and every fiend it shall be safer in Babylon to do murder by open day than to whisper the name of that foul spirit before me!"

Avil-Marduk smiled grimly when the next morning they told him of the king's oath, taken in madness.

"Ah, well," declared the pontiff, "happy for pure religion if his Majesty keeps this pious frame of mind when heaven gives back health. Yet he did ill when he spared Daniel. The Jew will be harmless in only one prison—the grave!"

But long since Daniel had been thrust back into a dungeon, scarcely less noisome than that which he had quitted. Ten armed men stood by when they replaced the fetters, all fearful of some withering spell; and the sentries pacing the galleries mumbled incantations to Nineb and to Ilu, shuddering every time they caught a glitter from the terrible Hebrew's eye.

CHAPTER XXII

The Persian army lay in the plain before the captured Kutha. Far as the eye might reach, it touched only avenues of black camel's-hair tents, sprinkled with the gaudier red and blue of the princes' pavilions. The gloaming was at hand, the first stars budding; all around myriad red sparks were twinkling forth—the camp-fires of the host of the Aryans. Over their drink the stout Median footmen and Scythian horse-archers were roaring out pledges—"Confusion to Belshazzar and destruction to his city!" For if there was one thing the hearts of the soldiers lusted after, it was to see the walls of Imgur and Nimitti-Bel. But the army had waited inactive for days, and save for petty skirmishings had scarcely sped an arrow. "Negotiations," grumbled some wiseacres; and others would answer, "The Father (meaning no one less than their august king) will not cast away all hopes of saving Prince Darius." Whereupon comrades would shake their heads gloomily, "We shall see the prince, in this world—never!" Then the banter, even of veterans, would lag, for Darius was the darling of the army.

So throughout the black tents. And in that village of pavilions, of guardsmen and grooms and chamberlains, where the king found lodging, there was no common gloom that night. For Cyrus sat alone in the innermost tent, and refused all drink and food. This was the fortieth night, on which Isaiah had promised to return with Darius, and naught had been seen or heard of the Jew since he had quitted Susa. Atrobanes, "the bearer of the royal handkerchief," and the attendant with whom Cyrus was most familiar, had ventured once to enter the tent, and light the tall silver candelabra. There was the master on the high ivory throne, looking straight before him upon the rugs, combing his flowing beard with his right hand, while his left gripped hard on the jewelled hilt at his side.

"Lord," Atrobanes had ventured, kneeling, "the feast in the banqueting tent is ready. The Princes Harpagus and Gobryas and the other captains have come, for you deigned to command that they should eat meat with you this evening."

No answer. Cyrus was still looking straight before.

"Live forever, O king," began Atrobanes again. An angry exclamation cut him short. For Cyrus to be in wrath was so unwonted that the attendant trembled.

"Live forever? Are you mad? Is life so utterly sweet, that one may never long to lay it down?"

"Mercy, lord of all goodness; mercy!" protested the shivering servant.

"By Mithra, you are frightened." Cyrus laughed softly; it seemed more in melancholy than in mirth. "I meant nothing; I scarce knew that you were here. What is your wish?"

"Will the king condescend to be present at the feast appointed for to-night to the captains of the army?"

A weary sigh, and more silence. Then Cyrus replied, almost bitterly, "Would to Ahura I had not ordered it! How can I sit over wine this night? Yet I must not dishonour the princes. Go to the high steward and say that I can touch no food, though I thank him for his pains. Yet say that when the evening advances, and the wine is brought, I will come and sit with the captains."

"And the king requires nothing for himself?"

"Only this—that you leave me."

Atrobanes kissed the cushioned footstool at his master's feet, and vanished behind the heavy draperies. There was profound stillness, save for the vague hum of the busy camp and the clatter of plate and dishes many hands were bearing to the banqueting tent. The king sat for a long time motionless, the grip on the sword-hilt ever tightening. Then, letting the weapon rest, he fumbled in his bosom, drew forth a locket, and gazed on it as on treasure untold. "The locket of Atossa. It has been close against her own pure breast." He pressed it to his lips, once, twice, thrust it back in his mantle, slipped from the high seat, and began treading to and fro, his feet noiseless on the carpets.

"Live forever, O king, O lord of all goodness! Live forever!" As he repeated the words he was smiling, but not with mirth. "Praised be the All-Merciful, these flatteries are but flatteries, nothing more!"

Voices sounded at the tent door.

"I come to report to the king from Artaphernes, commander of the skirmishers."

"Unless you have definite news, his Majesty is not to be troubled."

"Wait, then; I have only to declare that our scouts bring in nothing."

The pacings of the king grew swift and feverish.

"Nothing, nothing; well, it was to be expected. Are you waxed so old, Cyrus, son of Cambyses, that you will pin your faith on an open face and a ready tongue? The Jew spoke fair, but is like all men of every race saving our own—a liar. If he but come within my power after betraying thus—"

There was a javelin standing against a tent-pole; the king grasped and almost poised it. But the royal mood shifted; Cyrus replaced the weapon, and ran on, communing with himself darkly:—

"I am lord of a million sword-hands; at my word nations sink down in ruin. Men worship me as being a god on earth. Holy Ahura, when Thou madest me king, why did I not cease to be a man; why could I not cease loving, losing, longing? The garment of life is woven of the same stuff, whether for the vilest slave or the lord of the Aryans. I have godlike powers, but I am miserable!"

A noise without—the sentries passing the watchword for the night, as they changed the guard, "Vengeance for Darius!" Again the king touched the javelin.

"Of course the Jew failed, and that without playing falsely. His project was a mad one. Darius has long since died under Belshazzar's torments. Died; ay, and by Mithra the *dæva*-smiter, the watchword shall not prove vain! Men call me merciful; but to the son of Nabonidus and all his perjured brood, Angra-Mainyu, the arch-fiend, and his demons shall seem more compassionate than I. But ah! though I slay all Babylon, I may not breathe life into one form once stilled, nor woo back a loved spirit with all the rubies of Ecbatana!"

Again a voice at the tent door, and Cyrus, recognizing, commanded, "Enter."

Hystaspes passed within. The prince was in his coat of shining scale armour, for years had not made him too feeble to keep the saddle. The short Persian spear was in his hand, the sword dangled at his thigh. The king attempted to brighten before his friend, and threw out boldly:—

"Well, comrade, has not the country been scoured, and all the farms so well sacked, that a man of your hale years need ride with the skirmishers?"

The other laughed, though none too heartily.

"The young hotbloods who lead your Majesty's cavalry troops are all valour and no prudence. An older eye is needed to see that Sirusur with his Babylonish chariots does not dash down on us unawares, and fling us, man and beast, into the Tigris."

"Caution, always caution," answered the king, with an impatient gesture, when the other attempted to salaam. "Come, you have no longing for the feast. Let tables be brought here. I have only promised to appear at the banquet when they serve the wine."

"Your Majesty is thrice kind; a thousand pardons, but for some reason I cannot eat. Perhaps I have ridden too long; as you say, I grow old."

But the king plucked him nigh roughly by the shoulder.

"No, you cannot eat, nor can I. Away with merry lips, when they speak from grieving hearts. Darius, your son, is not here. We were fools to trust the Jew, who has either failed or dealt falsely. Yet we must eat, must eat heartily—you and I—and all."

"Does the king command that I feast against my will?"

"Yes; for if Darius is dead, Belshazzar lives, and all the asps of his guilty kind. And we need all our strength for a vengeance, the fame whereof shall last as long as Mithra's car glows in the heavens."

"Ah! lord, not so bitterly. I am the father, yet I can bow to Ahura's will!"

"But I, the king, who sent Darius forth, and sped him to his death, find like submission hard. For the king shall answer on the Great Day for the blood of all his people!"

"I do not blame your Majesty."

"Nor does any man." Cyrus smote his own breast. "The voice that blames is here."

But as he spoke a strange sound was spreading in the camp, a roaring as of wind, though very far away.

"An alarm!" and Hystaspes started from the tent.

"Alarm? No such outcry; the soldiers are at some sport."

Yet still the sound was rising—was swelling nearer; and now they caught, as it seemed, the clamour of countless voices.

"Alarm surely! I must seek my post!" Again Hystaspes started from the tent; but the king gripped his arm with so tight a clutch that it brought almost pain.

"Hystaspes,"—Cyrus spoke in a hoarse whisper,—"this sound—comes it from men or from angels—is a shout of joy, not of fear!"

"'Here is only the king; within your father waits.'"

Then they stood side by side, those strong men, and listened; for a mighty tumult was swelling through the camp, passing onward, nearer, nearer, rising and falling like the wind-driven billow bounding across the deep. Now the distant encampment of the Tartar Sacæans was thundering, now the Bactrians and the Medes; closer now, it had reached the Persians, the core of the army, and the "Immortals," the royal life-guards, were tossing on the cry. Then through the cheering the two heard something else—riders galloping fiercely; and words came at last, the shout of the captains and lords about the tent of the king.

"The prince! The prince! Glory to Ahura!"

The high chamberlain had entered. When he salaamed he stumbled. His ready tongue spoke thickly.

"Font of all goodness," he began; but Cyrus did not hear. Straight through the door strode the king, and into the throng of officers in the tent without. They parted to either hand at sight of him, like sand before the desert gale. Inside the pavilion itself a score of joyous hands were plucking from his steaming beast a young man, who started, tattered, dust-covered as he was, to kneel before the sovereign. Started: but Cyrus beckoned him on, and spoke before them all:—

"*Here is only the king; within your father waits.*"

So Darius was gone, with no man following him. Then two more newcomers were led forward, and bowed themselves to Cyrus, who saw that they were Isaiah and a stranger, though clearly a Jew also.

"Lord," Isaiah was saying, "behold my pledge fulfilled. This is the fortieth night, and your eyes see Darius."

But Cyrus would hear no more.

"Stand up, son of Shadrach, for the pledge is indeed made good. Look on this man, captains of the Aryans; honour him as you would honour your king, for he has brought joy out of anguish, brought life out of death. Take him away, Hydarnes,"—with a nod to the "master of the royal dresses,"—"clothe him in a robe of state; give him the wine and dainties you would give to me; in the morning put the kingly tiara upon his head, mount him upon my sacred Nisæan charger, and lead him through the host, proclaiming to all men, 'This is the Jew who is honoured by Cyrus!'"

"Hail! all hail, Isaiah, justly honoured of the Great King!"

So thundered an hundred; yet when there was stillness, Isaiah answered humbly, yet boldly, "Lord, I despise not your gifts and your honours; but it was not for even this that Zerubbabel, my comrade, and I plucked the prince out of the dungeon and the clutch of Belshazzar."

Cyrus shook his stately head and smiled.

"Ah! good Jew," spoke he, "do you think the promises of the Persians are pledges graven on water? Fear not that your people will find the king of the Aryans aught but a father and a friend. But enough—you have ridden hard and far; rest for to-night shall be the first reward. Lead them away, Hydarnes, and give this other, Zerubbabel, ten talents also."

But Isaiah did not follow the chamberlain.

"Your Majesty,"—he fell on one knee,—"I bring you not Prince Darius only. I bring you this."

He drew from his girdle and proffered a tiny clay cylinder, scarce the thickness of two fingers. The king grasped it, eagerly as the drowning clutch after the float. They saw him read, and lo, a marvellous thing! the eyes of the master of half the nations were bright with tears. Thus ran the letter:—

"*Atossa in Babylon, to Cyrus, lord of the Aryans:*

"I know that you must be first the king and then the father. Yet when you sent me from Susa, did you send me to this—to loathsome bondage, to be queen in name only, to be the toy of a man of wrath and guile, and the pledge of a peace sworn only to be broken? Come to me, my father, for I am of your own proud blood. Let other kings' daughters learn a master's yoke; a child of yours must be the mistress, or must die. Heaven favouring, the noble Isaiah will save Darius, whom I love; but I, who cannot fly, can only pray for the hour when the swords of my people shall flash within this accursed city. Yet save speedily; for the time grows near when I shall be Belshazzar's bride in very deed. Farewell."

"Did you penetrate the harem of Belshazzar?" asked Cyrus, his voice unsteady.

"Yes, your Majesty; I have seen the most gracious princess. Belshazzar triumphs in holding the child of his arch-enemy captive. To force her to his bridal will be his joy. And in three months he will celebrate another feast—the wedding one year from the betrothal."

"Then in three months Babylon is to be taken?"

"The king has said. Belshazzar will risk little in the field. He boasts his walls will mock your armies seven years, and yet be strong."

"And you say that he boasts well?" urged Cyrus, shrewdly.

"Lord, I only know that speaking from human wisdom, there may be doors to Babylon Belshazzar little dreams of; and speaking from the voice within"—Isaiah's own voice rose, and he swept his hand proudly—"the promise of Jehovah is yet strong,—'I, who have prospered so far, and saved from so many perils, will still favour even to the end.'"

"And favour He will!" cried the king, as in a great gladness; "three months for the might of the Aryans to master the 'fiend-servers' and their mute brick and stone! Let Ahura lay on us a harder task!"

Then the chamberlains took the Jews away, and forth from the inner tent returned Darius, who knelt now at Cyrus's feet.

"Rise up," the king commanded; "you also need food and sleep. And in the morning—"

"What in the morning, lord?" cried the prince, now standing.

"In the morning you shall ride at the head of the van. But you have won the right to crave a boon—and ask it, whatsoever you will."

"My king,"—Darius's voice was trembling,—"you well know what I would ask."

Whereupon Cyrus only smiled once more, and lifted his hand as in an oath.

"By the light of Ahura I swear it, that when we have conquered Babylon and plucked Atossa from the *dæva's* clutch, you shall ask for her in marriage, and I will not say you nay."

Three nights later the burghers of Babylon, when they mounted their house roofs, as was their wont in the cool of the evening, saw a light that stilled the bravest boasters. East, west, and north the horizon glowed with a redness which shone ever brighter, ever nearer, till it climbed the heavens. Rising smoke was blotting out the stars. Men spoke together in whispers, as they stared and shuddered at the brightness: "The host of Cyrus. All the country villages are burning. Marduk be praised, the walls are yet strong!"

At next morn the city folk saw a sight yet more terrible. The plains were covered with innumerable black tents and pavilions, and horsemen more than the sands of the sea. The king of the Aryans was at hand, and with him all the might of the far East. Imgur-Bel and Nimitti-Bel were put to proof at last.

CHAPTER XXIII

Three months nearly had the host of the Persians lain under the walls of the capital. They had ravaged far and wide, had driven the country folk by thousands inside the defences; the thriving villages were become one blackened waste. But still the great Euphrates brawled through the massy water gates; still the battlements loomed unapproachable above the besiegers' heads! What had Belshazzar and his city to fear? The battering ram? Let Cyrus first bridge the network of protecting canals, drain the moats, drive the archers from the walls, and establish his enginery, and then he might beat for months on those mountains of brick and accomplish nothing. Did he trust to starvation? There was corn enough, yes, and daintier fare, to let Babylon hold off famine three long years; and besides, the gardens and orchards within the long circuit of the walls could in themselves supply a multitude. After the first fright was passed the Babylonians had ceased to tremble and gibber, when they thought of the foe without the gates. Trade was resumed in the bazaars; the scholars returned to their schools; the rope-walks, the carpet factories, and the brass foundries were again busy. Merchants counted impatiently the days when the interrupted caravan trade with Egypt and Syria might recommence. Plentiful stories were afloat that Cyrus was having vast difficulty in feeding the myriad mouths in his army; that the Persian generals were at strife amongst themselves; that revolt in Media and Carmania might send the invader home discomfited at any moment. Therefore the worthy city folk had advised one another "patience"; and behold, to-day, their waiting was rewarded! A royal crier was parading the length of Nana Street, and his proclamation was heard even above the plaudits of the crowds:—

"Rejoice! Rejoice, men of Babylon, city favoured by Marduk! Last night the noble Sirusur, 'Master of the host,' made a sortie from the Gate of Borsippa, and smote the Persian barbarians utterly, slaying hundreds, and taking many of their great princes captive. This morning Cyrus, the impious blasphemer of our gods, being utterly discomfited by the valour of his Majesty's army,—his generals deserting him, and his kingdoms of Media and Bactria having rebelled against his tyranny,—is raising the siege in all haste. His power is destroyed forever. Glory, glory to Bel-Marduk, to Istar, to Samas, whose favour is over Babylon! Rejoice! Rejoice!"

"Glory to Marduk! Glory to Belshazzar, favoured son of the almighty god!"

So the thousands had hailed the glad tidings, and rushed with one accord to the walls, to make sure of the news. Even so; the black tents of the besiegers were disappearing. Already the pavilion of Cyrus had vanished behind the plains; the retreat bore almost evidence of a rout.

"Follow after! Destroy them utterly!" advised the younger and bolder captains about the exultant king, while he surveyed the welcome scene from the Gate of the Chaldees. But Sirusur, the victor of the sortie, who next to Belshazzar's self had won most glory in the defence, only observed, with the prudent wisdom of the all-knowing Ea:—

"Leave them alone, your Majesty; the barbarians are at strife among themselves: they will soon turn their swords on one another, and so fight for us. Our army is weary with the siege, grant it some reward before we take the field to conquer Cyrus's provinces. Proclaim a great feast of thanksgiving throughout Babylon."

"And is it not one year to-morrow night," demanded the king, nothing loath, "since I betrothed Atossa, the daughter of Cyrus?"

"Even so, your Majesty," quoth Bilsandan the vizier, at the other elbow.

Belshazzar clapped his hands in right kingly glee.

"Praised be every god! Do you proclaim a feast over the city for to-morrow and to-morrow night. Let Babylon be one house of mirth, for it shall be her king's triumph and wedding-night together. Prepare the palace for a banquet such as no king before—no, not Nebuchadnezzar the Great—set for his lords and captains; there I will drink wine before all Babylon, and show forth the daughter of Cyrus, whom I take to wife."

Therefore for a second time the crier had fared through the streets, and all Babylon gave itself over to merriment.

None did so with a gladder heart than Itti-Marduk the great banker. That evening, when he sat with Neriglissor on his house roof, the excellent man was in a state of enviable content. Two days before he had sold out a huge granary of corn at half a shekel on the homer[11] above the price it would now fetch, the siege being over; and when Neriglissor had examined the entrails of three white geese, to see if his friend ought to risk a very profitable loan, the omens had been most happy—the livers so white, the hearts so very large, that some great advantage was foretokened, unless all faith in augury was bootless. Therefore from business they had passed to small talk.

"Happy evening for Babylon," Neriglissor was saying; "I did not think Cyrus would give us the back so readily."

"Or that Sirusur the general would prove so valiant, if the flying rumours had been true."

"Rumours?" demanded the old priest; "in Bel's name, what rumours?"

"Are you so ignorant at the temple, as not to know the talk of the city?"

"Will you slaughter me, by not telling?"

The banker grew confidential.

"My dearest Neriglissor, surely you know that there have been many tales afoot lately that, since the day of the great riot, and that scene in his Majesty's council where Sirusur the general and your own lord, Avil-Marduk, passed such bitter words, the two have been as cold friends as a lamb and a desert hyena. I have heard no less than two tales, one of which is proved false,—the gods know concerning the other, not I."

"Well, tell them: I am tortured by curiosity."

"The first is that Sirusur the *Tartan* and Bilsandan the vizier fear the hostility of Avil and his influence over Belshazzar so much, that, rather than see him wax in power, they prefer to open the gates to Cyrus."

"A lie! Sirusur's valour in the sortie proved it so."

Itti let his head come yet closer to the priest's as they sat together; his gaze was shrewd and penetrating.

"And is this a lie also?—that Avil-Marduk, the worshipful priest of Bel, would not be greatly displeased if some hap of fate were to set him on the throne of Nebuchadnezzar? By Samas, you are startled!"

Neriglissor was smiling uneasily. "Have you the eyes of Nergal, dear Itti? Well, you are a good friend, and know the meaning of that hard word 'silence.' His Majesty is childless, thus far; he is the last of his line; if by some dispensation of heaven,—which Ramman forefend,—if Avil-Marduk were to be summoned to the throne—"

The banker broke the other short with a dry chuckle. "Ah! then I did not hear old-wives tales merely. Sirusur and Bilsandan would have good cause for quaking with Avil wearing the purple cap. But the king weds the Persian,—there may be an heir."

Neriglissor rolled one eye in his head. "Many things can befall before an heir is born to his Majesty."

"Ha!" laughed the other, "so be it, if trade is not disturbed, and Avil-Marduk remembers that he yet owes me twelve talents, be he king or priest."

So the gossip ran in the town, and in the palace there was one continuous carnival. Belshazzar sat on his throne in the great audience hall; two tame lions crouched at right and left, but he, in his kingly majesty looked the noblest lion of them all. Before him had come the captains of thousands and of hundreds, to pay obeisance and listen to the royal words of praise, or even receive some crowning mark of good will—a chain of gold hung round their necks by the monarch's own hand.

Then, next to Belshazzar, all paid court to Avil-Marduk, who stood more modestly in a corner of the great hall, while the noblest of the princes salaamed to him, and wished him "a thousand sons and a thousand daughters;" for it was hardly more an hour of triumph for the king than for Avil. His policy of mingled caution and boldness had been completely vindicated. His influence in the royal council would be supreme. Never had Babylon stood so clearly in the zenith of glory. And now that the power of Cyrus seemed broken, to what bounds might not the dominions of the Chaldee reach? And Avil-Marduk was saying within his crafty heart, "The city may ascribe the triumph to Belshazzar if they will, the wise will confess it won by me." Only one thing marred the high priest's bliss. Sirusur the *Tartan* and Bilsandan the vizier gave no compliments, only dark frowns, when they passed him; and Avil spoke again within himself of a certain ambition that boded little good for general or minister, or even king.

But the hopes and fears of his underlings had little place in the heart of Belshazzar that day, when he dismissed the levee, and his parasol and fan bearers followed him into the harem of the palace. Hardly had Igas-Ramman the guards-captain departed after reporting that the last of the Persian host had vanished in such haste as to leave much valuable armour and camp furniture, when Mermaza came before the king with a tale that made his smooth face beam with complacent mirth.

"Let the king's heart be enlarged, his liver exalted. Know, my lord, Marduk sends no fair thing singly. May your slave speak?"

"Say on." The king was smiling, too, for he saw Mermaza had some wondrous good fortune to relate.

"Lord," quoth Mermaza, smirking, "have you forgotten the daughter of Daniel?"

"Forgotten? By Istar, am I like to forget those stars, her eyes? or how her accursed father has hidden her, despite all search?"

"Wrong, my king." Mermaza brushed his stiffly pomatumed curls on the leopard's skin at Belshazzar's feet. "I and my eunuchs have discovered. A shy partridge, but she is snared."

"Nabu prosper you, fellow! How did you secure her? When? Where?"

Mermaza's smile grew yet more honeyed. "Lord, your slave can tell the story quickly. Daniel hid the maid with his friend Imbi-Ilu at Borsippa; but when that traitor fled to Cyrus, he gave the maid into the keeping of one Dagan-Milki, a schoolmaster who owed Daniel some debt of gratitude. To-day in the rejoicings one of the older scholars, well laden with palm-beer, chattered somewhat in the ears of Ili-Kamma, the slyest rat amongst all my eunuchs. Said the lad, 'Our master has a strange maid in his family, and her manner is thus and thus.' Ili comes to me; together we go to the school and house of Dagan-Milki. And behold! Dagan lies in the inner prison, and Ruth, the daughter of Daniel, waits now the good pleasure of Belshazzar, the ever victorious king!"

Belshazzar gave a laugh that almost set Mermaza to trembling; for it was safer sometimes to hear the roar of uncaged lions, than such burst of royal mirth. But the eunuch had naught to fear.

"I thank you, rascal; by every god I thank you! Truly, Marduk sends all things good at once; let him keep back some now, that his later store may not be exhausted. Where is the maid?"

"Already here in the harem. I have commanded that she be dressed in a manner pleasing to your Majesty."

"And she has lost none of her beauty—she is fair as on that day when Darius (curses light on the Persian!) beguiled me into letting her slip through my grasp?"

"She has lost nothing; nay, rather, in one year her bud has blown to full blossom; she is doubly fair."

"Again I give you thanks. Lead me to her." But the king paused an instant: "One thing also,—command that Atossa be brought to me, when I am with the Jewess in the harem."

Atossa had been on the palace roof that afternoon, where she had spent many a long hour during the siege,—gazing toward the lowering walls, and praying for the moment so long delayed, when Aryan steel should be flashing on the summits of those ramparts. And now Mermaza had come to her, declaring: "Rejoice, my lady! for all Babylon rejoices. Cyrus raises his siege; his host melts away like snow in the springtime!"

Then Atossa had stared hard at the eunuch, wasting no tears on such as him. "Another lie, serpent! Earth will turn to fire ere the host of the Aryans turn the back from a war once begun."

"Nevertheless," answered Mermaza, with an unusually lowly salaam, "you will find your slave's words do not err."

Full soon the shouts of gladness and the tidings that the under servants brought into the palace told the Persian that Mermaza had indeed spoken well; and right on the heels of this great bitterness trod a summons from Belshazzar to appear before him without delay. A fearful outburst rewarded the eunuch who brought it.

"Get you gone! Tell Belshazzar that Atossa will love to see your Chaldean 'Maskim' more gladly than him."

"Lord," explained the myrmidon, who knew how to soften tart messages to the king, "the Lady Atossa is much indisposed; she prays to see you later."

"Much indisposed!" roared Belshazzar, clapping his thigh. "Yes, by Nergal, she and all her race need more than an Egyptian doctor's physic for their ills! Bring her hither, by force if needs be!"

No disobeying this; Atossa was brought to the king. She found Belshazzar in one of the cool, softly lighted, high-vaulted chambers of the harem; he was lolling on the crimson cushions of his couch, in one hand his constant companion of late—a wine-cup. But what Atossa was swiftest to see was a young girl seated on a footstool at his right elbow,—a slender, graceful thing, but shivering, and glancing furtively this way and that like some trapped creature watching for escape. Only the flutter of the fans of the inevitable corps of attendants broke the silence, when Atossa was led before the king. She made no motion or sound; only looked straight before her, with stern, glassy eyes, as if seeing all, yet seeing nothing.

Belshazzar raised himself and tilted the goblet to his lips.

"Your health, my queen; may it be happier than that of your valorous father."

The hot colour in Atossa's cheeks was the king's sole answer; he drained, and thrust back the cup into the ever watchful cup-bearer's hands.

"Lady," began he again, a trifle more soberly, "you have fought against the bridle, but the Chaldee's curb is too strong. To-morrow you become indeed my wife. One year in Babylon is time enough to forget Susa. You are of us now."

"I Babylonish?" demanded Atossa, and in the last word there was a whole weight of scorn. But Belshazzar only let his eyes half close in easy good humour.

"You are a comely maid, even though Cyrus be your father. I do not repent his sending you to Babylon; for Istar's self might stand beside you, and flush with shame. Be you who you may, you shall become my 'first queen'; and if you are but reasonable, you will find your least wish a law to the Chaldees, no sorry thing even to a princess of the Aryans. Not so?"

"So I am to be first queen?" spoke Atossa, pointing with a finger; "but this woman—who is she?"

Belshazzar pinched the smooth arm of the maid at his side.

"Look up, my queen! The lady does not remember the day when her marvellous archer friend Darius saved you from the lion. Never since then have my soul's eyes lost sight of you, my flower, though your father hid so carefully; and I have plucked you at last! The Persian is the lily, and you shall be the rose in my sweet nosegay!"

Atossa caught the girl roughly under the chin, and looked into her face. "Excellent taste, my king," she taunted; "so this is the maid who is to divide honours with me. Is her father the Pharaoh, or Nadab the boatman?"

The girl shuddered out of Atossa's grasp.

"You forget," quoth Belshazzar, ogling from one woman to the other; "her father is no boatman, by Nergal! though, like your own, scarce now on good terms with the god of good fortune. He is Daniel, the one time civil-minister."

All the anger vanished from Atossa's face instantly.

"Were you not Ruth, who was betrothed to Isaiah the Jew?" asked she of the girl, who only nodded dumbly, for fear had stolen her power of speech.

"And what does the king require of her?" spoke the Persian, almost haughtily; "possessing me, does he not possess enough?"

"Fie!" answered he; "because I keep the swiftest Elamite bay in my stables, must I own no other charger? You need not fear her as a rival in power. You shall be queen, and she?—" he lifted the dark curls on the

Jewess's soft neck, "we shall find her place when some lucky god gives back to her her tongue."

Ruth cringed and shivered under the touch; more than ever she seemed the dumb, netted creature. But Atossa took her by the hand.

"Your Majesty," said she, more mildly than before, but losing none of her lofty tone of command, "surely you have made merry enough with your two slaves for to-day. Let me take the daughter of Daniel with me, to my chambers."

"Let the king so favour his handmaiden." It was the first word Ruth had spoken. And Belshazzar declared, with another great laugh:—

"So be it. Go your ways. Teach this wench speech, Atossa, and I thank you. But one last command,—let the Jewess be present at the feast of triumph; for if you are to shine as Istar, the other great goddess, Beltis, must not fail."

Once in the private chambers of Atossa, Ruth cast herself on the tiles at the princess's feet and burst into a flood of tears.

"O lady! if you have any power indeed, give one favour, a speedy death, and end my pain! Better black Sheol than to hear again the voice of Belshazzar!"

But the Persian, stronger and maturer, raised her up, and held her head against her own breast.

"Peace, peace. Lamentation binds up no broken hearts, else would mine have ceased its grieving long ago."

"Ah! merciful mistress," cried the Jewess, falling again on her knees, "forgive your slave; what freedom is this that I have shown before your face? Forgive—"

"I forgive nothing; there is naught to be forgiven," answered Atossa, with a wan smile. "We are equals in the wretchedness of our lot. Whether your plight or mine is worse, Ahura knows, not we."

"Ah! God is weak," groaned the Jewess, "else why has Belshazzar thus been suffered to blaspheme Him and to prosper? The king has hounded my lover from the city, has flung my father into a dungeon, and soon will take his life. Just before you came to us, Belshazzar said unto me, 'Forget your Jewish god, my pretty, for I will teach the nations how helpless is the demon the Hebrews and Persians serve.' Once I was strong, once I bade Isaiah risk all for our God, and count nothing for Him too dear. But now,—I am not of kingly blood, as you, O lady,—I can only know that to all seeming Marduk has conquered Jehovah."

Atossa pointed from the window, beyond the green foliage of the "paradise" about the palace, beyond the *ziggurats* and the towering walls.

"How can these things be? I do not know. Ahura-Mazda is all-wise and all-good. That should suffice, were we but perfect as His 'Ameshaspentas.' But this I know: beyond those walls are Cyrus and Darius and Isaiah; and while those three live, let these Babylonish swine grunt their boastings, I know that hope is not ended."

"But Cyrus departs. His princes disobey him, and turn against him."

Atossa pointed again toward the window. "Cyrus departs? Little you know my father, or the princes of the Persians, and our Aryan fealty. Other kings have cried 'victory' when they warred with Cyrus—but those kings, where are they?"

"Then you still hope?" almost implored the Jewess.

"Yes, because Ahura still sends Mithra the 'fiend-smiter,' into the heavens, pledge of His favour; and because Cyrus, lord of the Aryans, is Cyrus still; and Darius, son of Hystaspes, is Darius still."

"Yes, lady," cried Ruth, still quivering, "hope is sweet; but I have long hoped, and hoped in vain; and it grows hard. To-morrow is the feast, and after the feast Belshazzar will possess us utterly."

"The time truly is short"—Atossa's eyes, for the first time that day shone with tears; "yet if Ahura willeth, one last moment shall yet bring low this Babylon and its most evil king."

"But we?"

Atossa shook her head impatiently.

"We are only women, made to trust and bear. We can only wait his will."

CHAPTER XXIV

Nightfall again; and again a feast at the same hour when one year earlier Belshazzar had given a banquet to the daughter of Cyrus and proclaimed her his prospective bride. At early dawn all Babylonians had awakened to eat, drink, and make merry. Every beer-house had reëchoed with drunken revel. No business in the bazaars, no priests chanting their litanies on the temple-towers. The great merchants had thrown open their doors to the most distant friends, who were welcome to enter and quaff a deep-bellied flagon. By noon half Babylon was in drink: drunken sailors roaring along the quays, drunken priestesses at their orgies with tipsy youths in the groves of Istar, drunken soldiers splashing their liquor as they stood guard on walls and gates. Cyrus was gone. The siege was at an end. What need of watch and ward? One would have thought the city had forgotten Marduk and Samas, to adore the one god, Wine!

As the first twilight spread, the multitudes commenced to surge through the open gates of the palace. Long before the proper feast was prepared the royal stewards had brought skins of the rarest vintage from the palace cellars, and emptied them into the great silver mixing-bowls which stood in every corner of the vast courts, with a busy eunuch by each, handing forth goblets to great and small—for all Babylon could call itself Belshazzar's guest that night. The walls of the courts had been hung with gay stuffs curiously embroidered; over each of the courts rippled a vast awning of Sidonian purple, hung by a clever system of pulleys, making the huge space one banqueting chamber. And under this canopy, as everywhere else in the king's house,—save the inner harem,—jostled the shouting, rioting multitude, maddened with drink: ass-drivers, gardeners, artisans, women, children even, pressing around the eunuchs and stretching forth eager hands for the goblets, with only a single cry: "Wine! Wine! More! More!"

In and out through this human whirlpool ploughed Khatin the giant headsman; other pates might whirl with the cheer, not his, though none had seen the bottom of more cups that night than he.

"One year to-night," the executioner was braying, "since the betrothal feast; you recall your dear friend Khanni was with us then. Pity his Majesty bade me end his services four months since!"

"Peace; speak not of it!" groaned the eunuch Nabua, who dragged, very tipsy, on Khatin's arm.

"Silence, then, if you wish. Well, to-morrow I trust to say farewell to those Persian noblemen taken in the sally—stout lads, all of them!"

"But Darius has slid through your clutch," hiccoughed Nabua, snatching a honey-cake from a table, grasping and swallowing almost as one act.

"Darius? Yes, all the gods have won a grudge from me by that. But I shall be repaid. Avil-Marduk will have a free course against the Jews now. I doubt not to chaffer with that surly oaf, old Daniel, before another Sabbath."

"Sure of this?"

"So Mermaza whispered in my ear to-day. Imbi-Ilu is no longer in the city, to raise riots in the Jew's behalf. Avil has sworn Daniel's death. Not even his Majesty could save him, if he wished."

"The procession! The king! Way! Way!" bawled many. "To the great court!" Hardly did Khatin with all his might win an entrance to this huge enclosure, so vast was the crowd. Where save in Babylon was a like banqueting space! One hundred and fifty cubits long, one hundred broad; walls to the height of five men; the pictured walls of enamelled brick, the castellated and gilded parapet above; the great purple awning on high; the giant winged bulls at the many entrances,—this was the scene that glowed under the light of six score silver lamps hung from the awning, and as many resinous, red torches flaring in the sockets on the wall.

Straight across the lower half of the court stretched a rope barrier, cutting off the vulgar herd. Above, a bevy of eunuchs were making the last arrangements for the feast, setting innumerable chairs and stools beside the low tables, or hanging a great bower of dark cypress above the high couch on the dais at the end, where Belshazzar would take his wine, viewing and viewed by all.

Suddenly the brawl even of drunken voices was hushed.

"Hark! The king and all his captains!"

Nearer and nearer was approaching the clangour of cymbals and of kettle-drums; then out of the din burst the wailing of flutes and the blare of the war-horns. A louder crash,—fifty harps and zithers were joining. Into the court came filing two long lines of spearmen in silvered armour, who swept the multitude to right and left, then halted, leaving a long lane for the royal procession. After the soldiers marched the musicians, handsome men, each wearing the tall, peaked mitre of his guild: and after these a company at sight whereof every onlooker craned his neck, and a loud "ah!" arose.

"The Persian prisoners," grunted Khatin in Nabua's ear; "to-night they shall see his Majesty's triumph. To-morrow they shall die. Hah! They strut haughtily enough!" Then he howled aloud as the captives came nearer,

"Fine plunder, my merry sirs, are you finding in Babylon; sad your dear lord Cyrus is not near you now!"

But the pinioned Persians were led straight forward. Cords had been fastened to rings in their lips, by which their guards could drag them. Around the necks of many dangled unsightly objects—the heads of comrades whose bodies had fallen into the Chaldees' hands. A thousand jeers flew around them; but no Persian repaid with so much as a shake of the head or a curse. Even the most drunken of all that throng felt a small mite of respect, if not of pity, for these men, who showed their foes that where an Aryan could not conquer, he at least knew how to die. Silently they were arrayed inside the barriers, to await the royal pleasure. And now all forgot them, as, with more musicians accompanying into the court, marched the priests of Bel-Marduk, bearing glaring flambeaux. The ruddy light flickered on the white dresses and sleek goatskins of the priests, and their mitres set with bullocks' horns. The company ranged itself before the soldiers, that the king might pass up a lighted way. Loudly now rose their triumph song—for was this not the night of Bel-Marduk's own victory?

"O Ruler Eternal! O Lord of all being!

Smiter of the foes of Belshazzar thy servant:

Who stillest the ragings of Cyrus the Persian:

Hast broken his spear, hast shattered his quiver:

Confounding his god and the vile Jewish demon:

We praise thee, and with us all Babylon worships!"

The chant ended with a terrific clap of cymbals and thunder of drums. Then the wonted cry was spreading: "The knee! the knee! Hail! Hail! Belshazzar!" Soldiers again: the chosen sword-hands of the guard, the golden scales of the armour flashing: scarlet pennons trailing from every spear-head. Behind them on a lofty litter rode Belshazzar the king,—never more kingly than now, never arrayed before in costlier robes and tiara. And at sight of him a great shout rose spontaneously from the multitude.

"A god and not a man! Marduk appears on earth! Happy Babylon—your king was begotten in heaven!"

Belshazzar looked neither to one side nor the other, the faces of the stone bulls more mobile than his. "The king was indeed half god—what part had the son of Marduk with the life of vulgar men!" so his thought ran.

Under the firm steps of twelve great noblemen moved the litter. Right behind was a second, not so high, yet lofty also, and she that rode therein exposed to common sight. And now there was a titter here, a taunt there, and yonder silence.

"The daughter of Cyrus!" "Joyful day for her!" "Away with the chalk-white Persian!"

White indeed was Atossa, but Belshazzar gave the multitude no less heed than she. Where better to show her Aryan pride and courage, than before these *dæva*-worshippers!

"Fie, Persian wench!" hissed the tipsy Nabua, "your eyes turn green as a cat's with rage!" But a great hand clapped ungently upon his mouth.

"Peace, fool," Khatin whispered hoarsely. "Persian or Chaldee, I know a true man or a true maid. Where is the Babylonish hussy who could bear herself in Susa thus?"

Three more litters, bearing Tavat-Hasina, the stately queen-mother, Avil-Marduk, and the Jewess Ruth. Both women, like Atossa, shone with jewels that twinkled under every torch; but Avil was clad in perfectly plain robes and fillet,—strange contrast to the gay-robed company about. He met the gaze of the multitude with his wonted stare and smile, arrogant almost as his royal betters. But the Jewess was quaking like aspen behind her purple and crimson. She said nothing; but her great eyes were wandering all about, well telling the terror that had sunk too deep for tear or cry.

Then behind the litters came the lords and captains of the Chaldees, two by two, and more gilded armour, gem-crusted helmets, brilliant mantles and surcoats; stately men all, who had anew given their Babylon the proud title of "Lady of Kingdoms," for they were the first warriors before whom Cyrus, the terrible Aryan, had turned away in defeat.

Belshazzar had stretched himself on the high couch, the ladies and pontiff took the chairs set at his side, the captains were seating themselves below at the many small tables. Yet the king's eyes wandered about, inquiringly. "Where is Sirusur the general?"

Whereupon Bilsandan the vizier approached with a profound salaam.

"River of Omnipotence! the *Tartan* asks me to beseech that he be pardoned. He lies unwell in his own house; much service and the reopening of an old wound drive him to his bed."

"Lord," quoth Avil, *sotto voce*, to his master, "Sirusur was anything but ill this noon. To my mind—"

But Bilsandan interrupted nigh testily: "Priest, you sniff for treason as a hound for a hare! Is it conspiracy for the king's generals to be stricken with the sickness-demon?"

"Nevertheless," objected the priest, "let a messenger be sent to Sirusur's palace—"

But the vizier sneered boldly: "My dear pontiff, not one 'double-hour' since I saw him on his bed, with five wizards from your own temple preparing incantations over him. Shall we not rather vow three steers that he come from their clutches safely?"

"Samas protect Sirusur from the 'five fiends,'" laughed the king. "I mourn his absence, but he is forgiven. Enough delay! Let the feast begin."

Instantly, as by magic, the tapestries upon the walls were brushed aside, revealing doorways, whence a long procession of eunuchs filed into the hall, each bearing a silver dish or basket; and soon fish and flesh of every manner were piled upon the dishes of the king's guests. Nor were the throngs below the rope barriers forgotten; here, too, food was served until man and child could take no more.

The music rose and fell in swaying rhythm and cadence; and now and again the choir of Bel would burst into their song of praise to god and king, raising their pæan louder, louder, until the canopies quivered:—

"Bel-Marduk, sovereign of archers,

Bel-Marduk, spoiler of cities,

Bel-Marduk, lord of all gods,

Bel-Marduk, who rulest forever;

Thee, thee we praise!"

After the carp and pigeons had vanished, lo! amid shout and creaking, four flower-wreathed cars were wheeled into the court, each groaning with the weight of a roasted ox. Then the company—as if they had starved before—fell to feasting with true glutton's zest. From time to time Belshazzar would deign to command Mermaza to bear to this or that captain a morsel of meat carved from the king's own plate,—a rare mark of favour to the happy soldier thus commended.

So at first the feasters devoured in silence; then when even the hunger of the mighty men of the Chaldees began abating, the talk ran swiftly. Vainly Belshazzar strove to force the Jewess into speech. The Persian answered the king only curtly. Then at last he stretched forth his mighty hands, plucked Ruth by the arm, and drew her close to his couch.

"Hail, daughter of Cyrus! do you not hate your rival?" cried he.

But Atossa only answered, though the flush on her cheek grew crimson:—

"I pity the lord of the Chaldees."

"Pity?" Belshazzar stared at the Persian.

"Yes, verily! What save pity for a king who uses his power more to torture helpless women than to perform right kingly deeds?"

Belshazzar thrust the Jewess away with a curse. "Allat possess you, girl! Why is your touch so icy cold?" Then fiercely to Atossa, "Speak out, Persian; what mean you?"

"Mean?" Atossa leaned forward from her own seat, and met his angry glare unflinchingly; she spoke in a whisper, yet a whisper that could be heard for far around: "I say that if it were Cyrus who had won the victory you boast, he would not be lolling over a stalled ox and wine, but in the field, grinding to dust his fleeing enemies. But I speak as a Persian barbarian—the Chaldees are wiser. Their watchmen drink and sleep snug to-night, knowing that the Aryan's power is broken utterly."

Belshazzar gave a laugh so loud that every feaster kept silence before the king. "Bravely sped are your arrows, lady! I praise you! Were your race as valiant with the sword as you with your tongue, scarce would we be feasting here. Yet look on those captives yonder, choicest princes of Cyrus's host. Where is his power if he suffer *such* to be taken?"

"Beware to boast; the Persian memories are long. They will not forget revenge in a year or a generation."

"Long truly if they would wait the crumbling of Imgur-Bel and Nimitti-Bel!" But here the king halted, for Bilsandan approached his couch once more.

"May the king's liver increase, his heart find rest!" saluted the vizier. "I crave his compassion. A messenger from my palace: my youngest daughter lies grievously ill—a sudden torment sent by the 'Maskim.' Be gracious, and suffer me to quit the feast."

Belshazzar frowned. "You and Sirusur both away? I like it little. Yet go; I can refuse no boon to-night."

But the vizier had another request. "Lord, these Persian captives are a doleful sight at so gay a feast. Command that they be taken away."

The king nodded carelessly. Bilsandan whispered to the prisoners' guards and was gone; a moment later the captives were removed also, followed by the hoots of many. Mermaza, who was serving the royal party, laid his head beside Avil's for an instant.

"First the general and then the vizier. Strange! I would stake five wine-skins these excuses are lies!"

"I believe you," was the guarded answer; "but what mischief can hatch to-night? Yet I mourn that the king dismissed Bilsandan so readily."

"Ha!" interrupted Belshazzar; "enough of fowl and oxen; bring on the wine. Wine, the true gift of the gods, is the crowning of the feast!"

The music crashed again. The nimble eunuchs cleared away the viands in a trice, and as quickly brought in the great mixing-bowls of chased gold and silver. One huge tankard of perfumed Damascus they set beside the king; and Avil, taking a jewelled cup, stood pouring libation and praying loudly: "Grant, O Istar, O Nabu, O Bel, mighty deities whose power is over Babylon, that Belshazzar your servant may reign ten thousand years. Let his foes stumble, their weapons break, their bodies grow fruit for his sword. And so will we offer you sacrifice forever!"

Then on one knee Mermaza passed to Belshazzar another cup; and the monarch raised it with the cry: "Away with the 'care-demon' and his kind this night. This is the time appointed by Nabu for glee. When has Babylon shaken off a foe like Cyrus the Persian? Drink, men of Babylon, drink to the present glory and the coming triumphs of your king!"

"Wine! Wine!" from every captain and sword-hand; and the goblets went back to the waiting eunuchs in a twinkling.

Atossa had never seen Belshazzar so riotous before. He seemed to have let the mad spirit of the hour gain utter possession of him.

"Drink!" he shouted again, "drink! He is traitor who does not measure seven goblets." Then, turning to Atossa, he thrust his own cup into her hand. "I have been cruel, lady,"—his voice sank into hoarse soothing,—"cruel, because hitherto you have been Persian. But to-night you are become Babylonish by becoming my wife. We strike hands in a truce. Peace is better than war. Bel-Marduk is your god now, not Ahura the helpless. Are you not 'Queen of Sumer and Akkad'? Ask whatever you will, if in reason, and I will not refuse. But drink you with the rest,—drink to the triumphs yet to be won by Belshazzar your husband, whose glories are all yours."

Mechanically Atossa tasted; put the goblet away. But Belshazzar still in his mood ran on: "Yes, you are a great king's daughter, and worthy to be my wife, though Persian born. As for this Jewess here," with a leer at Ruth, "she shall learn to love me, when her father and his cursed god are all forgot. The fiends blast me; why can I not drive the thought of that drivelling Hebrew from my mind? To-morrow Khatin ends him, or I am no king."

But to the threat and curse neither Ruth nor Atossa answered, for the iron had long since entered deep into their souls.

Already the first set of mixing-bowls were emptied; the eunuchs bustled in with others. The rounded bottoms of the silver goblets, making it impossible to lay them down, forced rapid drinking. Avil sat and quaffed in silence; but once or twice paused to cast sinister glances toward the vacant seat of Bilsandan. "A care, good vizier," spoke he to his own heart, "beware; the time is not far when I will brush you and the general from my path, as I served Daniel and Imbi-Ilu; and then if aught of mortal fate befell the king—"

But these forecastings were broken by the entrance of a great corps of harem girls, clothed in gauzy dresses of all the tints of the rainbow. While the harps tinkled softly they came before the king, to the space cleared at the foot of the dais, and sped about in sensuous dances, raven locks flying, smooth brown limbs twinkling, while they wove their figures. And again and again their delicate voices joined with the priests' in the great chorus to Bel, bestower of all Babylon's bright glory:—

"Bel-Marduk, who rulest forever,

Thee, thee we praise!"

The music throbbed faster and faster, the players breaking into ever madder melodies, as though their music was answering to the mounting and throbbing of the wine. Belshazzar had sunk back on his couch in contented revery, scarce watching the dancers. What king of the Chaldees before him had opened his reign with a fairer triumph? Already to Belshazzar's vision the artists were portraying upon the palace walls, in imperishable stone and enamel, the mighty deeds of the all-victorious son of Nabonidus. Already before the king's mind Media, Armenia, Egypt, and farthest Tartary lay conquered. Nay, the barbarous tribes of the Greeks beside their distant sea should learn to pay tribute to the monarch of "Babylon the Great." But the king's dreaming ended when Avil touched his elbow and whispered in his ear. And at the next interval in the dances Belshazzar had a command for the chief of the eunuchs:—

"Hasten. Bring us the captured vessels, sacred to the gods of the nations I and the great kings my fathers have put to shame. For we will drink from them to the deities whose favour is upon Babylon."

An expected order, and quickly obeyed. The eunuchs put in the hands of the captains, the harem girls, and the musicians, innumerable fresh goblets of gold and silver, of many and curious patterns. But to Belshazzar Mermaza bore three golden drinking-cups, each huge and crusted with jewels. Then the king took the first and raised himself from the couch before the vast throng. What with his tiara, his own fair stature, and his lofty seat, he seemed a god indeed.

"Again, lords of the Chaldees!" he commanded, "drink again! I hold the goblet used by Pharaoh Necho, in worship of Ammon-Ra, his god. Nebuchadnezzar took it in the great battle of Karkhemish. Where is the power of Ammon against our Babylonish gods?" Belshazzar held the glittering goblet on high. "Rise, Ammon, god of Egypt, rise! Thou art mocked! Display thy power!" Perfect silence, and the king shouted again, "Drink then with me, since Ammon lies helpless, a pledge to our great Istar, 'the Lady of Battles'!"

"Hail! Hail to Istar!" from a thousand, and they drank the pledge.

A second goblet was in Belshazzar's hand; and again he called: "Look—a vessel taken from the temple of Assur in Nineveh, when our fathers sacked the city. Rise, Assur,—rise, god of Assyria! Thou art mocked.—Helpless also—drink therefore again, a pledge to our Samas, 'the Glory of the Heavens'!"

"Hail to Samas, the undying sun god!" was the tumultuous answer. But the king had not ended.

"Look, warriors and princes! I hold the goblet taken from Jerusalem, from the temple of the impotent demon the shambling Jews and flying Persians fear. When did Jehovah save Zedekiah the Hebrew out of the Chaldee's power? And how now shall Cyrus, who cries to him under the name of Ahura, find deliverance from my hands? For Cyrus has turned away ashamed, his vassals fail him, his god is helpless, his power is broken! Victorious war is before your king, and empire never won before!"

"Victory! Victory to Belshazzar, the favoured of Marduk!" so the vast company cried; and the king yet a third time uplifted a goblet.

"Rise, Jehovah, or Ahura,—whatever be thy name,—rise; thou art mocked!" Again the pause and stillness, then the shout of the king: "Rise, rise! thou who art boasted all-powerful. I defy thee, I laugh thee to scorn."

The great cup was nearing his lips. "For the third and last pledge, men of Babylon—to Bel-Marduk, whose power waxeth forever; who shall be praised a thousand ages after the Persians' and Hebrews' god is forgotten! To Bel-Marduk, lord of lords, and god of gods, drink!"

But as every man lifted his own wine-cup, and the shout of the pledge was on his tongue, there was suddenly a silence. The goblet fell from the royal fingers. They saw terror flash across the king's face as he looked upward; and each beheld something moving against the plastered wall....

"They saw terror flash across the king's face as he looked upward."

CHAPTER XXV

Since first dusk the army of Cyrus had been in motion: the horse-archers of Tartary, the Hindoo infantry, the Persian lancers. The army marched in silence, no kettle-drums thundering, no war-horns blaring, the commands sent softly down the long line, from officer to officer. When the last bars of light had flickered out in the west, there had come a halt; bread and wine were passed among the men, the horses were watered in a canal: and Orasmasdes, chief of the Magians, shook incense into the portable altar carried beside the king, and offered prayer. Softly yet clearly rose the song in praise of Mithra, the great minister of Ahura-Mazda:—

"His chariot is borne onward by Holiness.

The law of Ahura shall open the way for him;

At his right hand speeds Obedience the holy,

At his left hand flies powerful Justice,

Behind him drives lie-smiting Fire!"

When the chant was finished the General Gobryas rode up beside the royal chariot.

"Lord of the Aryans, what shall be the battle-cry to-night?"

And Cyrus, leaning from the car, made answer, "Give this battle-cry to the host, as it shall enter Babylon,—'For Ahura, for Atossa!'"

The officer bowed, vanished in the deepening gloom. Cyrus turned to his charioteer. "Forward!" he commanded softly.

The reins shook over the white Nisæans. As the chariot moved onward, the thousands made haste to follow. Once Atrobanes, the "handkerchief-bearer," who cantered beside his lord, ventured remonstrance.

"Will not your Majesty take your litter? My lord is not so young as once. If he drive all night, he will grow weary."

Cyrus stood erect upon the car, taller seemingly than ever.

"Peace, good friend; the king of the Aryans has at least the strength to ride when his children are marching, and with such a prize before!"

"True," quoth the other, as he rode beside, "even your Majesty does not often stretch forth his hands to take a Babylon."

"Do you think I ride for Babylon this night?" demanded the king, almost angrily.

But Atrobanes did not reply; he knew the guerdon of all the deeds that night would not be "The Lady of Kingdoms" but the Lady Atossa.

So onward in the darkness, the trailing host keeping wondrously still. They had wound wisps of hay around shield and scabbard and over the horses' hoofs to deaden all noise. As the night advanced, the sense of awe sank deeper. Even the beasts gave no whinny; only as one clapped an ear close to the earth would he have caught the jar and rhythm of many men marching. The sky along one horizon was just beginning to overcast and hide a few stars. Soldier muttered to soldier, "There will be a storm,—lightning and thunder." But for the hour all the elements kept silence, with no wind creeping across the plain or lifting the lifeless pennons.

Cyrus had ridden long without speaking, when the muffled canter of two horsemen sounded, approaching from ahead. A moment later Darius and Isaiah were reining beside the monarch's car.

"You meet nothing? no alarm? no watchers?" asked the king in a whisper.

"None, lord," answered Darius; "we rode to the shadow of the outer wall; there was no sentry to challenge us."

"The stillness may be ominous," remarked Cyrus, shrewdly—"a pretended carelessness to lure us under the walls, when Belshazzar can fling wide his sally-ports and dash on us with his thousands. And you did grievous wrong in perilling your lives so near."

"Am I not a Persian too, your Majesty?" answered the prince in his pride; "have I not learned to dare and to do from you and from none other?"

"True," they knew Cyrus was smiling, "but Belshazzar may nevertheless have set a trap."

"Then the Babylonians' guile is deeper yet," replied Darius; "you do not see, my lord, in the darkness, who it is Isaiah has mounted behind him."

"A deserter from Babylon?"

"Imbi-Ilu, the exiled pontiff of Borsippa, just come from the city. Let him speak for himself."

The chariot halted, while a figure leaped to the ground from behind the Jew, and salaamed before the king.

"May every god shine on your Majesty," Imbi reported; "at no small peril your slave disguised himself as commanded and entered Babylon. He has communicated with Bilsandan the vizier, and Sirusur the *Tartan*. They accept your Majesty's promises, and rejoice to become your servants,—the more because Avil-Marduk works hourly on Belshazzar to gain their ruin. The guards on the gates have been withdrawn by Sirusur, the rest of the garrison is nigh drunken to a man. My priests at Borsippa swear they will not fail."

"The garrison drunken? Is Belshazzar mad; does he think my power shattered so utterly?" asked Cyrus, marvelling.

"Be that as it may, my king," interposed Isaiah, "while we awaited Imbi-Ilu under the walls, we heard from within nothing else than the sound of music and of revelling. The Chaldees are not Persians. Their god is the wine-cup, if the truth be told. Jehovah has caught them in their wickedness. He has led them into the net prepared by His servants."

"So be it," remarked Cyrus; then to the priest he hinted sternly, "Your friends will do well to keep troth. Let there be treachery in this, and I swear by your gods and by mine, I will lift your head from your shoulders!"

The Babylonian was not discomposed. "And I accept the warning; if I or my priests of Nabu play false, do to me as you will. But if Babylon is taken—"

"You shall not fail in your reward," declared Cyrus, "on the word of a Persian king; I renew my promise of the high priesthood of Bel-Marduk in Avil's stead."

"Forward then," urged the Chaldee; "let the king possess his city."

The charioteer made the lash whistle, the car whirled forward. The shadow of the great walls was above them now; speed, not silence, demanded; the guards about the king pricked with the spur to keep beside. Darius spoke again to Cyrus:—

"Lord, Imbi-Ilu tells us that at midnight Belshazzar quits his bridal feast."

Cyrus shot a glance up at the heavens, where the advancing clouds had not yet quenched all the starlight.

"By the movement of the stars, it lacks three hours of midnight," he answered.

"We must therefore take all Babylon in three hours. Away with prudence; haste, oh, haste!" cried the prince.

But Cyrus spoke back to him, "If so Ahura willeth, in three twinklings of an eye we could yet save Atossa!"

But, notwithstanding, they heard the king's great voice swell out in a shout that was music in the ears of all the army.

"Forward, men of Iran!"

It was the word that let the hounds slip from the leash, that uncaged the lion. Directly above their heads was the beetling rampart; they saw the glassy shimmer of the broad canal under the vanishing stars, and they heard—from within the vast bulwark, even as Isaiah had said—the sound of mirth and of harping. The footmen burst into a run, every horseman pricked deeper, while one shout, though in many tongues, echoed against the fortress.

"The Father! The Father! Let us die for Cyrus our king!"

Then the battlements surely quivered while a second shout smote them, "For Ahura, for Atossa!"

The echoes died; no battle-cry from behind the walls pealed in answer. The column was skirting the southern rampart, when yet another messenger flew up beside the king.

"I come from the Princes Harpagus and Hystaspes; their troopers are in station before the northern city. They attack as soon as the uproar proclaims that the king is assaulting."

No answer from Cyrus, for the van was beside the water-gate of the great canal of Borsippa. The column perforce had halted. The last stars had fled. It was very dark. The walls above seemed barriers lifted to the very gates of heaven; undefended, might not Belshazzar's city mock its mightiest foe? The canal was creeping through the dark cage-work of the bronze water-gate. For an instant was stillness, while king and soldier waited; and then, all vaguely, they saw the great fabric of metal rising, crawling like a sluggish monster from its slimy bed. Unseen chains and pulleys strained, grated; the gate rose higher; now the canal coursed freely under, now it was lifted to the height of a mounted man. Close under the wall lay a causeway, wide enough for a single cavalryman to enter. Nimitti-Bel was unsealed!

Out of the darkness appeared figures and flickering torches.

"Live forever, O king," spoke Sirusur the betrayer, "the city is sunken in mirth and drunkenness. Forward boldly—you will dash the wine-cup from Belshazzar's own hand."

Cyrus started to descend from the chariot.

"A horse," he commanded abruptly; "there is no space for the car to enter."

But at his words one cry of protest arose from Darius and all the officers, "The king will not *himself* enter the city!"

"Not enter?" Cyrus's voice became stern and high. "Am I not king? To whom may I give account?"

None stirred to obey him. Moments were rubies; the monarch was swelling with anger.

"Have I not commanded? I can yet be terrible to the disobedient. I am still the 'Giver of Breath' to all Iran!"

But the others stood mute and motionless. The preciousness of the hour made Cyrus blind to all save his desires. He bounded from the car, and snatched a mounted officer with a giant's clutch.

"Down! Your horse!" he commanded thickly. The man was helpless in that grasp, but suddenly a dozen hands were put forth upon the king himself.

"Lord," said Gobryas, the senior general present, "we cannot suffer this thing. Your Majesty must remain without the gates till your slaves have mastered the city."

The king struggled to be free.

"Must? Not even you may use that word to me. As Ahura liveth, you shall die for this madness."

But the others did not release him.

"Lord," repeated Gobryas, "when your Majesty wills, I bow my neck to the stroke; but till then, I love the 'Light of the Aryans' too well to see it quenched, even at its wish."

"But I implore you—" protested the king, for commands were useless.

And Gobryas answered, "We love the king too well even to heed his prayers."

Cyrus gave one bitter groan, but he remounted the chariot and said no more.

"Advance," entreated Sirusur; "every instant gives Belshazzar chance to take alarm, and my work is undone!"

"We will enter," spoke Darius; and in the faint torchlight they saw Cyrus bow his head. Then every officer bent low in the saddle, saluting the king. The host behind was fretting and wondering at the strange delay. But once more the king's command rang out strong. "Forward, my children! And swiftly—your father prays it!"

"For Ahura, for Atossa!"

So thundered Darius, and as all the rest rolled on the cry, he sent his steed at headlong gallop straight through the narrow portal; after him Isaiah, after him the choicest of the Aryan cavalry. Within the gate the priests of Nabu met them with more horses and torches to guide them on their way; for the Borsippa folk's hatred of Avil-Marduk passed their dread of the Persian. Darius glanced over his shoulder,—the gate had been forced wide open, the sword-hands and lancers of his people were pouring in by tens, by hundreds. The gate of Imgur-Bel opened wide for them. Let Belshazzar defend his inner barrier as he might, the strongest were lost him. The night was darker yet, the storm was rumbling nearer. But far away, down the long vista of Nana Street shone a dull redness against an inky sky—the torches and bonfires of the palace, where the Lord of the Chaldees sat at feast.

Darius pressed the spur until his good beast almost screamed with the pain.

"The City of the Lie is ours!" he cried to Isaiah, who flew beside him, while a thousand raged close behind. "Ours! And Belshazzar is ours!—and Atossa!"

CHAPTER XXVI

There on the wall the letters glowed, right under the torch-holder; glowed like ruddy fire, the whole dread inscription spreading in one long, terrible line under the eyes of king and nobles. While Belshazzar looked, his bronzed cheeks turned ashen. The awful hand had vanished the instant the sentence was written,—gone—whither? The lord of the Chaldees gazed upon his servants, and they—back at their master, while none spoke. But the letters did not vanish; their steadfast light burned calmly on. Then came another fearful deed; for Belshazzar caught the golden cup that had fallen from his hand, and dashed it against the wall. A great square of the plaster fell, but lo! the letters were burning still. Then new silence, while every man heard the beatings of his heart and thought on his unholy deeds.

But the stillness could not last forever. Belshazzar broke it. The pallor was still on his face, his knees smote together, his voice quivered; but he was kinglier than the rest, even in his fear,—he at least was brave enough for speech.

"Ho! captains of Babylon! Why do we gape like purblind sheep? A notable miracle from the gods! Some new favour, no doubt, vouchsafed by Marduk!"

No one answered; all strength had fled from the stoutest sword-hand. Belshazzar's voice rose to a sterner pitch, as he faced the array of priests.

"What mean these letters? They are not the characters of the Chaldee. Their meaning? Here are learned men, wise in every tongue. Translate to us!"

Still no answer; and the king's wrath now mastered all his fears.

"Fools!" his hand was on his sword-hilt; "Marduk has not added to the miracle by smiting all dumb." He confronted the "chief of the omen-revealers," who stood close to the dais.

"Here, Gamilu, this falls within your duties. Look on the writing. Interpret without delay; or, as Marduk is god, another has your office!"

Gamilu, a venerable pontiff, lifted his head, and stared at the inscription. He mumbled inaudibly, but the royal eye was on him. With vain show of confidence he commenced:—

"Live forever, lord of the Chaldees! A fortunate sign, on a doubly fortunate day! This is the word which Bel, the sovereign god, has sent to his dearly loved son, the ever victorious king, Belshazzar—"

But here he stopped, bravado failing. Thrice he muttered wildly, then grew still. The king's rage was terrible. "Juggler! you shall learn to mock me. Nabu destroy me too, if you are living at dawn!"

The luckless man fell on his knees, tearing his beard: his one groan was, "Mercy." Belshazzar heeded little. "You other priests,—you the chief 'demon-ejector,'—do you speak! The meaning?"

A second wretch cast himself before the king. "Pity, Ocean of Generosity, pity! I do not know."

The king wasted no curse. "You, Kalduin, 'master of the star-gazers,' who boast to be wisest astrologer in Babylon,—look on the writing. I declare that if you, or any other, can read these letters, and make known to me the interpretation, he shall be clothed in scarlet, and a chain of gold put about his neck, and he shall be third ruler of the kingdom, next to Avil and myself."

But Kalduin also fell on his knees, groaning and moaning. Belshazzar turned to Avil-Marduk, who had not spoken since the apparition, and who was still exceeding pale. "Avil!" the accent of the king was icy chill, "if you are truly the mouthpiece of your god, prove your power. Interpret!"

Then came a wondrous thing, even on that night of wonders. For the chief priest, to whom Babylon had cringed as almost to the king, cowered on the rugs by the royal couch. "Lord! Lord!" he moaned in fear, "I know not. I cannot tell. Mercy! Spare!"

Belshazzar shook his kingly head as might a desert lion, he alone steadfast, while a thousand were trembling.

"And is there no man in all Babylon who can read this writing?" was his thunder.

There was a rustling beside him. From her chair the aged queen-mother, Tavat-Hasina, leaned forward. "Your Majesty," she whispered, from pale lips, "live forever. Let not your thoughts trouble you. There *is* a man in your kingdom in whom is the spirit of the holy gods."

"What man?" demanded Belshazzar. Every eye was on the queen, who continued:—

"In the days of your father, light and understanding like the wisdom of the gods were found in him; and King Nebuchadnezzar made him master of the magicians and soothsayers, because an excellent knowledge and interpretation of dreams and dissolving of doubts was found in him."

"Ay! The man! His name!" The king snatched her wrist roughly. Many voices reëchoed, "The man! His name! Send for him! Send!"

The queen-mother looked steadily into Belshazzar's eyes.

"The name of the man is Daniel, whom the king called Belteshazzar; now let Daniel be called, and he will show the interpretation."

But the words were like fire thrust into the king's face. He recoiled from her; the ashen gray came back to his cheeks. "Not Daniel! I will never see him! I have sworn it! Not he! Not he!"

So cried the king. But from all the captains rose one clamour:—

"Send for Daniel! He is the only hope. He alone can reveal. Send! Send!"

Avil found courage to rise and whisper in the royal ear, "Let all Babylon burn, ere the king craves one boon of this villanous Jew!"

"Never! I will not send," cried Belshazzar. But as he saw again that burning line, he grew yet paler.

"Daniel! Daniel! We are lost if the writing is longer hid! Send for the Jew!"

The captains were waxing mutinous. Scabbards clattered. Would the feast end in rebellion? Belshazzar addressed Mermaza. "Eunuch, go to the innermost prison and bring Daniel hither without delay."

"Hold!" cried Avil, at the top of his voice; "what god can speak through *his* lips? Is the king of Babylon sunk so low—"

"Read and interpret yourself, priest," bawled an old officer; and from fifty fellows rose the yell: "Away with Avil-Marduk. It is he who angers heaven!"

"Shall I go, lord?" questioned Mermaza, and Belshazzar only nodded his head.

Then there was silence once more, while monarch and servants watched those letters burning on the wall. Presently—after how long!—there were feet heard in the outer court, the clanking of chains; then right into the glare and glitter came Mermaza, followed by two soldiers; and betwixt these an old man, squalid, unkempt, clothed in rags, the fetters still on wrist and ankle. But at sight of him a hundred knelt to worship.

"Help us, noble Jew! Make known the writing, that we may obey heaven, and may not die!" One and all cried it. But Daniel heeded nothing until he stood before the king.

As Belshazzar rose from his couch to speak, a cry broke forth from Ruth. "My father! My father! Help me! Save me!" Almost she would have flown to his arms, but he outstretched a manacled hand, beckoning away.

"Not now, daughter. On another errand have I come." Then to the king, "Your Majesty, I am here."

Belshazzar tried vainly to meet the piercing eye of the Jew. His own voice was metallic, while he groped for words.

"Are you that Daniel, of the captive Hebrews, whom Nebuchadnezzar brought out of Judea?" Where were the king's wits fled, that he asked this of the man so long known and hated? A stately nod was his reply.

"I have heard that the spirit of the gods is in you, and light and understanding and excellent wisdom. And now the wise men and astrologers have been brought to read this writing, and to interpret, but they could not. And I have heard that you can make interpretations and dissolve doubts." The king's voice faltered; he would have given a thousand talents not to be driven to speak the rest. "Now, if you are able to read the writing, and make known the interpretation, you shall be clothed in scarlet, and have a chain of gold about your neck, and be the third ruler of the kingdom."

No response: Daniel looked straight upon Belshazzar, and again Belshazzar strove to shun the captive's gaze.

"Will you not speak?" demanded the king. "Speak! or you are beaten to death!"

Was it triumph or pity that lighted the old Jew's face? "Death? My times are in mightier hands than yours, O king. Answer truly—will you have me speak? For this is not the word of Bel."

All saw Avil leap up, as if in creature fear; but Belshazzar at least faced Daniel steadily, with all save his eyes.

"Answer me truly—be it good or ill. But answer!"

The king stretched forth his hands to the Jew, imploring. The prophecy was fulfilled; Belshazzar the king supplicated Daniel the captive! The old man's form straightened; he swept his gaze around that company, every eye obedient to his. His voice was low, yet in that silence each whisper swelled to loudness.

"Let your gifts be for another, O king; give your rewards to another, but I will read the writing to the king, and make known the interpretation."

Then he told the tale all Babylon knew so well, how when the mighty Nebuchadnezzar hardened his heart in kingly pride, madness smote him, and made him no better than the beasts, till after living seven years thus humbled, he came to himself, and knew that the Most High was above all kings. And by the time the tale was ended the silence was so great, that even the sputtering torches were loud to hear. Daniel stood directly before the dais; the chains rattled as he stretched forth a finger, and pointed into the king's face.

"But you, O Belshazzar, have not humbled your heart, though you knew all this; but have lifted yourself up against the Lord of Heaven; and they have brought the vessels of His house before you, and you, and your lords, and your women have drunk wine in them; and you have praised the gods of silver, of gold, of brass, iron, wood, and stone, which see not, nor hear, nor know; and the God in whose hand your breath is, and whose are all your ways, you have not glorified. Then was the hand sent from Him, and this writing was written."

The finger pointed toward the glowing characters upon the wall. "And this is the writing that was written: *'Mene, Mene, Tekel, Upharsin.'* And this is the interpretation: *'Mene'*—God has numbered your kingdom and finished it. *'Tekel'*—you are weighed in the balances and are found wanting. *'Upharsin'* which is otherwise *'Peres'*—your kingdom is divided and given to the Medes and the Persians."...

... A fearful cry was rising; captains were on their faces, groaning to Samas, to Istar, to Ramman: "Save! Save from the wrath of Jehovah!" The workings of Belshazzar's features were terrible to behold. Thrice he strove to speak,—his lips moved dumbly. Then, as the king looked, lo! another wonder. The fiery words were gone, and only the shattered plaster showed where they had burned. "Woe! Woe!" all were moaning; but the vanishing of the letters gave back to Avil his courage. He leaned over, whispering to the king. In an instant Belshazzar uttered a hideous laugh.

"Good! By Istar, the Jew has me fairly on the hip! Clever jugglery, I swear, to contrive a trick that could chase the blood from the cheeks of the stoutest captains of the Chaldees! Show me the conjurer; I will pardon and reward. A clever jest, my princes, a clever jest."

The shout died away in profound silence. The king grasped a goblet once more. "By Nabu, the jest is so well played, you still wander for wits. Daniel must have reward. Ho! Mermaza; the robe of honour and the chain of gold. Off with these rags and fetters. Behold in Daniel the third prince of the kingdom. Set a new seat on the dais. A health to his Highness!" He drained the cup, then in a darker tone, directly at the Hebrew: "This is the promised reward. But when at midnight I quit the feast, if your prophecy is not fulfilled, you die the perjurer's death, for mocking thus your king."

Daniel answered nothing. The eunuchs pried off his fetters, put on him the robe and the golden chain. They set him in a chair beside Belshazzar, offering a jewelled goblet. He took it, tasting only once. Avil had risen, in vain effort to fuse the company with the same mad merriment affected by himself and the king.

"I congratulate Prince Daniel, my colleague in government! Another health to him, and to our 'ever-to-be-adored' Queen Atossa. Strike up, harpers; raise the triumph hymn to Bel once more."

With reluctant fingers the musicians smote harp and zither, the choir of priests and maidens lifted quavering voices,—sang a few measures,—the weak notes died away into ghastly stillness. Every eye crept furtively up to the square of shattered plaster. Then, as if in desperation, and bound to hide his mastering fears, a "captain of a hundred" motioned to a eunuch.

"Wine, fellow, wine, heady enough to chase these black imps away! Let us drink ourselves to sleep, and forget the portent by the morning."

"Wine!" echoed all, "more wine! Surely the Jew has lied. Forget him!"

The revels were resumed. The torches flared above the king of the Chaldees and all his lords draining their liquor,—beaker on beaker,—in one mad, vain hope—to drown out their own dark thoughts. The fiery apparition had vanished from the plaster only to glow before the uncertain vision of each and all. Soon rose drunken laughter, more fearful than any scream or moaning.

Avil at least kept sober. Once he turned to Mermaza.

"What are these flashes? The lamps cast shadow. And this rumbling?"

"A storm approaches, though still far off."

"Foul omen at this season!" answered Avil, and under breath—scoffer that he was—he muttered a spell against the "rain-fiends."

Atossa sat on her own high seat, watching, waiting, wondering. One can hardly say whether she had hopes or fears. She had not spoken since the miracle. What followed she remembered as she would recall a dim memory of long ago. Daniel was sitting by her side. Once she ventured, despite Belshazzar's frown, to speak to him.

"My father, the spirit of the holy Ahura is on you. Tell me, shall we be saved, you, and Ruth and I, from the power of these 'Lovers of Night'?"

And Daniel, calm, unblenching, sober, amid a hundred gibbering drunkards, answered with a confidence not of this world: "My child, we shall be saved. Doubt it not; but whether we be saved in this body, or depart to see Jehovah's face, He knoweth, not I. But His will is ever good."

The king interrupted boisterously, with unveiled mockery:—

"Give wisdom, noble Daniel. Shall I rebuild the walls of Uruk or spend the money on new canals at Sippar?"

The Hebrew made the king wince once more, as he looked on him,

"Lord of Babylon, think no more on walls and cities. Think of your past deeds. Think of the Just Spirit before whom you must stand."

"Verily, Jew," sneered Avil, "you will play your mad game to the end."

"To the end," was all the answer; but neither king nor pontiff made mock of Daniel again.

Deeper the drinking, madder the revelling. From the outer palace rose the laughter of soldiers and the city folk. The priests of Bel at length gathered courage from their wine. They roared out their hymn, and the dancing girls caught up red torches,—brandishing, shrieking, dancing, one lurid whirl of uncaged demons. The officers put forth their hands time and again for the beakers which the eunuchs could not fill too fast. In the reaction after the portent, the scene became an orgy. The king's cheek was flushed, his voice was loud and high. Tavat, the queen-mother, quitted the feast; and Atossa would have given all she possessed—how little!—to be suffered to follow. She had hardly tasted the cups pressed on her. She was utterly weary. The gold and jewels on her head seemed an intolerable weight. Oh, to be away,—to have that scene blotted out, even by death's long slumber! Her head fell forward. Ahura was kind. Did she sleep? Suddenly Belshazzar's voice aroused her.

"Midnight, the feast ends; and you, O Jew, have lost!"

The king was standing. The lamps were smoking low; the noise of the feasters failing, as the wine accomplished its work. The tipsy priests had quavered out their last triumph song:—

"Bel-Marduk, who rulest forever,

Thee, thee we praise!"

Belshazzar addressed Mermaza. "Eunuch, deliver Daniel the Jew to Khatin for instant death. His mummery turns to his own ruin. *Now* truly let his weak god save!"

Even as he spoke there was a strange clamour rising in the palace without: a headlong gallop, a shouting, not of mirth but of alarm. None yet heeded.

"Your Majesty," Daniel was answering steadily, "suffer me only this: let me embrace my daughter Ruth."

The king nodded. "Be brief, for you have vexed me long!" Then, turning to Atossa: "Ah! lady, Queen,—at last! to the harem! you are my wife!"

Atossa knew she was being taken by the hand; she saw all things dimly as through darkened glass. Nearer the gallop without, louder the shouting, and through it and behind a jar and a crashing,—not of the elements surely! Daniel had clasped Ruth to his breast. His words were heard only by her and by Another. The king gestured impatiently. "Enough! Away!—" But no more; there was a panic cry at the portal, the howl of fifty voices in dismay; and right into the great hall, over the priceless carpets, through that revelling throng, spurred a rider in armour, two arrows sticking in target, blood on crest, blood streaming from the great wound in the horse's side. Up to the very dais he thundered; and there, in sight of all, the beast staggered, fell, while Igas-Ramman, the captain, struggled from beneath and stood before the king.

"*All is lost, lord of the Chaldees!*" and then he gasped for breath. But already in the outer palace was a fearful shout. "Arms! Rescue! The foe!"

Belshazzar tottered as he stood, caught the arm of the throne. His face was not ashen, but black as the clouds on high. "What is this, fool?" he called. And Igas answered, "O king, Sirusur and Bilsandan are traitors. The retreat of Cyrus was a ruse. By night his host has returned. Imbi-Ilu, the exile, has tampered with the priests of Nabu, and they have opened the Borsippa water-gate. Sirusur has withdrawn the garrisons from the chief defences; Bilsandan has released the Persian prisoners and with them overpowered the guard at the Northern Citadel. Prince Darius is speeding to the palace."

"And you, where did you fight?" demanded the king.

"We made shift to defend an inner gate. Treachery is all about. We were attacked in the rear. I fled with the tidings. The Persians carry all before them,—hear!" and hear they did; "the foe will come and none to stay!"

"None shall stay? Twenty thousand men of war in Babylon, and Belshazzar be snared as a bird in his own palace?" The king drew his sword, flinging far the scabbard.

"Up, princes of the Chaldees, up!" he trumpeted, above the shriekings all around. "All is not lost! We will still prove the Jew the liar! Whosoever dares, follow me! All Babylon is not turned traitor. We will make our streets the Persian's grave!"

Yet while he cried it a second messenger panted into the great hall.

"The outer defences of the palace are forced, O king! The foe are everywhere!"

But Belshazzar leaped down from the dais, and sped about one lightning glance.

"Here, Khatin, stand by these women and this Jew! See that they do not flee. I will yet live to teach them fear."

A crash without made the casements shiver. Belshazzar sprang forward. "At them, men of Babylon; all is not yet lost!"

And, spurred by his example, the feasters rushed after. The cups lay on the tables, the lamps flickered overhead, the storm wind was shaking the broad canopy, but Atossa knew only one thing—the raging din that ever swelled louder. Then a second crash, mightier than the first; and out of it a shout in her own tongue of Iran.

"For Ahura, for Atossa!"

The battle-cry of the Persians—and Atossa knew that Darius, son of Hystaspes, was not far away.

CHAPTER XXVII

Oh, the terror, the blind terror, which possessed the guilty, lustful city that night! the stupid guards staggering from their wine-pots; the priests, crazed with the lees, shrieking to Istar, to Bel, to Ramman, their strengthless hands catching at useless weapons. What drunken courage might do then was done. But of what avail? For treachery was everywhere. The citadel was betrayed; Imgur-Bel and Nimitti-Bel betrayed. The giant-built walls frowned down, but the massy gates were wide open,—and through them streamed the foe. Right down the length of broad Nana Street, under the shadow of the *ziggurats* and the great warehouses, had charged the Persian cuirassiers, the finest cavalry in all the East. Through the Gate of Istar poured Harpagus and the Median chivalry; through the Gate of the Chaldees swept Hystaspes with the "Immortals," Cyrus's own life-guard, the stoutest spearmen in wide Iran. They met files of tipsy sword-hands, men who fought without order, without commanders. The howls of the slaves and women were on every hand. The light of burning houses brightened the invaders' pathway; and so the Aryan host fought onward, brushing resistance from its way as the torrent sweeps on the pebbles, all ranks straining toward one point, the palace; for the hour of reckoning had come to the "City of the Lie."

Atossa sat upon the dais, looking upon the scene below. The great hall was still around her,—still the pictured walls, with the shadows darkening upon their enamels, as the lamps and torches burned lower. The tables were there, and the remnants of the feast; the floor was strewn with torn garlands and trampled roses,—but the company, the wanton dancing women, the sleek eunuchs, the lordly priests, the yet more lordly captains, where were they? Fled,—all save the last,—to the innermost palace, there to moan, while the noise of the avenger was nearing.

Atossa arose, shook herself, stared once more about the hall. At the foot of the dais lay the dead charger. On a seat at her side sat Ruth, her head bowed on her hands, her lithe form quivering with fear. Beside his daughter was the old Hebrew, calm, steadfast, seemingly passionless, looking straight before, as if his sight could pass through wall and battlement, beholding the far-off peace of the upper heavens. But in the outer palace what was not befalling? Never before had Atossa heard the clangour of men at war; but she was a great king's daughter. Should the child of Cyrus fear when her own people knocked at the gate thus loudly? The awful roar grew louder each instant. Louder the Aryan war-cry, "For Ahura, for Atossa!" And still the despairing shout was answering, "Save, O Marduk, save!" For the Babylonish lion, though at his death, must die as a lion.

As the din surged in and out like some raging sea, the princess heard her own name alone shouted. Dared she believe she knew the voice?

"Atossa? Atossa?"

Then a new crash that drowned all else, and the whirl of a thousand feet. Men and women, cursing, howling, were rushing back into the hall. In an instant the empty scene became a chaos of forms, all the gibbering palace folk fleeing thither.

"Lost! The gate is carried! The palace is taken!"

So cried those not frenzied past all speech. But Atossa heard with an awful gladness. This was the hour of her triumph; the destroyers were the servants of her father, their leader the man she loved. Let, then, the Babylonian hounds whine and cringe at doom. What cared she?

But the end had not yet come. Another voice was thundering in the Chaldee, Belshazzar's voice:—

"Rally again! All is not yet lost. We will defend the palace room by room!"

"Forward, sons of Iran!" sped back the answer; and a shout followed it at the very entrance of the hall.

"For Ahura, for Atossa!"

"Darius!" cried Atossa, "Darius! Here am I!"

Her scream was drowned in the chaos of battle. And then for the first time fear smote the princess. Outside those doors fought the son of Hystaspes, perilling himself in the press,—and for her sake. She could contain herself no more.

"Darius," she shrieked again, "I come! Save!"

She leaped from the dais; in her madness she would have plunged into the riot below, when a heavy hand fell on her; she struggled, was helpless. Above her towered Khatin.

"It is commanded, lady," quoth the headsman, gruffly, "that you abide here, till the king order otherwise."

"Fool!" she cried, shrinking at his impure touch, "do you seek death? A moment more and your life is in my power. Release, and you shall live."

"Ah, my bright-eyed rabbit," answered he, dryly, unmoved by all the terrors about, "I have sent too many better men than I to the 'world-mountain' to dread myself the journey thither. All the Chaldees have not turned traitor, nor have I. Wait."

He forced her back upon her seat, and stood guard beside her. Drunk or sober, the nobles of Babylon proved their lordly birth that night. Twice Atossa's heart sank when a triumphant cry rang through the palace:—

"Glory to Marduk! Drive them forth! Victory!"

But each time the Persians swept back to the charge; and still the clamour rose. Well that all the death was hid from Atossa, or, king's daughter though she was, her woman's heart would have broken. How long might this last? The swarm of frenzied palace folk was growing denser. They sprang upon the dais, threatening Atossa, in their witless fear, but gave back at sight of Khatin's bared sword-blade. Then forth rushed a single man, Avil-Marduk, his face blanched, his teeth a-chatter, and cast himself at Daniel's feet.

"Save, generous lord! Save me from death! For you are merciful, and the Persians will hear you! Beseech your Jehovah that He may not let me die!"

Before the Jew could answer Khatin dragged the suppliant from his knees. "Peace, babbler; if Marduk is a great god, let *him* save; if not, die like a man. But take not even life from one you have reviled, like the God of Daniel!"

"But I am sinful, unfit to stand before Ea and his awful throne. I shall die in my iniquity!"

"I only know you are no fitter to live than to die," answered the implacable headsman; and he cast the priest headlong from the dais. Ruth had lifted her head, and stared about vacantly, till her gaze lit on the Persian. Then she flung herself into the arms of Atossa.

"Ah! lady," she cried, the hot tears falling fast, "I see all as in a frightful dream! When will this tumult end? I can bear no more!"

But Atossa answered in her queenly pride:—

"Peace, Jewess, be strong. For this is the hour for which we cried to Ahura together. He is trampling down the 'People of the Lie,' and this sound arises from the men we love."

But as she spoke the mob below swayed with new terror. For a third time the great palace quaked. The door was again darkened by many men—and in their midst they saw the king....

Belshazzar was covered with blood, whether his own or the foeman's, who might say? His mantle was in tatters, the tiara smitten from his head, on his arm a shivered shield. The king staggered, then the sight of Atossa upon the dais seemed to dart new power through his veins. He steadied, swept his weapon around in command to the officers who pressed by.

"Rally again!" cried the king; "we have still thousands around the walls and throughout the city. Prolong the defence till dawn, and we may yet conquer!" His majesty and presence stayed the panic-stricken captains, who had been streaming past him into the wide hall.

The king surveyed the room one instant.

"We can defend this hall until the garrison may rally. There is still hope; drive forth this rabble, and barricade the doors!"

The guardsmen swept the eunuchs and women from the hall. They fled, the thunders of the gale, now at its height, drowning their moanings. Ever and anon the dying torches cast shadow while the lightnings glared. Then came the crash of the hail and rain, beating down the canopy, quenching half the lights, and adding gloom to terror. All this in less time than the telling. Belshazzar himself aided in piling the tables and couches in heaps against all the doors save one, through which the Chaldees were sullenly retreating, marking their pathway by the Persian dead. Once again Atossa leaped from her seat; despite her brave words to Ruth, more of this chaos would strike her mad. She slipped from the grasp of Khatin, and flew toward the entrance. For the instant all were too intent on their fearful tasks to heed.

"Darius! I come!" cried she, in her Persian, and a shout without was answering, when a clutch, mighty as Khatin's, halted her. She was in Belshazzar's own hands.

"Back, girl! I am still the king, and I command!"

But Atossa struggled desperately. "Away! Take me away!" rang her plea. "Slay this instant if you will, but I can bear no more!"

"Take her to the dais," shouted the king to two guardsmen; "watch her preciously; her life is dearer to us now than gold."

The two had need of their strength, but she was thrust again to her hated station. This time cords were knotted around her arms, and she was held fast. She looked to Daniel. There he sat, serene and silent, the only calm object in that scene of furies.

"Father," she moaned, "pray to Khatin, to any, that they strike once, and let me die! All the *dævas* are loose and drive me mad!"

"Peace, my child," he spoke mildly, yet amid all that storm she heard him; "we shall full soon know what is the will of God!"

But she had started despite the bands. The last Babylonians had been brushed from the portal, a rush of feet, a battle-cry the loudest of the night; and right in the entrance, sword in hand and looking upon Atossa, was the son of Hystaspes, at his side Isaiah, at his back the stoutest veterans of Cyrus the conqueror.

There was silence for an instant, while the foes glared on one another. Then the Babylonish officers by sheer force drew their king behind them, and formed in close array before the dais. The last stand!

"Stand fast, Chaldees!" rang the voice of Igas-Ramman; "let them touch the king only across our bodies. While he lives Babylon is not truly lost."

The Persians were entering slowly, grimly. Their prey was in their clutch; they were too old in war to let him slip by untimely triumph. The rain beat down in one continuous roar, amid ceaseless peals of thunder. Yet despite the elements they heard the clamour of distant conflict; at the temple of Bel, at the palace of Nabupolassar, the fight was still desperate.

"While your Majesty lives," muttered Igas in the royal ear, "there may be yet rally and rescue. Let us fight to the end."

Darius had advanced from his company, halfway across the hall, as if he alone would walk upon the swords of the Chaldees. He addressed the king.

"Live forever, Lord of Babylon! Live forever. I have bayed a fairer game, this night, than an aurochs or a lion; but I have brought him to the net at last. Too noble, truly, to slay. Let him be wise; he will find my master merciful."

"Yield to Cyrus? Let the dogs eat first our bodies!" so cried Igas, and all the Babylonians yelled like answer.

Darius did not retire. "We Persians honour kings, though once our foes. Crœsus the Lydian is Cyrus's friend. Be wise,—Bel your god may not save you. Craft and strength alike have failed. Yield on fair quarter. Do not sacrifice these gallant men—"

But he ended swiftly, for the king had leaped upon the dais, and his voice sounded amid the thunder. "Look! with all your eyes look, Persians! Behold the daughter of Cyrus." Atossa had been upborne upon his strong arms and those of Khatin, and stood upon the royal couch before the gaze of all. And at sight of her a tremor thrilled through the Persians.

"The princess in Belshazzar's clutch! Woe! Ahura deliver!" groaned many a grizzled sword-hand, who had slain his man that night; but the king swept on: "I say to you, that as the first arrow flies, or sword-stroke falls, the blade enters the breast of the child of Cyrus. Get you gone, and that instantly, if you would not see her die!"

They saw the steel glancing in Khatin's hand, no idle threat. And for a moment longer, Persian and Chaldee looked on one another, while the storm screamed its wild music. But now Atossa spoke, her voice clear as Belshazzar's:—

"And I, daughter of your king, command that you hold back in nothing for my sake. For to an Aryan maid of pure heart death is no great thing, when she knows behind it speeds the vengeance."

"Not so! We may not!" moaned Persian to Persian; and Darius sprang back among his men.

"Lord," cried a captain from the rear, "the garrison is rallying. A little longer, and many companies come to Belshazzar's aid. We may yet be undone!"

Darius had flung away his target; his hands had snatched something—a quiver, a bow. He leaped before them all, while Belshazzar's voice again was rising:—

"Back, Persians; or as Bel is god of Babylon, the maid dies, and you are her murderers!" He sprang down from beside her, leaving Khatin standing.

But the prince drew the shaft to the head, and sent his eye along the arrow. Did he level at Atossa's own breast? So thought she, with all the others, and her cry rang shrilly:—

"Shoot! In Ahura's great name, shoot! Death at your hands is sweet!"

They saw her close her eyes, and strong men turned away their faces. One deed to slay a peer, in heat of battle; another, to see a lover strike down his bride! But Belshazzar, looking on his foe, was startled,—*he had seen him shoot before.*

"Strike!" he commanded Khatin, "swiftly!"

They saw the long blade move, and heard the whiz of the arrow. Right through the headsman's wrist sped the shaft, just as the stroke fell. The sword turned in impotent fingers, and fell upon the floor. And still Atossa stood.

She trembled, moved, made to spring from her station: but Darius's voice in turn was thunder:—

"Move not! There alone is safety, where I cover you! And now—on them, men of Iran!"

There, lifted up above them all, remained Atossa, the arrow of the "King of the Bow" upon her, and no Chaldee so lustful after death as to leap beside her, and to strike.

The Persians had sprung upon their prey and never relaxed their death grip; but the Babylonians ringed round their king with a living wall, and fought in silence, for all was near the end. Then the rush of numbers forced the defenders away from the dais. Atossa saw the arrow of Darius sink, saw him bounding forward, but saw no more; for in mercy sense forsook her,— she felt two strong arms, and then for long lay motionless as the dead.

The prince laid her upon the royal couch at the extremity of the dais; beside her he set Ruth, who had long since ceased crying, through very weight of fear. Back to the combat then, and the last agony of the king, when from under the shivered tables crawled one who groaned, and kissed his feet—Avil-Marduk. Darius spurned him; the next instant two tall Medians were hauling the wretch away—a noble spectacle he would be for triumphing Ecbatana, before they crucified. But a nobler spoil remained. Darius flung himself upon the Chaldee nobles. Igas-Ramman was down, and Khatin, whose left arm had smitten many a foe while his right hung helpless. The king still fought, ten swords seeking his life, and he parrying all,—none of his conqueror race more royal than he in this his hour of doom. Suddenly the desperate defenders turned at bay, and charged their foes with a mad fury that made even the stoutest Aryans give ground. One final lull, in which they heard the beating of the rain. Then right betwixt raging Persian and raging Chaldee sprang a figure,—an old man in hoary majesty, Daniel the Jew.

"Peace!" and for that instant every man hearkened. "Your god is helpless, O Belshazzar, your idol mute. Your power is sped, but bow to the will of the Most High. He will still pity the penitent. Do not cast your life away."

But at the word the king lifted his last javelin.

"Be this my answer to your god!"

The missile brushed the white lock on the old man's forehead, and fell harmless.

The Babylonians retreated sullenly to the wall, set their backs against it. Then, with death in the face of each, with the shattered plaster frowning down on them, those men who had fought so long and well to save their king and city, raised their song,—the pæan of the vanquished, to the god whose power that night had passed:—

"Bel-Marduk, sovereign of archers,

Bel-Marduk, spoiler of cities,

Bel-Marduk, lord of all gods,

Bel-Marduk, who rulest forever,

Thee, thee we praise!"

At the last note the Persians closed around them, and each Chaldee as he stood fought to the end, selling his life full dear; but about the king the strife raged fiercest, for Darius had commanded, "Slay not! Take living!" Long after the last of his servants had sped from the fury of man, Belshazzar beat back all who pressed him. The spirit of his fallen god seemed to possess the king; he fought with Bel's own power. But the sword was beaten from his grasp. Twenty hands stretched out to seize him; he buffeted all away, leaped to one side, and, before any could hinder, drew the dagger from his girdle and sheathed it in his own breast. He staggered. Isaiah upbore him. The king saw in whose arms he was, then his eyes went up to the shivered plaster. The Hebrew felt a spasm of agony pass through Belshazzar's frame.

"Bel is dead!" he cried, his voice never louder.

"Bel is dead! O God of the Jews, Thou hast conquered!"

Then came a dazzling bolt. The wide canopy fell. The rush of rain drowned every torch, and all was blackness.

Darius groped his way beside Belshazzar, and spread his mantle across the king's face to shield it from the rain.

"Cruel and 'Lover of the Lie,'" spoke the prince, "he was yet a brave man and a king; therefore let us do the dead all honour!"

Soon the great court was empty, the victors gone, the vanquished cold and still. But till dawn the tempest held its carnival above the towers of the palace. And the winds had one cry, the beat of the rain one burden, to those who were wise to hear, a burden heavy with long years of wrong:—

"Babylon the Great is fallen, is fallen, is fallen! The Lady of Kingdoms is fallen, is fallen, is fallen! She will oppress the weak no more, will slay the innocent no more, will blaspheme God no more! Fallen is Babylon, the Chaldees' crown and glory."

In a greater Book than this is written how Cyrus the Persian made good his vow to Isaiah, and restored the Hebrews to their own land, raising Jerusalem out of her dust and ashes. Elsewhere also is told how Darius and Atossa fared together onward until the son of Hystaspes sat on Cyrus's own throne and gave law to all the nations. And to Isaiah Jehovah granted that he should become a mighty prophet among his people, and see rapt visions of the "King-who-was-to-be." But as for Babylon the Great, the traveller who wanders through the desert beside the brimming Euphrates looks upon the mounds of sand and of rubbish, then thinks on the word of the Hebrew poet and prophet of long ago:—

"And Babylon, the glory of the kingdoms,

Shall be as when God overthrew Sodom and Gomorrah.

It shall never be inhabited,

Neither shall the Arabian pitch tent there;

Neither shall shepherds make their fold there;

But wild beasts of the desert shall lie there,

And owls shall dwell there,

And satyrs shall dance there,

And wild beasts of the islands

Shall cry in their desolate houses;

Her days shall not be prolonged."

FOOTNOTES

[1] The chief god of Babylon, properly named Bel-Marduk, was often called indifferently simply Bel or Marduk.

[2] Twenty per cent annually.

[3] Such copy-books have been actually preserved to us.

[4] The *gur* was about eight bushels.

[5] The Babylonians observed a seventh day as sacred, much after the Jewish fashion. It was likewise called "The Sabbath."

[6] Often, though incorrectly, written "Zoroaster."

[7] The Persian "hell," conceived of as in the extreme north; a land of pitiless cold.

[8] Sirius.

[9] Ten P.M.

[10] Saturn.

[11] About three bushel.

NOTE TO THE READER

The author has not been unmindful that certain record tablets give a narrative of the capture of Babylon, in some points differing from the Bible account in the Book of Daniel. The reasons for preferring the latter to the profane narrative are too many to be discussed here; but it is not improper to point out that the "Chronicle Tablets" were written with a political end to serve,—to soothe the feelings of the conquered Babylonians, by representing that Babylon surrendered voluntarily to Cyrus. This is hardly likely; but it is very probable that the city was taken by treachery among the priests and not by assault.

I have ventured to give the name of Isaiah to the great "Prophet of the Captivity," whose writings are found in the last half of our present "Book of Isaiah." It has been well conjectured that his name was also Isaiah, which resulted in the combining of the two independent prophecies into one book.

VALUE OF MONEY

(according to Sayce)

Shekel	$ 0.75
Maneh	45.00
Talent (silver)	2700.00

Gold was worth ten times as much as silver, weight for weight.